D1083517

Stay the Rising Sun

To the men and women of "The Greatest Generation"

We owe them so much

And to all the officers and sailors who trod the historic decks

of USS *Lexington*, CV-2: You made a difference.

STAY THE RISING SUN

THE TRUE STORY OF USS *LEXINGTON*, HER VALIANT CREW, AND CHANGING THE COURSE OF WORLD WAR II

PHIL KEITH

ZENITH
PRESS

Quarto is the authority on a wide range of topics.

Quarto educates, entertains and enriches the lives of our readers—enthusiasts and lovers of hands-on living.

www.quartoknows.com

First published in 2015 by Zenith Press, an imprint of Quarto Publishing Group USA Inc., 400 First Avenue North, Suite 400, Minneapolis, MN 55401 USA. Telephone: (612) 344-8100 Fax: (612) 344-8692

quartoknows.com
Visit our blogs at quartoknows.com

10 9 8 7 6 5 4 3 2

ISBN: 978-0-7603-4741-6

Library of Congress Cataloging-in-Publication Data

Keith, Philip A.
  Stay the rising sun : the true story of USS Lexington, her valiant crew, and changing the course of World War II / Phil Keith.
    pages cm
  Includes bibliographical references and index.
  ISBN 978-0-7603-4741-6 (hc w/jacket)
  1. Lexington (Aircraft carrier : 1927-1942) 2. World War, 1939-1945--Naval operations, American. 3. World War, 1939-1945--Campaigns--Pacific Area. 4. Coral Sea, Battle of the, 1942. I. Title.
  D774.L4K45 2015
  940.54'5973--dc23
                    2014042180

Project Manager: Madeleine Vasaly
Acquisitions Editor: Elizabeth Demers
Art Director: James Kegley
Cover Design: Kent Jensen
Layout: Helena Shimizu

Printed in the United States of America

"It follows then as certain as that night succeeds the day, that without a decisive naval force we can do nothing definitive, and with it, everything honorable and glorious."

—President George Washington to Marquis de Lafayette
November 15, 1781

"I can imagine no more rewarding a career. And any man who may be asked in this century what he did to make his life worthwhile, I think can respond with a good deal of pride and satisfaction: 'I served in the United States Navy.'"

—President John F. Kennedy, Bancroft Hall
US Naval Academy
August 1, 1963

"Praise the Lord and pass the ammunition!"

—Lieutenant Howell Maurice Forgy, Chaplain, US Navy
USS *New Orleans (CA-32)*
Pearl Harbor, December 7, 1941

Conversations quoted in his book are based upon the firsthand recollections of one participant or the other or notes written down by reporters and other individuals who were actually involved or spoke directly with the participants. They come from some of the books listed in the bibliography, personal diaries, blog entries, and articles written about the events depicted in this book. Since most of the quotations are from the recollections of one party or the other and, as we all know, time has a habit of morphing experiences into shapes that could differ from actual events, it is of course impossible to say if the actual words quoted are 100 percent verbatim. I like to use bits of conversation when they can be reasonably verified, since it tends to inject life into events that would otherwise be a dry recitation of facts. I have tried very hard to ensure that all conversational passages used square with the facts and do justice to the lives and actual experiences of the speakers.

CONTENTS

Dramatis Personae
(with rank and responsibilities at the time of the action described in the text)

Names in *italics*: killed in action, Battle of the Coral Sea

The 1920s
Rear Admiral David W. Taylor, Chief, Bureau of Construction and Repair
Captain Albert W. Marshall, Commanding Officer, USS *Lexington* (CV-2),
    December 14, 1927–August 22, 1928
Captain Frank D. Berrien, Commanding Officer, USS *Lexington,* August 22,
    1928–June 30, 1930

The 1930s
Captain Ernest J. King, Commanding Officer, June 30, 1930–May 31, 1932
Captain Charles A. Blakely, Commanding Officer, May 31, 1932–June 12, 1934
Captain Arthur B. Cook, Commanding Officer, June 12, 1934–April 6, 1936
Captain Aubrey W. Fitch, Commanding Officer, April 6, 1936–April 13, 1937
Captain Leigh H. Noyes, Commanding Officer, April 13, 1937–June 18, 1938
Captain John H. Hoover, Commanding Officer, June 18, 1938–June 17, 1939
Captain Alva D. Bernhard, Commanding Officer, June 17, 1939–June 13, 1940

Pearl Harbor to Coral Sea
Admiral Ernest J. King, Chief of Naval Operations, Washington, DC
Admiral Husband E. Kimmel, Commander in Chief, Pacific Fleet, February 18, 1941–
    December 17, 1941
Vice Admiral William S. Pye, Commander in Chief, Pacific Fleet, December 17, 1941–
    December 31, 1941
Admiral Chester W. Nimitz, Commander in Chief, Pacific Fleet, December 31, 1941–
    December 14, 1945
Vice Admiral Wilson Brown, Commander, Task Force 3
Rear Admiral Aubrey W. "Jake" Fitch, Commander, Task Force 11
Captain Frederick C. Sherman, Commanding Officer, USS *Lexington*, June 13, 1940–
    June 24, 1942[1]
Lieutenant Edward H. "Butch" O'Hare, Fighter Pilot, VF-3, USS *Lexington*
Lieutenant Junior Grade Marion W. Dufilho, Fighter Pilot, VF-3, USS *Lexington*

Battle of the Coral Sea
Rear Admiral Frank J. "Jack" Fletcher, Commander, Task Force 17
Rear Admiral Thomas C. Kinkaid, Commander, Task Group 17.2 (Attack Group),
    Flag Aboard USS *Minneapolis* (CA-36)
Lieutenant Howell Forgy, Senior Chaplain, USS *New Orleans* (CA-32)
Rear Admiral William W. Smith, Commander, Cruiser Escorts

Task Group 17.3 (Support Group)
Rear Admiral John Gregory Crace, Royal Australian Navy, Commander
Captain Howard D. Bode, Commanding Officer, USS *Chicago* (CA-29)

Task Group 17.5 (Carrier Air Group)
Rear Admiral Aubrey Fitch, Officer in Tactical Command (OTC), USS *Yorktown* (CV-5)
Commander Harry B. Jarrett, Commanding Officer, USS *Morris* (DD-417)
Lieutenant Commander John K. B. Ginder, Commanding Officer, USS *Anderson* (DD-411)
Lieutenant Commander Glenn R. Hartwig, Commanding Officer, USS *Russell* (DD-414)
Lieutenant Commander Arnold E. True, Commanding Officer, USS *Hammann* (DD-412)

USS *Yorktown*
Captain Elliott Buckmaster, Commanding Officer
Lieutenant Commander Oscar Pederson, Commander, *Yorktown* Air Group
Lieutenant Commander William O. Burch Jr., Commanding Officer, VS-5

---

1. Although lost on May 8, 1942, USS *Lexington* was not officially struck from the list until June 24, 1942.

Lieutenant Commander James H. Flatley Jr., Commanding Officer, VF-42
Lieutenant Commander Joe Taylor, Commanding Officer, VT-5
Lieutenant John J. "Jo Jo" Powers, Bomber Pilot, VB-5
Lieutenant Milton E. Ricketts, O-in-C, Engineering Repair Party

USS *Lexington*
Captain Frederick C. "Ted" Sherman, Commanding Officer
Commander Wallace M. Dillon, Executive Officer (until January 18, 1942)
Commander Morton T. Seligman, Executive Officer (January 18–May 8, 1942)
Commander James R. Dudley, Navigation Officer
Commander Walter W. Gilmore (SC), Chief Supply Officer
Commander George L. Markle, CHC, Senior Chaplain
Commander Wadsworth J. Trojakowski, DC, Chief Dental Officer
Lieutenant Commander H. R. "Pop" Healy, Damage Control Officer
Lieutenant Commander Alexander F. Junkers, Chief Engineering Officer
Captain Ralph L. Hauser, USMC, Commanding Officer, Marine Detachment
Lieutenant Thomas J. Nixon III, Damage Control Assistant
Lieutenant Charles Williams, Supply Corps, Assistant Supply Officer
John B. Brandt, Chief Boatswain's Mate
Corporal Vincent Anderson, USMC, Battery No. 4
Private Jesse Rutherford Jr., USMC, Battery No. 4
Stanley Johnston, Embarked War Correspondent, *Chicago Tribune*
"Admiral Wags," Cocker Spaniel, Captain's Mascot

USS *Lexington* Air Group
Commander William Bowen "Bill" Ault, Commander, Air Group
Lieutenant Commander Robert E. Dixon, Commanding Officer, VS-2
Lieutenant Commander Weldon L. Hamilton, Commanding Officer, VB-2
Lieutenant Commander Paul H. Ramsey, Commanding Officer, VF-2
Lieutenant Commander James H. Brett Jr., Commanding Officer, VT-2
Lieutenant Noel M. Gayler, Executive Officer, VF-2
Lieutenant (Junior Grade) William E. Hall, Scout Pilot, VS-2
Aviation Ordnanceman 2nd Class Walter Hassell, VT-2

Task Group 17.6 (Fueling Group)
Commander John S. Phillips, Commanding Officer, USS *Neosho* (AO-23)
Chief Watertender Oscar V. Peterson, USS *Neosho*
Lieutenant Commander Willford M. Hyman, Commanding Officer, USS *Sims* (DD-409)

Task Force 16
Vice Admiral William F. "Bull" Halsey, Commander

From Tarawa to Tokyo
Captain Felix Stump, (First) Commanding Officer, USS *Lexington* (CV-16)
Captain Ernest W. Litch, (Second) Commanding Officer, USS *Lexington*

Imperial Japanese Navy, Coral Sea Commanders
Vice Admiral Shigeyoshi Inoue, Commander, Imperial Japanese Navy, Fourth Fleet
Vice Admiral Takeo Takagi, Commander, Carrier Striking Force
Rear Admiral Chūichi Hara, Carrier Division 5, Officer in Tactical Command (OTC)
Rear Admiral Aritomo Gotō, Commander, Covering Group/Main Body Support Force
Rear Admiral Sadamichi Kajioka, Commander, Port Moresby Attack Force
Rear Admiral Kōsō Abe, Commander, Port Moresby Invasion Force
Captain Ishinosuke Izawa, Commanding Officer, Light Carrier *Shōhō* ("Happy Phoenix")
Captain Takaji Jōshima, Commanding Officer, Fleet Carrier *Shōkaku* ("Soaring Crane")
Captain Ichibei Yokokawa, Commanding Officer, Fleet Carrier *Zuikaku* ("Auspicious Crane")
Lieutenant Commander Kakuichi Takahashi, Shōkaku, Air Group Commander
Lieutenant Kenjiro Nōtomi, Commanding Officer, *Shōhō* Carrier Fighter Unit,
Lieutenant Takumi Hoashi, Commanding Officer, *Shōkaku* Carrier Fighter Unit
Lieutenant Masao Yamaguchi, Commanding Officer, *Shōkaku* Carrier Bomber Unit
Lieutenant Tatsuo Ichihara, Commanding Officer, *Shōkaku* Carrier Attack Unit

List of Acronyms

ANZAC	Australia–New Zealand Army Corps
AO	Auxiliary Oiler, a refueling ship, as in USS *Neosho*, AO-23
AVP	Auxiliary Patrol Support Ship, a specialized ship to support patrol plane operations, as in USS *Swan*, AVP-7
CA	Heavy cruiser designation, as in USS *Chicago*, CA-29
CAP	Combat Air Patrol
CC	Battle cruiser designation, as in USS *United States*, CC-1
CINCUS	Commander in Chief, United States (superseded by CNO designation—see below)
CINCPAC	Commander in Chief, Pacific, commander of all Navy forces in the Pacific
CO	Commanding Officer
COMBATFOR	Commander, Battleship Forces
COMSOPAC	Commander, Southern Pacific, commander of all US Navy forces in the South Pacific
CLAG	Commander, *Lexington* Air Group
CNO	Chief of Naval Operations, top admiral in the US Navy
CV	Aircraft carrier designation, as in USS *Lexington*, CV-2
CVN	Nuclear aircraft carrier designation, as in USS *George H. W. Bush*, CVN-77
CYAG	Commander, *Yorktown* Air Group
DD	Destroyer designation, as in USS *Morris*, DD-417
FDO	Fighter Direction Officer
GQ	General Quarters, the highest-alert level aboard a ship
HMAS	His Majesty's Australian Ship, as in HMAS *Australia*
HMS	His Majesty's Ship, as in HMS *Victory*
IFF	Identification: Friend or Foe, electronic means of identifying aircraft on a radar display
IJN	Imperial Japanese Navy
LSO	Landing Signal Officer
MC	designation for US Navy officers assigned to the Medical Corps (usually qualified doctors), as in Cmdr. H. M. White (MC), USN
MIA	Missing in Action
MO	Japanese navy code designation for the Port Moresby Invasion Force
NAP	Naval Air Pilot, an enlisted (non-commissioned) aviator
OOD	Officer of the Day, the officer in charge of the current watch section aboard a US Navy ship
RAN	Royal Australian Navy
RMS	Royal Mail Ship, as in RMS *Titanic*
ROTC	Reserve Officer Training Corps
TF	Task Force
UO	Utility/Observation aircraft
VB	Designation for a bombing squadron
VF	Designation for a fighter squadron
VMF	Designation for a US Marine Corps fighter squadron
VP	Designation for a patrol squadron
VT	Designation for a torpedo squadron
XO	Executive Officer, the second in command

PROLOGUE

1100 hours, May 8, 1942. The Coral Sea, five hundred miles east-southeast of New Guinea and four hundred miles east-northeast of Australia's Great Barrier Reef.

A US Navy–Royal Australian Navy Joint Task Force, centered on the aircraft carriers USS *Lexington* and USS *Yorktown*, prepared to battle an Imperial Japanese Navy Strike Group with the fleet carriers *Shōkaku* and *Zuikaku*. The opponents had been searching for each other for several days. On May 7, they finally made contact. The Japanese suffered the loss of a light aircraft carrier, along with three dozen aircraft. The Americans were bloodied as well: an extremely valuable fleet oiler became a floating wreck, and one destroyer sank with the loss of nearly all hands. Yet these were only the opening skirmishes. The commanders of the opposing fleets believed that May 8 would finally bring on the general engagement they had been anticipating.

The Japanese intended to clear a path for their troop transports and landing parties, already at sea and intent on capturing Port Moresby, New Guinea. The Allies wanted to stop the Japanese thrust aimed at the front door of Australia. The coming fight would be a contest of major strategic significance. It would be the first time in the history of naval warfare that aircraft carriers would contend against one another. The opponents would never set eyes directly on each other; instead, they would rely on their aircraft to conduct a battle that would take place over distances of a hundred miles and more. Just before noon, unbeknownst to either battle group, all four carrier air wings were in flight and heading for their opposite numbers. All the strikes would arrive at their targets nearly simultaneously.

On the bridge of USS *Lexington*, the captain craved a cigarette, but the smoking lamp was out—rightly so, considering that ammunition was flying everywhere and flammable materials, like aviation gas and noxious fumes, were omnipresent.

Captain Frederick C. Sherman's ship was taking a terrible pounding. Known throughout the fleet as an expert ship handler, Sherman could dock the massive bulk of USS *Lexington*, all 888 feet of her, without the use of tugboats. But today, all the zigs, zags, and maneuvers he could devise could not keep pace with those of his Imperial Japanese Navy opponents. With the eye of a master tactician, Sherman noted with clinical dispassion that the Japanese pilots savaging his ship had developed a nearly foolproof way to make sure their torpedoes struck home. They had devised a pattern wherein two separate flights of aircraft would simultaneously approach *Lexington* from the starboard and port quarters, off the bow. They would drop their torpedoes in unison. No matter which way the helmsman turned the rudder, he would be steering the ship's broad flanks directly into one spread of torpedoes or the other. If he did nothing, of course, they could all strike home.

Watching as the current flock of Kates[4] bore down on him, Sherman chose starboard. The huge vessel shuddered and heeled to the right, but not quickly enough. At 1118, a powerful Long Lance torpedo slammed into *Lexington*'s port bow. At 1120, another struck her port side, amidships. *Lexington* was equipped with torpedo blisters,[5] and the ship's builders had assured Sherman that the old girl could absorb nine torpedo hits, maybe as many as a dozen, before getting into serious difficulty. He was praying they were right.

Lexington had faced these kinds of air attacks before, but not at this intensity. Admiral Aubrey Fitch, consulting with his boss, Adm. Frank Fletcher, had decided to launch almost the entire *Lexington* air wing in a winner-take-all assault against the Japanese carriers nearby. This had left Sherman with only a handful of fighters and scout planes to form a combat screen for his ship. The few Wildcats and Dauntlesses in the air above him were quickly overwhelmed by the waves of enemy aircraft that had been launched against both *Lexington* and the nearby *Yorktown*.

Sherman could see *Yorktown* in the distance. Although he loved his ship, he was, at that moment, quite jealous of its captain—his friend and fellow Academy classmate Elliott Buckmaster—and the newer, faster, more maneuverable *Yorktown*. Buckmaster was obviously having an easier time dodging the Japanese attacks being flung against his vessel.[6]

Sherman was desperate for some of his planes to return and help drive off the relentless Japanese, but the *Lexington* pilots were still over one hundred miles away, hammering at their assigned targets. The best he could hope for

---

4. "Kate" was the US designation for the Japanese Nakajima B5N single-engine torpedo bomber.
5. Blisters were rounded, longitudinal metal extensions of the ship's hull, welded in place just below the waterline and specifically designed to absorb some of the impact of torpedo hits and prevent the breaching of the hull.
6. *Yorktown* would successfully evade all eight torpedoes launched at her that day, and a number of bombs—all except one, which plunged through her flight deck and exploded below, killing sixty-six men.

was that his vast array of deck guns, and the nearby cruisers and destroyers screening him, could keep his tormentors at bay.

Sherman glanced skyward again and saw more black dots approaching, growing larger, diving lower. *Oh my god . . . here come the bombers. . . .*

Goddamn knee knockers, Cmdr. Mort Seligman cursed to himself as he stumbled down the passageway, groping for the next ladder.[7] As XO (executive officer) and a veteran carrier pilot, he had spent a great deal of time aboard flattops, but avoiding the raised metal flanges between the ship's hatches during high-speed runs and zigzags was nearly impossible, even for an experienced sailor. The result was often a painful whacking of the shins, and he had just suffered one.

The ship was shuddering and shaking as she raced across the Coral Sea at her top speed of thirty-three knots. Every sweep of the chronometer seemed to bring a swerve from port to starboard, then back again. Navigating the miles of waxed linoleum slithering beneath his feet under these conditions required a gymnast's agility. All attempts at maintaining a constant balance were impossible. On top of the mechanical jitterbugging, a cacophony produced by the ship's guns was rattling the bulkheads—and Seligman's nerves.

Commander Seligman had just left the hospital ward, where mounting casualties were overwhelming the medical staff. He was headed to report to the captain on the bridge. To get there, he'd have to claw up more levels amid pure chaos. The ship was constantly rolling one way and then the other, swaying and bucking, trying to avoid the bombs and torpedoes the Japanese were hurling in the ship's path. First he had to reach the hanger deck. Once there, it would be a sprint across that open cavern to another set of ladders that led to the flight deck, where he could gain access to the island. Inside the towering island superstructure, there were three final ladders to climb. This would put him on the signal bridge, where the captain was directing the ship's defense.

The passageways were empty, except for the rescue parties bringing the wounded below for treatment. Every man on the ship had been at his assigned battle station since 0500 that morning. As XO, Seligman's job at GQ (General Quarters) was to roam the ship, reporting all dangerous or important situations to the captain.

The ship's intercom had blared out the warning "Enemy aircraft inbound!" just after 1113. Seligman had been in the belly of the ship, in Central Station. It was from this wide, port-to-starboard compartment, buried deep within the bowels of the ship, that Lt. Cmdr. "Pop" Healy and his crew of

7. "Knee knocker" is navy slang for the raised metal flange at the bottom of a "hatch" or doorway in a ship's passageway (hallway). Although a nuisance, they are essential to maintaining the ship's structural integrity. They also provide a solid lip for securing any doors that might be attached to the hatches. The doors, in turn, are critical to sealing off compartments and maintaining watertight integrity.

damage-control specialists would react to any damage. This was the nerve center of the ship, connected to every space by sound-powered phone, wires, or buried sensors. From Central, Healy could reach out and flip a switch to direct the closing of a valve, shut down a compromised pump, or deal with just about anything that threatened the integrity of the ship's critical systems. For large disasters, such as serious hull punctures or dangerous fires, Healy had five repair teams at his beck and call. These highly trained damage-control experts acted as flying squads, applying their different technical specialties wherever they were needed most.

As the first attacks began, along with the chatter of the ship's guns, Seligman felt everything change. The air became electric, almost blue, and the men stubbed out their cigarettes. They braced for the emergencies they knew would come. Even from this sheltered space, the rumble of the guns and the metallic pinging of bullets rattling off the ship's sides could be heard easily. When enemy ordnance fell into the water and exploded nearby, it popped the men's ears, rattled their teeth, and made them feel like they were inside a big bass drum.

Seligman was no coward, but tendrils of sweat rolled down his spine and a sudden claustrophobia gripped him. He did not want to be in Central any longer. It could be a death trap if another torpedo came roaring into the side of the ship; two had done so already. He was an aviator, after all, and he craved air—daylight. No one noticed him fade into the back of the compartment. He quietly opened the hatch, stepped outside, re-dogged the latches, and jogged away.

On his way topside, he decided to check on the ship's hospital. Maybe, Seligman hoped, "Doc" White had broken open his supply of medicinal brandy. A shot of liquid courage wouldn't hurt, he reasoned. He had a stash of whiskey in his stateroom, but that space would be an impossibly hazardous trek right then.

The spacious medical ward looked like a trauma unit when Seligman stuck his head in the door. A nearby gurney contained a still form, completely covered by a blood-soaked sheet. Pharmacist's mates dashed about the space, carrying bandages and medicines. Low moans emanated from some of the racks (beds). A tortured soul shrieked "Mama!" from somewhere in the rear. The doctors were overwhelmed, so the ship's dentists had been pressed into triage as the casualties mounted. Seligman knew the coppery smell of blood and the fecal smell of death and it always turned his stomach.

"Gangway, sir!"

Seligman stepped aside as two sailors, members of the ship's band and stretcher bearers during crises, stumbled through the hatch half carrying, half dragging a wounded marine. The man's clothes had been torched away and his skin was a mass of second- and third-degree burns. A patch of charred dermis sloughed away and plopped grotesquely onto the deck. The stench of cooked flesh was the final straw, and Seligman decided he could forego the brandy.

He was halfway up the ladder to the hangar deck when a violent explosion slammed into the port side of the ship. His hand was ripped from the left rail. Somehow, he held on with his right as his body was flung outward from the ladder and suspended in midair. He fell back against the right rail painfully and lost his grip. He fell to the bottom of the ladder, some four to five feet, and landed in a heap. *God, that was close!*

As the reverberations from the explosions abated, Captain Sherman became anxious for information on the damage. *Lexington* had swallowed at least two torpedoes on the port side and suffered two bomb hits. The inclinometer showed she was already listing to port. The captain shouted at his talker. He needed to be in touch with Lieutenant Commander Healy in Central Station. Healy came up on the line and reported that he'd have the six-degree list neutralized within the hour. He was already counter-flooding a number of starboard-side compartments and his repair crews were plugging the holes. Sherman felt somewhat reassured.

Before signing off, Healy barked into his handset, "Captain! One more thing!"

"Yes, commander?" Sherman yelled back.

"I strongly advise, if you're going to be taking any more torpedo hits, that you take them on the starboard side."

Despite the dire situation, even Sherman had to chuckle. If his damage-control officer was that flippant about their status, then things were probably going to be OK.

One hundred and twenty miles to the northwest, CLAG[8] Cmdr. Bill Ault was in serious trouble. The Zero he had tried to avoid during his dive on the Japanese carrier *Shōkaku* had nailed him. He had managed to release his single thousand-pound bomb and had scored a direct hit, squarely in the middle of the flight deck, but the burst from the Japanese pilot's 7.7-millimeter gun had peppered his plane with slugs and flying metal. His left hand and leg had been hit, and although the blood loss was manageable, the stinging in his arm and his reduced mobility made flying difficult.

His gunner, Aviation Radioman 1st Class Bill Butler, was gravely wounded, possibly dead. Ault had not been able to raise him on the intercom for several minutes. After their Dauntless dive bomber had been hit, Butler

---

8. Commander, Lexington Air Group: the officer in command of all the squadrons aboard the carrier.

reported he was "shot through" and bleeding "all over." Ault could smell a fuel leak, and one of his gauges was already bouncing on empty. There was not enough gas to get back to *Lexington.*

His choices were grim. He was a sitting duck for any other Zero that might come by. His machine was barely flying, and he could not engage in any evasive maneuvering. If he escaped detection, the best he could do would be to make it back to within thirty or forty miles of the ship. Then he and Butler would have to ditch and hope that one of *Lexington*'s escort ships could pick them up if they survived the ditching.

Ault radioed *Lexington.* He managed to raise Air Ops but quickly discovered that they were in a bind of their own. He did give a brief sit rep (situation report) indicating he was having difficulty figuring out his position and that he did not have enough fuel to get back.

Before signing off, Ault closed with, "OK, people, if we don't make it back, I want you to know we put a thousand-pound bomb right on that flattop."

Private Raymond Miller's battle station was Battery No. 4, a section of three five-inch anti-aircraft guns positioned on *Lexington*'s port side. As a "second loader," it was his job to pass the live rounds from the ammunition locker for Gun No. 10 to the primary loader on the firing step for the gun.

Captain Sherman had sounded General Quarters at 0552, and since then the marines had been standing by their guns, helmets on, wearing their heavy, flash-proof clothing, growing hotter and more impatient as the tropical heat bore down. They watched as the first waves of the carrier's outbound attack force had taken off around 0900 and headed away from the ship. The few planes that remained for the defense were launched at 1100, and soon thereafter the ship's loudspeakers announced that Japanese aircraft had been spotted on radar, inbound.

Vincent Anderson, who as of this writing lives in Palm Desert, California, was a young corporal also assigned to Battery 4, Gun 10. Several of the Japanese attackers slipped through the protective screen of aircraft and pounced on *Lexington.* It was about 1115.

"The sound of all of our guns firing was deafening," Anderson recalls, "and suddenly we felt violent, vibrating blows to our ship."

These hits were the two torpedoes that struck "Lady Lex," in short order, right after 1119; the first was such a violent shock that both the ship's elevators jammed in place. Fortunately, they were in the "up" position, or the deck would have been rendered unusable. Worse: the fracturing effects of the blast started a series of small leaks in the aviation gas storage tanks and fuel lines along the port side. Aircraft fuel began to seep out and its deadly vapors were spreading everywhere.

The second torpedo struck directly opposite the bridge. The primary port water mains—critical for firefighting—were ruptured and three of the eight portside boiler rooms were flooded. The engineer, Cmdr. Alexander Junkers, was forced to reduce speed to just over twenty-five knots.

Two of the attacking Japanese torpedo planes were hit by *Lexington*'s guns, and went down immediately. Two more of the attackers flew down the port side of the ship, and as they swung away their rear machine gunners sprayed Battery No. 4 with a hailstorm of bullets. The man standing to Corporal Anderson's left was shot through the head and killed instantly. Three more of the men working the gun on his right were wounded. Anderson couldn't believe he hadn't been struck. Behind him, Private Miller had taken several slugs and was bleeding profusely. He refused to leave his post and doggedly continued to heave the heavy five-inch shells from the locker beneath his feet to the men still alive and manning the gun.

~

The hands of the clock swept toward noon on May 8, 1942, the final day of the Battle of the Coral Sea. The battle's outcome still hung in the balance. Eight hours later, the proud "Queen of the Flattops" would be on the sea bed, some two thousand feet below the surface, taking 216 of the ship's brave crew with her.

This is the story of that valiant ship, USS *Lexington*, CV-2. At the keel level, she started her service life as a battle cruiser, but the design was ultimately abandoned and seven years later she left the dock as the navy's first true aircraft carrier.[2] Commissioned for service in 1928, everything she did set a precedent. The rapidly advancing concepts of naval air warfare would be developed and tested from her flattop deck. Naval aviation, in turn, would play a pivotal role in winning World War II, especially in the Pacific. All future carriers would be designed and built around the lessons learned from the *Lexington* class of carriers.[3]

But USS *Lexington* was much more than the first of her kind. She was a "tradition," built on reverence for those seminal events in American history that took place on Lexington Green and in the streets of Concord in 1775. CV-2 was actually the fifth ship in US Navy history to bear the designation *Lexington*. Her valor in combat would rouse the men and women

---

2. *Lexington*'s only predecessor, USS *Langley* (CV-1), had originally been USS *Jupiter* (AC-3), a coal refueling ship. *Jupiter* was converted to an experimental flattop in 1920. At the outbreak of World War II, she was no longer an aircraft carrier: she had been converted once again, in 1938, to a seaplane tender. On February 27, 1942, while on a mission to ferry Allied aircraft to Java, *Langley* was badly damaged by Japanese dive bombers. The crew was forced to abandon ship. *Langley* was torpedoed and sunk later in the day by US Navy destroyers to prevent her falling into enemy hands.
3. There were only two in the class: *Lexington* and her sister ship, USS *Saratoga*, CV-3.

from the very same Massachusetts shipyard where she was built, scant miles from where the Minutemen stood at Lexington Common, to beg the navy and President Roosevelt to give them the honor and the task of building another *Lexington* to replace the one lost at Coral Sea. That ship, CV-16, would become the fabled "Blue Ghost" that would storm the Pacific "from Tarawa to Tokyo," pummeling the Japanese in revenge for the loss of the first Lady Lex.

Even after CV-2 was sunk, she continued to contribute to winning the war. Because of remarkable seamanship, over 90 percent of her crew survived. These men went on to other ships, many of them into new aircraft carriers. They took their hard-won experiences and used them to train their new ships and crews.

Ultimately, CV-2 was lost because of faulty design, not Japanese torpedoes and bombs. While enemy ordnance inflicted the damage that caused the fires that consumed the ship, it was the lack of proper gasoline storage, insufficient firefighting equipment, and the use of extensive flammable materials in her construction that ultimately doomed her. These lessons were swiftly incorporated into the newer carrier designs.

The air wings of the two American carriers that fought at Coral Sea had flown into combat independently of one another. The air wings from the Japanese carriers engaged at Coral Sea had fought as one coordinated unit. This was another valuable lesson, and fortunately the US Navy began learning from it in time for the Battle of Midway, one month later.

Lady Lex is the fulcrum of a two-hundred-year story arc. The tale stretches from the first USS *Lexington*, a brigantine commissioned for service in the Continental Navy, to the "Blue Ghost," CV-16, the ship that became the longest-serving aircraft carrier in US Navy history (1943–1991).

This book will focus on the stories and reminiscences of the remarkable men who sailed CV-2 into the Coral Sea in May 1942. Together, that ship and her crew truly changed the course of World War II.

CHAPTER 1

QUEEN OF THE FLATTOPS

HEARING A SOFT KNOCK on the outer office door, Rear Adm. David W. Taylor glanced up from the stack of working papers and ship drawings on his desktop. The wardroom bell clock on Taylor's wall chimed a muted four bells: six o'clock civilian time. It was rapidly becoming dark outside his window and a chilly rain, flecked with sleet, was threatening.

"Excuse me, Admiral," boomed the voice of his chief yeoman, piercing the quiet. "The photograph you wanted to see is ready."

Striding across the highly polished oak floor as confidently as he would a quarterdeck, the master chief approached the admiral's desk and stood stiffly at attention, grasping a large manila envelope.

"Stand at ease, Master Chief. Let's see what you've got."

The oversized image had been taken a week earlier and was scheduled, pending his signature, to be released to the general media via the navy's news service. Taylor was sure a fair number of newspapers would publish the photo, since the reverberations from the recently concluded Washington Naval Conference[9] were still rattling the foundations of parliaments around the world. The photo he held in his hands was a graphic representation of one of the conference's major agreements, and it foreshadowed the future of the US Navy, certainly, and probably the futures of several other navies around the globe.

In the frame stood three senior navy admirals, including Taylor, and three members of the House of Representatives, congressmen who had played significant roles in setting out the policies that had emerged from the Naval Conference. In front of the six men, on a large coffee table, sat a scale model of the newly designed *Lexington*-class aircraft carrier. Above

---

9. November 12, 1921, to February 6, 1922.

that model, which was held at the bow end by Taylor and the stern end by Rear Adm. John K. Robison, chief of the Bureau of Naval Engineering, was another model, this one a to-scale rendition of USS *Lexington* as CC-1, a battle cruiser. Thanks to the new Washington Naval Treaty, the battle cruiser as a concept was dead. The six ships of the *Lexington* battle cruiser class would never be built, even though three of them were already under construction.

Taylor laid the photo on his desk. "That'll be all, Master Chief, thank you. Wait. I'd love some coffee."

"Right away, Admiral." With that, the yeoman turned smartly on a heel, and left the office.

Everything is changing, Taylor sighed to himself, *and nothing will ever be the same.*

David W. Taylor was born on March 4, 1864, the very day Abraham Lincoln delivered his Second Inaugural Address and Ulysses S. Grant was promoted to lieutenant general in command of all the Union armies. Taylor was from Louisa County, Virginia, however, so these events may not have seemed as historically significant deep in the heart of the Confederacy.

Seventeen years later in a different era of peace and unity, Taylor entered the Class of 1885 at Annapolis. At the Naval Academy, he amassed a record of scholarship that has yet to be equaled. He graduated first in his class, became a naval constructor (engineering officer), and was sent to the Royal Naval College in England, where, once again, he broke every record for academic achievement. With his intellectual gifts, there were many avenues he could have explored, but he stayed true to his calling (marine engineering) and the navy, where he achieved flag rank and completed nearly forty years of active service.

In March 1922, Taylor was a year away from mandatory retirement. He had compiled a superior record and a number of personal decorations and medals, and he had led the navy through a new era of naval construction and change. He developed and built the first experimental (model) ship basin in 1898 and set standards for ship design and fabrication that are still in use today: the Taylor Standard Series, last revised in 1998.

At the apex of his career, Taylor steered the US Navy's ship design and building program through some very stormy waters, which had begun roiling immediately after the sinking of the RMS *Titanic*. Taylor, by then a senior captain and one of the US Navy's most innovative maritime thinkers, was brought in as an expert witness in the investigation. It had become clear to Taylor, and to many other analysts, that as hulls grew more massive and propulsion systems more powerful, there would have to be substantial changes in materials and in construction techniques.

The Royal Navy, in particular, began to push the boundaries as it watched the German and Imperial Japanese navies build bigger, faster, more powerful ships. After the Japanese crushed the Russian fleet at the Battle of Tsushima in 1905, the Royal Navy went all out in a quest for more power, bigger guns, and faster ships that sailed on longer, lighter hulls and carried less armament. The British wanted to move away from the large, lumbering, but heavily armed and armored battleship but not all the way over to the lighter, more agile, speedier, less powerful cruisers. The result was a hybrid, appropriately dubbed the battle cruiser, a design concept that contained the best elements of both classes.

The most active proponent of the battle cruiser was the Royal Navy's enigmatic first sea lord, Adm. "Jacky" Fisher. As Fisher looked around the naval world of the early twentieth century, he saw a continuing role for battleships; but for conducting heavy reconnaissance, for close support, or for commerce raiding and pursuit, he needed something different. He wanted warships capable of sinking any ship "fast enough to catch them, and run from any ship capable of sinking them." In other words, Fisher wanted a battle cruiser: a hull type capable of destroying any cruiser afloat while dancing away from all the dreadnoughts.

The first iteration of the Royal Navy's battle cruiser program was the *Invincible* class, consisting of three ships: *Invincible*, *Inflexible*, and *Indomitable*. All three were commissioned and launched in the 1908–1909 timeframe. Each carried a powerful array of four turrets, two fore and two aft, each with two twelve-inch guns. Top speed was twenty-five knots, which allowed these battle cruisers to outrun everything else on the high seas. Each ship was 567 feet long and 78.5 feet wide and required a crew of 784. The main armor protection was six inches of steel, giving them slightly more than half the protection of the new and revolutionary *Dreadnought* battleships being built concurrently.

The next battle cruisers to slide down the ways were the ships of the *Indefatigable* class. Actually, the Royal Navy ordered only one ship in this class, *Indefatigable* itself, but two more were built, one for the Royal Australian Navy and one for the Royal New Zealand Navy. *Australia* and *New Zealand* were slightly longer (590 feet) and a little broader in the beam (80 feet) to improve hull stress when their big guns were working. These battle cruisers, slight modifications of the *Invincibles*, came into service between 1911 and 1913.

The next to last of Britain's pre–World War I battle cruisers were two ships dubbed the "Splendid Cats" by the tars who manned them, *Lion* and *Princess Royal*. Perceived deficiencies in the *Invincible* and *Indomitable* classes were corrected in the *Lion* class; moreover, England felt it needed to respond to the new German *Moltke*-class battle cruisers, each more power-ful than the Royal Navy's previous battle cruiser designs. A naval arms race was underway.

Lion and *Princess Royal* were more battleship than cruiser. At twenty-seven-plus knots, they were two knots faster than their predecessors; they mounted the new 13.5-inch main guns in four batteries of two each; and they were beefed up in terms of armor protection to a more robust nine-inch armor belt. Their length crept up to seven hundred feet with an eighty-eight-foot beam.

The very last battle cruiser to join the Royal Navy before hostilities began in 1914 was the single-ship class consisting of *Queen Mary*. She was the fastest battle cruiser afloat, at twenty-eight knots, and also the biggest, at 703 feet long and 89 feet wide. Her wartime crew requirements had ballooned to 1,275 officers and men. They would be firing eight of the big 13.5-inch guns and a host of smaller-calibers and torpedoes.

Admiral Taylor watched all of the developments of America's closest naval ally with a keen eye. In 1914, on the cusp of the coming war, Taylor was promoted to rear admiral and placed in charge of the Navy's Bureau of Construction and Repair. He held that post for the remainder of his career (until 1923), and in this job he had vast authority over and ultimate responsibility for what the ships of the US Navy would look like in the decades ahead. Even though President Woodrow Wilson had pledged that America would stay out of any conflict in Europe, Taylor, and many of the US Navy's leaders, privately believed that it was only a matter of time before American sailors were firing up their boilers, too.

The Great White Fleet of President Theodore Roosevelt's "Big Stick" policy had proven that America was a player in world affairs, at least at sea. The fourteen-month circumnavigation of the globe by the US Navy's Atlantic Fleet[10] had gone off with very few hitches and minimal mechanical problems. Sixteen battleships and their support vessels with fourteen thousand officers and sailors steamed forty-three thousand nautical miles, making twenty port calls on six continents. It was an unprecedented tour de force at sea. Lessons learned by the ship's crews in gunnery, seamanship, logistics, navigation, and planning would set the course for naval policy and training for many years. There was one major drawback to the exercise, however: all sixteen battleships were pre-dreadnought types and therefore obsolete, even though most of them were less than a decade old.

In August 1914, the US Navy was the third largest in the world with 914,218 tons in the water. By contrast, Germany, the second largest navy,

---

10. December 1907 to February 1909.

weighed in at 1,304,640 tons and Britain, as the number-one seagoing force, had 2,713,756 tons. Germany and England were frantically building battle-ships, battle cruisers, cruisers, and submarines. The US Navy had only four battleships under construction, no battle cruisers, no armored cruisers, and only a few submarines. The predominant US naval construction effort was concentrated on destroyers and submarines.

The strategic planners in Britain and Germany were looking ahead to set-piece battles at sea between capital ships. American naval strategists were looking more toward coastal protection via long-range, shore-based guns and protection of commerce via submarines and destroyers. The ships needed for one strategy were far different from the other. Nonetheless, as the Great War exploded in Europe, Admiral Taylor and others in the Navy Department watched for trends in the hope that they would have enough time to react.

$\sim$

The Naval War College in Newport, Rhode Island, had, since 1887, promoted an annual series of war games to test current theory and practice. Although mostly played out in a landlocked laboratory, these games, during the first decade of the twentieth century, were beginning to show gaps in the navy's abilities vis-à-vis the emerging navies of the other great powers. When the war-gaming scenarios were translated to actual fleet exercises, it was apparent that the US Navy lacked the ability to track enemy fleets in bad weather, could not concentrate its forces to eliminate an enemy's battle fleet, and was ineffective in combating commerce raiding at sea. It began to dawn on the navy that there was a role for a battle cruiser in its order of battle.

Royal Navy experience at sea in 1914 and 1915 finally convinced US Navy planners that a new approach was necessary. During the December 8, 1914, Battle of the Falkland Islands, the British battle cruisers *Invincible* and *Inflexible*, along with three armored cruisers and two light cruisers, obliter-ated a German armored cruiser squadron, including *Scharnhorst*, *Gneisenau*, two other light cruisers, and two auxiliaries.

Less than two months later, on January 24, 1915, another similar action took place off Dogger Bank in the North Sea. This time, it was a more evenly matched affair of battle cruisers versus battle cruisers. The Royal Navy, intercepting a secret German navy signal, jumped a German squadron, which immediately broke away and tried to head to port. The faster British battle cruisers *Lion*, *Tiger*, *Indomitable*, *New Zealand*, and *Princess Royal* took on the German cruisers *Blücher*, *Seydlitz*, *Moltke*, and *Derfflinger*. The older, slower *Blücher* got the worst of the British 13.5- and 12-inch hammer blows;

she turned turtle and sank with the loss of nearly eight hundred sailors. The Germans got some blows in, however, and nearly destroyed *Lion*. The outcome was considered a Royal Navy victory, but in truth, it was a very near thing. Nonetheless, the reputation of the battle cruiser was enhanced yet again.

When the German submarine U-20 torpedoed and sank RMS *Lusitania* on May 7, 1915, drowning 128 Americans, the storm of war finally arrived in the United States. Congress, in June 1916, authorized a massive new construction program for the US Navy, including six new battle cruisers, designated as the *Lexington* class.

Yet, despite initial successes at the Falklands and Dogger Bank, 1916 brought unmitigated disaster to the British battle cruiser squadrons—not all of it caused by enemy action.

At the Battle of Jutland on May 31, 1916, the Royal Navy lost *Invincible*, *Indefatigable*, and *Queen Mary* and almost lost *Lion*. Three battle cruisers blew up, which probably had as much to do with poor ammunition handling and too rapid a rate of gunfire as anything the enemy did. Only a handful of the men in each crew survived. *Lion*, flagship of British Adm. David Beatty, was on fire and in danger of blowing apart herself, and probably would have done so except for the heroic actions of a Royal Marine artillery officer named Maj. Francis Harvey.

Harvey, although mortally wounded, ordered the magazine of *Lion*'s Q turret to be flooded. This action prevented the tons of cordite stored there from detonating. Although he succumbed to his injuries seconds later, his dying act may have saved more than a thousand lives, and it prompted Winston Churchill to later comment: "In the long, rough, glorious history of the Royal Marines there is no name and no deed which in its character and consequences ranks above this."[11]

These shocking losses gave Chief Constructor Taylor pause, though he faced another, more immediate challenge. The German U-boat fleet was wreaking havoc with Allied shipping, and this took first priority for available funds and construction facilities. During the period from early 1917 through the end of the war, the US Navy built and launched dozens of submarines and destroyers, all to combat the U-boat threat.

In late 1917, Taylor once more turned his attention to battle cruisers. The Royal Navy sent Taylor a bright, young constructor, Stanley Goodall. He arrived with a full account of the disastrous experiences suffered by the British Fleet at Jutland and, most fortuitously, a complete set of blueprints for the Royal Navy's most ambitious and exciting new construction project, the battle cruiser HMS *Hood*.

---

11. Stephen Snelling, *VCs of the First World War: The Naval VCs* (Charleston, SC: Sutton Publishing, 2002), 108.

Hood made unfortunate history for her tragic loss in May 1941, when she was blown to bits by the German super-battleship *Bismarck*, yet on her completion in 1918, she was a model of power, speed, and armored construction. Historians have argued whether she was a battle cruiser or a "fast battleship"; nonetheless, several of her then-innovative designs went into the revised plans for the *Lexington* class. Rear Admiral Taylor directed his staff to update their blueprints and add bigger guns, take away some of the armor protection (in favor of speed), add additional torpedo tubes, and beef up the top speed to thirty knots. These changes would ultimately make *Lexingtons* even heavier than the new *South Dakota*–class battleships while mounting the very same sixteen-inch guns. Last, the armor would be sloped—that is, set at angles other than vertical—so that enemy shots would theoretically bounce off the hulls.

With a great deal of anticipation, Taylor submitted the new *Lexington* designs to the General Board of the United States Navy on June 3, 1918. The board, dominated by senior admirals who had risen to command and prominence in the era of the sturdy, plodding, big-gun battleships, declined to approve any of the modifications. The board was also concerned that the new blueprints would set back the much-delayed 1916 Naval Construction Program, already approved and funded. In essence, board members wanted what had already been agreed to, and they wanted to implement the program before a postwar Congress changed its mind. In May 1919, the board directed Chief Constructor Taylor to proceed with the *Lexingtons* as originally planned, with only minor structural modifications.

Taylor had his marching orders, and even if he didn't necessarily agree with them, he was a pragmatic and wise enough officer who knew when to salute and say, "Yes, sir!" The hulls for the original *South Dakota*–class battleships were laid down on March 15, 1920, and construction of the *Lexingtons* began with the proposed USS *Constellation*, CC-2, on August 18 of the same year.

With thousands of workers toiling in a half-dozen shipyards, working on six battle cruisers, the tides shifted once again in late 1921.

History has not been kind to the twenty-ninth president of the United States, Warren G. Harding, but one bit of his legacy attained global significance: the Washington Naval Conference of late 1921 and early 1922. Called by Harding, it involved the United States, Great Britain, France, Italy, China, Japan, Belgium, the Netherlands, and Portugal. The focus of the conference was the Pacific Basin and East Asia, and the invited countries were those with significant interests in those regions. The conference was held outside the scope of the newly formed League of Nations because the United States had declined to join the body that its previous president had worked himself to death to achieve.

The conference was motivated by the horrors of the Great War and the hope that squabbles over territories and natural resources in the Pacific arena could be precluded. The organizers believed that one way to avoid trouble would be to forego the arms race that would be necessary to dominate that part of the world. There were also practical motivators, such as saving taxpayer money and capitalizing politically (at least for Harding) on a general desire for peace.

Over three months of negotiations, the attendees came to a general agreement. Yet the conference, engineered by the United States, was a subterfuge. The United States had broken the diplomatic codes used by the Imperial Japanese delegates, and the US secretary of state, the brilliant Charles Evans Hughes, knew what the Japanese minimum and maximum positions would be on any aspect of the treaty. Since the key nation-players at the conference were Britain (already siding with the United States) and Japan, this gave Hughes a tremendous advantage. The end result was a sweeping agreement to limit an arms buildup that would give any of the signatories naval advantage in the region. The pact, when signed in February 1922, essentially preserved the peace in that part of the world until Japan broke the agreement in 1936.

The Navy Department greeted the treaty with profound dismay: there would be a ten-year maximum limit on tonnage for battleships, 525,000 tons each for the United States and Britain and 315,000 tons for Japan. To meet those limits, fifteen current battleships would be decommissioned and scrapped. This provision caused more than one wag to comment that the Washington Conference sank more battleships than all previous wars combined. The entire *South Dakota* class of battleships would be abandoned along with all the *Lexington*-class battle cruisers. Several of the battleships were already more than one-third completed. Of the battle cruisers, only the hulls *Lexington* and *Saratoga* were more than one-quarter completed. The navy would be left with eighteen capital ships, all dreadnought-type battleships, most of which would form the core of the battleships the Japanese attacked at Pearl Harbor. The US Navy could not, under the Washington Treaty, build any additional capital ships except as replacements for hulls that had been decommissioned and scrapped. It was a devastating blow for Chief Constructor Taylor, the commanders of the various fleet commands, and even the stodgy old General Board.

There was one small silver lining, however: an allocation of tonnage for "aircraft carriers" was added to the general tonnage restrictions. The aircraft carrier was, at the time, a new concept, but the Royal Navy had laid down the first ever keel-up, purpose-built aircraft carrier in 1918, the HMS *Hermes*, followed quickly by the Imperial Japanese Navy's *Hōshō*, or

"Phoenix in Flight."[12] At the time of the conference, the US Navy was experimenting with its first aircraft carrier, USS *Langley*, CV-1, a converted coaling ship with a remodeled flattop deck. If the Japanese and British were building aircraft carriers, then the United States wanted to keep pace with these developments.

Under the terms of the treaty, the United States and Britain would be allowed 135,000 tons for aircraft carrier hulls and the Japanese 81,000 tons, with no single aircraft carrier hull going over 27,000 tons.[13] This would allow the US Navy to build five 27,000-ton carriers.

Chief Constructor Taylor, with two battle cruisers already one-third complete, was in favor of converting something he already had in hand rather than starting from scratch. However, both the *Lexington* and *Saratoga* hulls were designed to weigh out at 43,000-plus tons. He could surely eliminate the massive sixteen-inch guns called for in the original plans, as well as some of the armor plating, but the lightened hulls would still top the 27,000-ton limit.

Enter Assistant Secretary of the Navy Theodore Roosevelt Jr. Young Teddy was able to finagle a modification to the treaty that would allow each of the five big navies to convert two existing hulls to 33,000-ton aircraft carriers. Even this added weight would not accommodate a powerplant capable of creating a sustained thirty knots, which was the desired benchmark. Teddy pressed a little harder and got Chapter 11, Part 3, Section 1, Article D modified to allow the weight of the aircraft carriers to include, without penalty, 3,000 additional tons per ship for torpedo blisters and "anti-air attack deck protection." This addendum would allow the two hulls enough tonnage to fit all the desired specs—and still fit through the Panama Canal.

~

Another knock on the door frame. The master chief had returned carrying a tray holding a steaming mug of coffee, sugar, milk, and a sterling silver spoon.

"Ah, thank you, Master Chief. Just what I need."

"Anything else I can do for you, sir?"

Taylor stirred his coffee, staring at the picture in his hand. "Yes, please have my aide step in. I'll need him to deliver this immediately."

The master chief disappeared again.

One particular face in the photo had caught Taylor's eye—the third admiral, standing in the background, wearing a slight smile. *Ah, Bill*

12. The *Hōshō* was actually completed ahead of the *Hermes*, thus claiming the title of the first keel-up designed and commissioned aircraft carrier.

Moffett, you sly dog. Your day is dawning. It looks like everything you predicted is coming to pass.

Rear Admiral William A. Moffett was first chief of the navy's newly formed Bureau of Aeronautics. He was junior to Taylor by five years and a graduate of the Naval Academy, Class of 1890. Although a blue-water sailor for a quarter century, Moffett had lately become entranced with the power and possibilities of naval aviation. He had established the first naval aviator training program when commander of the Great Lakes Naval Training Center during World War I. From 1918 to 1921, he was commanding officer of the battleship USS *Mississippi*, and while in that post he established a scout plane unit that could operate from the ship. *Mississippi* had launched some of the navy's first seagoing aircraft from catapults affixed to the top of one of her large gun turrets.

By the time Moffett had decided naval aviation was his passion, he was too old to qualify for flight training. He did, however, undergo Naval Aviation Observer training in 1921 and was awarded the silver wings for that designation. His longstanding personal friendship with Franklin D. Roosevelt, assistant secretary of the navy from 1913 to 1920, helped him secure the top position in the new Bureau of Aeronautics in 1921. The posting came with the temporary rank of rear admiral, made permanent by Congress in 1923.

Taylor flipped the photograph over, picked up a pen, and authorized its release. As he slid the picture back into its envelope, he gazed at the tableau one more time. How fitting, he thought wistfully, that he and Robison, representing the navy of yesterday, were holding the model of the old *Lexington* battle cruiser while Moffett waited in the background to take their places.

~

For the employees of the Bethlehem Steel Corporation's shipbuilding works in Quincy, the July 4 fireworks of 1922 would have an extra glow. Many of them had been diligently at work laying down the keel, strakes, and bulwarks of CC-1, the battle cruiser USS *Lexington*. They had started work in January 1921, and they were nearly a quarter complete when, in February 1922, construction was officially suspended. Hundreds faced layoffs, not only in Quincy but at the shipyards in Newport News, Camden, and Philadelphia, where the other five battle cruisers were in various stages of completion. Thankfully, two of the hulls had been saved and the crews at Fore River received the happy news on July 1 that their project would move forward.

Chief Constructor Taylor and his staff had a choice between modifying the battle cruiser designs and turning them into carriers or starting from scratch. Plans for a new type of carrier had been approved, and the cost for these new designs was not much higher than the cost of converting the half-finished battle cruisers. There was one important difference that was the determining factor. New carriers would be limited to 27,000 gross tons per hull, but conversion of any two hulls already under construction could go as high as 36,000 tons. More tonnage meant more aircraft, larger propulsion systems, and a longer flight deck. The navy, believing that bigger was better, opted for conversion: *Lexington* and her sister ship, USS *Saratoga* (CV-3), already 20 percent complete in the Camden, New Jersey, shipyard, would be reconfigured and move forward.

There were pluses and minuses involved in the conversion from battle cruiser to flattop. On the positive side, conversion would afford the ship better anti-torpedo protection. The original hull incorporated six medium steel protective bulkheads from three-eighths to three-quarters inch thick with cushioning spaces between. The redesign added torpedo blisters to that configuration.[14]

Since *Lexington* had originally been slated to carry massive sixteen-inch guns, there was plenty of space within the hull concept for big magazines to handle large amounts of the munitions that would be needed for her aircraft.

The long hull would offer: (a) enough room for two elevators, which would be used to get aircraft to and from the hangar deck; (b) more flight-deck space for parking and maneuvering aircraft; and (c) excellent runway space for the current aircraft designs. (There were no integrated aircraft catapults: early carrier aircraft could easily take off and land within the available deck space.)

On the negative side, due to the original slender cruiser design, the flight deck was pinched at the stern end, making the landing area narrower than the pilots would have liked. The narrow beam also cramped the available hangar space.

The propulsion system was massive for its day and consisted of sixteen boiler rooms that produced enough steam to power eight 22,500-horsepower electric motors. The turboelectric motors, in turn, drove four propeller shafts that propelled *Lexington* ahead at thirty-three-plus knots.[15] The powerplant had a unique feature: the reduction gear system allowed the electric motors to be reversed. *Lexington* could go almost as fast backward as it could forward. In at least one instance during her brief wartime

---

14. Torpedo blister: essentially, a lateral compartment at the waterline level that is isolated from the ship's internal volume. It is partly air filled and partly free flooding. In theory, a torpedo strike will rupture and flood the outer, air-filled component of the bulge and the inner, water-filled part will dissipate the shock and absorb explosive fragments, leaving the ship's main hull structurally intact. Transverse bulkheads within the bulge limit flooding throughout the entirety of the structure.

career, this ability saved a number of valuable aircraft from going into the drink.

The conversion design created armament quandaries as well. The Naval Board had not yet warmed up to the viability of the airplane as a weapons system capable of defending its own "nest." As a consequence, the senior admirals insisted that *Lexington* and *Saratoga* mount four batteries of twin eight-inch guns, two turrets afore and two aft of the ship's island super-structure. This was a concession to the big-gun navy thinking that still dominated the fleet.

Four big-gun batteries and an island superstructure added many tons to one side (starboard) of the ship, of course, and to compensate for their placement an offsetting weight was required on the opposite (port) side. The necessary ballast would be provided by the ship's fuel tanks, located near the portside boiler rooms. *Lexington* could bunker almost 6,800 tons of fuel oil, but only 5,500 tons of it was usable without dangerously offsetting the port/starboard weight and balance.

Most unfortunate of all the design compromises was, in fact, the place-ment of the ship's fuel and aviation gas tanks. In the original battle cruiser plans, there had been no need for aviation tanks, but once *Lexington* was repurposed, accommodation for tons of "av gas" had to be made. The tanks would have to be retrofitted into the shape of the hull, as it was already built. It was decided to place them on the port side, with the other internal fuel tanks, and vertically align them; that is, they would be filled from the top with gasoline and ballasted from the bottom with seawater. Since gasoline was lighter than water, the fuel would always float on top of the tank. As fuel was siphoned from the top, seawater, representing compensating weight, would flow in from the bottom.

This system worked beautifully for many years, until the fatal flaw in this design finally manifested itself at the Battle of the Coral Sea. The avia-tion gas tanks were mounted against the hull and held in place with sturdy brackets, but the attachments could not stand up to the pounding they would take when Japanese Long Lance torpedoes smashed into *Lexington*'s port side on May 8, 1942. Brackets failed, tanks cracked, and lethal gasoline vapors began to seep out, waiting for a spark.

On July 1, 1922, new orders signed in Washington, DC, were forwarded to the shipyard manager at Fore River to take the tarps off of *Lexington*. Her designation was officially changed from CC-1 to CV-2. Within days, the clang of hammers on steel and the electric crack of welding torches would reverberate across the reanimated giant.

---

15. As it turned out, during *Lexington's* sea trials, she achieved a speed of 34.6 knots, beating all the expectations.

JULY 1922–DECEMBER 14, 1927

FORE RIVER SHIPYARD

From the perspective of today's fast-paced lifestyles, the construction of *Lexington* seems agonizingly slow. From the restart date in July 1922, it took until October 3, 1925, to get her hull into the water. Even then, she was far from completed. The island superstructure, guns, elevators, and much of the internal finishing work had yet to be completed. On December 14, 1927, her official commissioning flags were finally hoisted. The elaborate ceremony, held at the Fore River Shipyard, attracted more than twenty thousand curious spectators and guests.

In truth, the schedule of her completion was quite remarkable. No ship like her had ever been built before in the United States. Just as today's super-carriers are outfitted with the latest technologies, Lady Lex was state of the art. Even today, aircraft carriers take about as much time to go from concept to commissioning. For example, CVN-77, USS *G. H. W. Bush*, was ordered on January 26, 2001, laid down on September 6, 2003, launched on October 6, 2006, and commissioned on January 10, 2009.

Lexington's first commanding officer was Capt. Albert Ware Marshall, a graduate of the Naval Academy, Class of 1896, who had spent most of his career afloat. In World War I, as commanding officer of USS *Baltimore*, a thirty-year-old cruiser that had sailed into Manila Bay with Admiral Dewey, Marshall and his crew were sent to the North Channel off northern Ireland to lay a deep mine field. The nine hundred mines that *Baltimore* set out were meant to deter the horrendous losses the Allies endured at the hands of German U-boats. It was dangerous and demanding work, and Marshall and his crew handled it flawlessly. For this service, Marshall was awarded the Navy Distinguished Service Medal.[16]

Marshall, like Admiral Moffett, was an early supporter of naval aviation. Men like Marshall were eager for senior positions in a postwar navy that would be shrinking in terms of ships and important commands. Aviation was "the coming thing" and it would likely open up additional command slots. Marshall became a naval aviation observer in 1925 and received his pilot's wings, as Naval Aviator No. 3300, in 1926. As a senior captain, experienced ship commander, aviator, and war hero, he would be in the front ranks for any important aviation assignments that might become available; thus, in 1927, he acceded to the captain's chair aboard *Lexington*.

Albert Marshall was the first of ten commanding officers who would take the helm of the Lady Lex. Remarkably, all ten of these captains would attain the rank of rear admiral. One commanding officer, Ernest J. King,

16. The DSM actually ranked higher in the Pyramid of Honor than the Navy Cross until 1942, when their precedence was reversed.

would rise to the top of the naval pyramid. Command of *Lexington* would become an almost guaranteed pathway to flag rank, and Captain Marshall would set the standard.[17]

Taking an aircraft carrier, especially the first of its kind,[18] from commissioning to active service in the fleet would require a great deal of discipline, tolerance, patience, and hard work. It would also demand a certain touch with public relations. In January 1928, Captain Marshall received aboard *Lexington* a large delegation of citizens from the town of Lexington, Massachusetts. The good folks of Lexington had pitched in and bought Lady Lex her traditional silver service,[19] slated to adorn the senior officer's wardroom, captain's table, and admiral's quarters.

JANUARY 5, 1928
EN ROUTE FROM FORE RIVER TO SOUTH BOSTON
Lexington proceeded down the Fore River, all ahead slow. It would be a short sail, less than ten nautical miles, from her "birth" place to the Navy Yard Annex in Charlestown.

It was a blustery day, with wind chills near the freezing mark. Even at her languid pace, there was more than enough headwind to launch the one airplane on her flight deck, a Vought UO-1 scout, flown by Lt. Alfred M. "Mel" Pride, USN. As Pride gunned his radial engine, the twenty-two-foot-long biplane rolled smoothly down the teak deck and floated into the air less than 100 feet from where the plane had been tethered, just aft of the forward elevator. It was the first takeoff from the deck of *Lexington*.[20]

Over the next fourteen years, thousands of naval aviators would conduct tens of thousands of takeoffs and landings from the same flattop deck. Unlike modern carriers, the flight-deck surface was wooden, a holdover from earlier days when the decks of navy ships were made of wood. Teak, which held up well in the marine environment, was preferred, and in the early twentieth century it was not yet an endangered hardwood. A second reason was to save weight. Although the teak on *Lexington* was laid over steel, the flattop deck was not a "hard," or structural, deck. The flight deck was, at that time, considered part of the superstructure and was not, therefore, as thick or as heavy as the main deck. *Lexington*'s main deck, and its first structural deck, was in fact the hangar deck. As the new *Lexington* set sail for the first time, her flight deck was a solid teak, painted in a reddish mahogany.

17. Command of an aircraft carrier today is still an almost automatic ticket to promotion to flag rank.
18. USS *Saratoga*, CV-3, *Lexington*'s sister ship, technically beat *Lexington* into commissioned service by a few weeks, but *Lexington* was the first to complete her post-commissioning trials and join the fleet.
19. Coffee urns, accompanying servers, assorted trays, and sterling silver.
20. Lieutenant Pride went on to become a four-star admiral, World War II hero, and commander of the Seventh Fleet. He died in 1988 at age ninety-one.

There were no integral aircraft catapults, either.[21] The aircraft that *Lexington* would initially carry were very light and capable of becoming airborne after very short takeoffs. Even armed with a heavy torpedo, or a thousand-pound bomb, the warfighting machines of the late 1920s and early 1930s could become airborne in a couple hundred feet, especially with a good twenty- to thirty-knot headwind over the deck.

Getting back aboard *Lexington* would require a pilot to catch one of four transverse arresting wires stretched across the aft section of the flight deck with the tailhook attached to the aircraft.[22] To prevent aircraft from sliding over the sides of the ship, *Lexington* was also equipped, in those early days, with longitudinal wires placed down the sides of the flight deck. (The longitudinal wires were gone by 1931 and the original electrical transverse system was replaced by a stronger and more reliable hydraulic system the same year.)

Her initial aircraft inventory was seventy-eight: the split was roughly eighteen aircraft in each of four squadrons. There was a bombing squadron and a scouting squadron (both using the same type aircraft), a torpedo squadron, and a fighter squadron. In addition, there might be a half dozen of other types of planes, such as observation, utility, or seaplanes. Later, the navy learned it could cram more aircraft aboard by winching spares to the ceiling of the hangar deck. By 1936, *Lexington* was carrying seventy-nine frontline aircraft and thirty spares.

Captain Marshall, bundled in his long, navy-blue greatcoat, strode from one side of the bridge to the other. The powerplant and all systems were performing just as they should. Several steam tugs shadowed the Lady Lex as she wound her way down the river, past the Washington Street swing bridge and out into Boston Harbor. The faint smell of brass polish, new paint, and fuel oil stirred the sailors' blood. The great ship was finally free of her builder's chains. Her flight deck stretched ahead of the bridge for another 350 feet, her bow nosed forcefully into the future.

She is a queen, indeed, Marshall mused, *the first queen of the flattops.*

Those first three months of 1928 were extraordinarily busy for *Lexington*. After that first short voyage, she went into dry dock for her final fitting-out and to have her first marine growth scraped from her hull. While at the Boston Navy Yard Annex, Captain Marshall and his crew received the startling news that they were being transferred to the Pacific. Originally, *Lexington* had been slated to become the flagship of the Atlantic Scouting Fleet. The Navy Department changed its mind,

---

21. *Lexington* and *Saratoga* were both equipped with a 155-foot flywheel catapult on the starboard side of the bow. This launcher was intended to fling seaplanes into the air but was hardly ever employed; in fact, by 1931, only five launches with this catapult had been attempted. It was ultimately removed in the upgrade to the ship performed in 1936.
22. Four more transverse wires, to make a total of eight, were added in 1934.

however, and issued orders for her to join the Pacific Battle Fleet, stationed at Long Beach, California. Instead of scanning charts of Newport Harbor, Captain Marshall was wondering if his new ship could squeeze through the Panama Canal.

CHAPTER 2

FLEET PROBLEMS
AND OTHER ADVENTURES
THE 1930s

FROM THE END of the Great War until the attack on Pearl Harbor, the US Navy enjoyed nearly twenty-three years of peace on the high seas. A lack of combat presents a problem for a standing navy in terms of keeping its forces both sharp and gainfully employed, and beginning in 1923, the navy decided to do something about these peacetime challenges.

The Naval War College had been conducting war games to train its senior officers since its establishment in 1884, but the games were held mostly on paper or in the theoretical confines of the college itself. Naval instructors wanted to take the games to sea and test the actual responses of the various operating commands. The Fleet Problems, as they were dubbed, used actual assets minus real bullets.

The Fleet Problems were usually held in the winter months or in the warmer, ice-free climates of the Caribbean, the Panama Canal Zone, or Hawaiian waters. There were exceptions: Problems XVI and XVIII took place partly in Alaska, and Problem XX was held in the Atlantic and the Caribbean. The "opponents" were almost always the Scouting Fleet, based in the Atlantic, and the Battle Fleet, from the Pacific.[23] Each force alternated from year to year in assuming the role of the defender or the aggressor.

In Fleet Problem I (1923), aviation, as a new technology, played only a small part. The sole aircraft carrier the navy possessed in the early Fleet Problem era was CV-1, USS *Langley*, and she was not ready to participate in the first exercise; instead, the battleships *Oklahoma* and *New*

---

23. The navy had been reorganized in 1922 into two basic fleets. The Scouting Fleet represented the Atlantic and consisted mostly of the older battleships. The Battle Fleet was stationed in the Pacific and comprised the newer battleships and the aircraft carriers.

York were given the roles of "constructive carriers." Each of these battleships was allotted a solitary seaplane, and each plane was to represent an entire carrier air wing—which surely had to stretch the imaginations of the umpires assigned to moderate the exercise.

USS *Langley* finally got involved directly in Fleet Problem II, but only as an observer. The few planes *Langley* carried (sixteen) were used to take photographs and simulate torpedo runs, but the overall impression left on the "Gun Club" admirals[24] was reportedly minimal. Poor *Langley* was barely even mentioned in the post-action reports. Another challenge for the former coal ship turned flattop was that she could make only sixteen knots on a good day, and as a result she could not keep up with even the oldest battleships. Until *Lexington* and *Saratoga* were able to join up for Fleet Problem IX in 1929, the role of the aircraft carrier in the exercises was generally undistinguished.

What follows is a very brief discussion of the participation of *Lexington* in those Fleet Problems that ended up having the greatest bearing on the development of naval aviation and carrier tactics. Due to the constant tension between the members of the Gun Club—who tended to be the older, most senior, and most influential officers—and those who were of the newer generation, the role of naval aviation during the Fleet Problems waxed and waned, depending on who was in charge. Nonetheless, several Fleet Problems were seminal to the evolution of carrier airpower.[25]

1218, JANUARY 25, 1929
FLEET PROBLEM IX, OFF THE COAST OF PANAMA

Captain Frank Berrien, the Blue Fleet ship *Lexington*'s second CO, was furious. The carrier had just emerged from a squall line and found herself right under the guns of the battleships of the Black Fleet. The on-board umpire ruled *Lexington* as "sunk" less than five minutes later. Berrien called for the ship's navigator, and not in pleasant tones.

A careful look at the plot and a review of the message traffic from the Blue ships shadowing the Black battleships showed clearly that *Lexington* had received bad information. The Black forces were actually seventeen nautical miles closer than *Lexington* believed. Even the twelve-knot speed advantage *Lexington* enjoyed over the older battle wagons could not get her out of range of their fourteen-inch guns before mock half-ton shells began raining down on her.

---

24. Those officers of the navy who favored battleships and surface warfare over aviation were dubbed members of the "Gun Club." Aviators were derisively called "Flyboys" or "Brown Shoes," due to the fact that flying boots were generally crafted out of brown leather.
25. For a complete and thorough discussion of the Fleet Problems, the reader is referred to the excellent book by Dr. Albert A. Nofi, sponsored by the Naval War College, titled *To Train the Fleet for War: The US Navy Fleet Problems, 1923–1940* (see bibliography).

The Blue Fleet's only aircraft carrier, assigned to help protect the Panama Canal from aerial attack, was out of the game. Or was she? Since the navigational error had not been *Lexington*'s fault, the umpires ruled that she could continue to sortie her planes, but her speed could not exceed eighteen knots. Captain Berrien and his crew had a new life.

Lexington's sister ship, USS *Saratoga*, was faring better—brilliantly, in fact. What "Sara" did, combined with the lessons learned by *Lexington* and her pilots in this Fleet Problem, would have a profound impact on the future of naval aviation.

While *Lexington* was dealing with the bit of bad luck she had been handed, *Saratoga* Capt. John Halligan Jr.,[26] in command, was racing toward the Panama Canal from the south. Also aboard Sara was Rear Adm. Joseph M. "Bull" Reeves.

Reeves was a hard-charging risk-taker who had earned his nickname fair and square. He had fought in the Spanish-American War and in World War I and had made a reputation as an aggressive cruiser and battleship commander. He had earned the Navy Cross in World War I as CO of the battleship USS *Maine*. In a bit of aviation irony, he had also been CO of USS *Jupiter*, the navy's first electrically propelled vessel (like *Saratoga* and *Lexington*) before it was converted into USS *Langley*.

Reeves was a rising star in the navy after the Great War and attended the Naval War College from 1923 to 1924. While at Newport, he became intrigued with the potential of naval aviation and requested a transfer to that branch. Like others of his era deemed too senior for pilot training, he qualified as a naval aviation observer in 1925 and was assigned as commander, Aircraft Squadrons, Battle Fleet.

Commodore Reeves spent 1925 through 1929 developing and putting into practice everything the navy was learning about naval aviation. He pioneered dive-bombing tactics, basic aviation sortie patterns from flight decks, the use of aircraft in scouting roles, and more. Fleet Problem IX gave Reeves his first chance to throw everything the navy had learned about the use of aircraft at sea into full practice.

In a move that would be debated for years, and ballyhooed in the popular press for months, Reeves boldly split *Saratoga* away from the main Black Fleet forces. Accompanied by a lone cruiser, she sprinted south, away from the exercise area. Reeves's goal was to go dark for as long as possible. Near the Galapagos, he reversed course and charged back, at full speed, directly toward the Panama Canal. Since disappearing, *Saratoga* had attained the status, with the Blue forces, of "out of sight, out of mind."

---

26. Halligan, first in his 1998 USNA class, was promoted to rear admiral in 1930. He was commandant of the 13th Naval District in 1934 when he died of a heart attack, age fifty-four, at Puget Sound.

Yet *Saratoga* did not go completely undetected. The destroyer USS *Breck*, acting as a Blue force scout, discovered *Saratoga* at 1613 on January 25. *Breck* made a recognition error, however, and assumed that *Saratoga* was *Lexington*. Cleverly, Reeves directed Captain Halligan to signal *Breck* to "fall in and take station astern," which *Breck* proceeded to do. As soon as the unsuspecting destroyer drew close enough, *Saratoga* unleashed her big eight-inch guns and blew the destroyer out of the water (to the umpire's satisfaction).

Early the next morning, back in striking distance for his aircraft, Reeves launched every airplane on the ship. By 0458, eighty-three fighters, bombers, and torpedo planes were in the air. It was a complete surprise for the defenders of the Panama Canal, made more embarrassing by the fact that the Blue Fleet commander had not even bothered to send out a single aerial patrol to search for *Saratoga*. The umpires ruled the Pacific end of the canal completely obliterated.

The impact of Fleet Problem IX was huge. Naval historian Thomas Wildenberg cites the following as support:

> Writing many years later, [Cdr.] Eugene E. Wilson, who had been one of Reeves' staff officers in 1929, would rightly state that *Saratoga*'s exploits during Fleet Problem IX marked "the first step in the development of the Carrier Task Forces which were so effective in the Pacific." This operation convinced naval aviators—and some surface warriors—that task forces built around carriers would be of importance in the future of naval warfare. . . . The most important conclusion drawn from the *Saratoga*'s raid was the impossibility of stopping a determined air attack once it was launched. Unfortunately, in the years to come, this lesson would be forgotten, by certain members of the so-called Gun Club—the battleship men who were unwavering in their faith in the supremacy of the big gun. Their preoccupation with refighting the Battle of Jutland instead of ensuring the security of the fleet contributed greatly to the disaster at Pearl Harbor. Evident to Reeves and to the carrier commanders who followed in his footsteps, was the reality that in any future engagement involving aircraft carriers at sea, the first carrier to locate and bomb the other would determine the outcome.

27. Wildenberg, 153.

DECEMBER 12, 1929

PUGET SOUND NAVAL SHIPYARD

"Enter!" Captain Berrien growled after the sharp rap on his day cabin door.

A nervous young radioman, second class, stepped into the captain's office, hat in one hand and a message hot off the radio set in the other.

Berrien looked up. "What is it, Sailor?"

The petty officer stepped forward and thrust the slightly crumpled transcription toward his captain. "This just came off the wire, sir. It's from the secretary of the navy himself!"

Berrien harrumphed, "Let's have it," and took the proffered paper. "Stand easy, son."

"Yes, sir," the radioman exhaled, assuming the at-ease position.

The captain scanned the message quickly. "Damn!" The nervous sailor jumped. "Have the duty chief get the engineer up here quickly! Dismissed."

Saluting, the petty officer ducked out and back into the passageway, racing to find the chief petty officer of the watch.

Ten minutes later, USS *Lexington*'s chief engineer, Lt. Cmdr. H. L. White, knocked on the captain's door. "You wanted to see me, sir?"

"Yes, come on in, Henry. Take a look at this nasty bit of business." Berrien handed White the message he had received minutes before.

White's eyes widened as he read the words, "Sir, he can't be serious!"

"I'm afraid he is. The request comes down from President Hoover himself, and the secretary, though he objected at first, has reluctantly ordered us to give it a try."

"When? And for how long?"

"Immediately and for however long it takes."

"Good lord!"

"Well, I suppose we might have brought some of this on ourselves. We've been bragging about these marvelous turboelectric engines for months. The press obviously got onto this and, well, here we are."

"I'm not even sure we can do this . . . it might fry the circuits . . . it might blow the powerplant. It could overstress the boilers. . . ."

"All we can do is give it a go, Commander. I'll brief the XO. You'd better get busy."

"Yes, sir." A thoroughly perplexed White went off mumbling to himself.

Berrien picked up his ship's phone and punched the button marked CONN. The executive officer, he knew, was up on the navigation bridge conducting a test.

The executive officer was Cmdr. Newton H. White, a pioneering naval aviator with original pilot's card No. 16 (and no relation to Engineer

---

28. White, USNA Class of 1907, was the first CO of USS *Enterprise*, CV-6. He retired as a captain in 1939 and became an insurance executive. He died in 1958.

White).[28] As soon as the XO arrived, he was invited in, Berrien asked him to be seated, and coffee was served.

"We've got a real challenge, XO," the captain sighed heavily.

"What is it, sir?" White inquired anxiously.

"Our fellow citizens, down the coast in Tacoma city, are in a real fix, it seems. The year-long drought has dried up their reservoirs. Tacoma runs on hydroelectric power, if you didn't know."

"I did not."

"The water levels are too low, it seems, to run their powerplants. The city is plunging into darkness. So is the army base at Fort Lewis. They want us to help."

"How, Captain? Disaster relief? Supplies?"

"Well, no. Power."

"Power? What power?"

"Our power. We are, after all, a floating, steam-driven powerplant. The city has made a plea, through the president, and the secretary of the navy, to borrow our turbines. They want to hook them up to the city's power supply and generate electricity."

White let out a long, low whistle. "Can we even do that?"

"I guess we're going to find out. Make preparations to get underway. We're steaming to Tacoma."

USS *Lexington* left Puget Sound and sailed the forty miles south to Tacoma, arriving on December 16, 1929. The next day she tied up alongside Baker Dock, the only Tacoma pier that could accommodate the 888-foot-long ship. In anticipation of *Lexington*'s arrival, the engineers and utility workers at Tacoma Power & Light had strung two miles of high-tension wires from their beleaguered powerplant to the quayside.

Chief Engineer White, his crewmen, and the civilian electrical workers jury-rigged a distribution platform with electrical connectors. They hooked it up to *Lexington*'s No. 4 main motor. There was one last worry plaguing Lieutenant Commander White—city power ran at sixty cycles. To equal that frequency, *Lexington*'s generator would have to run forty-five rotations per minute higher than its rated capacity. Fingers crossed, White threw the switch. As the additional revolutions were slowly applied, the wires hummed and the load held steady.

Within days after *Lexington* tied up at Baker Dock, the skies reopened. Rain poured down for weeks. By mid-January, the local cache basins and reservoirs were full once again and *Lexington* could pull the plug. During the thirty days *Lexington* was tied to Tacoma's electrical system, the ship supplied more than one-quarter of all the power needed by the city. The No. 4 motor generated 4,250,000 kilowatt hours. The city had agreed to pay the navy for its troubles, and the disbursing officer at Puget Sound was able to collect a tidy profit for the *Lexington*'s repair and maintenance fund. All totaled, it amounted to $59,881.91 in 1930 dollars.

MARCH–APRIL 1930

FLEET PROBLEMS X AND XI

It was unusual to conduct two massive Fleet Problems in one year, but the navy, in early 1930, with preapproved budget still left over after the stock market crash of 1929, decided to push ahead. Fleet Problem X's scenario pitted the Blue Fleet against the Black in a large exercise in the western Caribbean. *Lexington* was assigned to the Black Fleet, representing the aggressor forces, and *Saratoga* and *Langley* were attached to the Blue.

Neither force commander made any significant disposition in their plans for the use of his carriers as the members of the Gun Club were still in charge and Admiral Reeves was off on another assignment. The admiral leading the Blue Fleet made only one mention of *Lexington* in his operational orders: "When *Lexington* is located, attack *Lexington*." The admiral commanding the Black Fleet was less effusive. His directive for Captain Berrien was to locate *Langley* and *Saratoga* and then "await further orders." These so-called plans were not exactly ringing endorsements for the role of naval aviation.

As it turned out, these minimal orders were interpreted creatively, and the results were significant. *Saratoga* and *Langley* were told to steam as part of the main body of ships in the Blue Fleet. If there was to be a role for them, it would be to launch their planes and attack their opposite number—*Lexington*—after she was located. *Lexington*, on the other hand, was pushed out ahead of the main body of the Black Fleet and placed in a separate carrier group.

Accompanied by several destroyers, *Lexington* would act as a scouting force. Although the Black commander thought he was getting rid of a distraction, it would be the birth of the future carrier battle-group concept. What would become today's standard operating procedure for aircraft carriers grew out of the dispositions made in Fleet Problem X.

Lexington had, in effect, been given the ability to act independently. Once the "enemy" was located, *Lexington*—still enjoying the element of surprise—launched a preemptive strike against her opponents, "sinking" both carriers. She also used her freedom of movement and a speedy propulsion system to get away from the scene faster than she could be pursued.

The commander in chief of the US Fleet, Adm. William V. Pratt, wrote:

> A fast group, composed as this one was [*Lexington* and her destroyer screen], has all the elements for conducting a wide search; speed, if necessary, to retire

before superior strength; and the weapons [aircraft] to inflict a very serious blow on any suitable objects found—enemy carriers or battleships. . . . The aggressive use of aircraft to gain superiority over the enemy prior to the main engagement appears sound, provided one's own security is not entirely neglected. Aircraft carriers engaged in such operations are less likely to be located by the enemy than if they are tied to a cruising disposition with a more or less passive task of waiting to defend the fleet when it is attacked.[29]

All in all, Captain Berrien and his crew had a lot more to be proud of after this Fleet Problem than from their previous experiences in Fleet Problem IX. They did not have time to rest on their laurels, though, because Fleet Problem XI was looming.

This time, the Blue and Black fleets would be competing for domination of the Caribbean and South America. The exercise assumed a war had been underway for several months between the United States, allied with Central America and the larger, northern Caribbean islands, and the southern Caribbean nations in league with South America. A two-week armistice had allowed the various forces to scatter their assets across the Caribbean. *Lexington* started the exercise in St. Thomas; *Saratoga* was in Barbados; and *Langley* was in port at Trinidad.

At 0800 on April 14, 1930, all ships sortied from wherever they were anchored and headed for Jamaica, where the scenario would be played out. Various games of cat and mouse occurred over the next several days with no major engagements. As in Fleet Problem X, *Lexington* was placed in a separate carrier/scouting group, but this time she was with cruisers in addition to destroyers.

On the morning of April 17, *Lexington* had scout planes aloft, looking for the Black Fleet, *Saratoga* in particular. They did not find her but did uncover two of the Black Fleet's three submarines, "sinking" one and thus proving another useful aspect of carrier maritime patrol. During the same morning, *Saratoga* intercepted radio traffic from *Lexington* and was able to triangulate enough bearing information to launch two attacks. Unfortunately, *Lexington* did not have a fighter patrol in the air. After some discussion, the chief umpire awarded a twenty-four-hour penalty to *Lexington*, effectively granting air superiority to the Black Fleet for the remainder of the exercise.

Although Fleet Problems X and XI were not initially focused on the challenges and opportunities provided by the employment of aircraft carriers (especially in a battle group), the exercises ended up focusing squarely on exactly that. It was almost as if, by their very nature, these

---

29. Report of the Commander in Chief, reel 13, 37.

ships and their aircraft became magnets of unpredictability and power. The after-action report stated that there were interesting opportunities that might "lie ahead" in the employment of carrier battle groups:

> [T]he possibilities lie before us in the employment of this group in distant operations for information; in exercising partial control of the sea before complete control is established; in tactical scouting; in whittling down the enemy's strength; and possibly in other ways we do not now visualize. This question is of the highest importance for study and exercise in the Fleet.[30]

FEBRUARY 1931

FLEET PROBLEM XII

Lexington's next skipper, Capt. Ernest J. King, got to participate in the two Fleet Problems that were arguably the most crucial in terms of prewar carrier aviation (XII and XIII). One was a near disaster for King and *Lexington*, the other a triumph, and both influenced King as a future chief of naval operations (CNO) and leader of the Allied Forces in the coming war.

In Fleet Problem XII, which began on February 16, 1931, the Blue Fleet was defending the Panama Canal and a hypothetical second Nicaraguan Canal from the aggressor Black Fleet. In this challenge, however, a complicating factor—a third fleet, the Brown—entered the mix. Brown Fleet was the naval force of a European nation whose allegiance was unknown at the start of the exercise and up for grabs by either Blue or Black, depending on the circumstances.

Blue Fleet had both *Lexington* and *Saratoga* along with zeppelin *Los Angeles*, seaplane tender USS *Wright*, battleship *Arkansas*, and several cruisers and destroyers. The Black Fleet had *Langley*, which would be its only air support. Due to the makeup of the opposing forces, the national press, which in the 1930s followed these exercises much like it does football playoffs today, were already dubbing these the "battleship versus aircraft carrier" exercises. The navy didn't use the same dramatic terms, but it was no secret that part of the exercise was to see how a head-to-head confrontation would shake out. The Brown Fleet was a paper fleet only, to be used by the umpires as they saw fit.

At the beginning of the exercise, Admiral Reeves, who was back from his detached duty and in charge of the Blue carrier division, divided his forces, sending *Lexington* south to guard the Panama Canal and keeping *Saratoga* in the north to patrol the approaches to the Nicaraguan Canal. Reeves anticipated that the Black admiral would use one of Reeves's old

30. Report of the Commander in Chief, reel 13, 63.

tricks against him as in Fleet Problem IX, when Reeves had sent *Saratoga* on a feint and then turned her around to bomb the Panama Canal. Reeves sent King and *Lexington* speeding off to the Galapagos area to make sure there were no Black forces lurking at his back. He need not have worried.

The Black forces relied on the power of their battleships. They spilt themselves into two nearly equal squadrons and charged east. The two divisions would each attack one canal and their defenders head-on. The northern Blue force, with *Saratoga*, sailed west in search of its opponents. Without the benefit of shipboard radar, which would not be available for another decade, the force overshot its objective and the Black northern division, undetected, got in behind the Blue. Reeves finally figured out the situation, using radio intercepts and scout planes, and turned his fleet around, but *Saratoga* was forced to play catch-up.

Meanwhile, down in the south, seaplanes from *Wright* discovered the advancing Black southern division as they charged toward the Panama Canal. Airship *Los Angeles* also scouted and reported Black's position to King on *Lexington* before being "shot down." King, sailing at nearly flank speed, finally got into range of the Black Fleet and launched his scout bombers and torpedo planes. However, the *Los Angeles* position report was off by thirty-five miles and several degrees of bearing. Since *Los Angeles* was then "dead," she could not correct her mistake. The *Lexington* pilots figured it out, corrected their strike vectors, and made their attacks. They bore down on *Langley* and took her out of the problem.

The navigational error made by the airship then presented another challenge—the speedier and more fuel-efficient scout bombers could get back to *Lexington* safely in the remaining daylight. The slower, thirstier torpedo bombers could not. By the time the torpedo planes arrived back at *Lexington*'s position, it was dark. Captain King ordered every light on *Lexington* illuminated so the pilots could see the ship. Thus, some of the very first night carrier landings were recorded and every one of the pilots made it back safely.

To the north, *Saratoga* and her Blue mates steamed through the night to close the gap between themselves and the aggressor Black Fleet. They were too late. By the time they arrived the next morning, the Black forces were already in position. *Saratoga* launched scouts but simultaneously also launched its attacking force of sixty-two planes, hoping the scouts would find the Black Fleet and the attacking force would then be able to swoop in. The scouts failed to locate the Black ships, and the entire launch was forced to return to *Saratoga* and refuel. Finally, on the second try, the scouts located their opponents. But by that hour, most of the damage had been done. The attacks were allowed to go on, however, for training purposes.

The air attacks continued into the next day, but problems with launches and recoveries, mostly due to the inability to coordinate timing between faster and slower aircraft, kept the effectiveness of the air attacks to a minimum. In addition, it was shown clearly that a single carrier, operating without sufficient support ships, was not able to overcome an opposing force of big guns. It seemed that the argument between battleships and carriers was settled, and not in favor of aviation.

Yet despite the errors in navigation, coordination, and allocation of forces, it could no longer be denied that airpower was an ascending factor. The officers in charge of the exercise also understood that they had stacked the deck by allocating all ships of one type to one force rather than parceling them out on a more balanced basis.

USS *Lexington* was still steaming off the coast of Panama, wrapping up training exercises and preparing to return to Long Beach, when a devastating 6.0-magnitude earthquake struck the capital city of Managua, Nicaragua, on March 31, 1931. Thousands of buildings toppled, upwards of five thousand were killed, and fires broke out all over the city.

The United States Marine Corps had maintained a presence in Nicaragua ever since the so-called Banana Wars of 1912. The Managua garrison, with only two navy doctors, was overwhelmed with casualties, both civilian and military. They called for help.

The duty petty officer in communications finished copying down the message and raced off to find the communications duty officer, who was listening to the shortwave in the next compartment.

"You better look at this, sir. Just came in from Op Nav."

Lieutenant Junior Grade Robert A. Heinlein, USNA class of 1929, *Lexington*'s assistant communications officer, took the message and quickly scanned it.

Heinlein had been listening to a broadcast from Mexico City about the earthquake. He initialed the message as required, stuck it on a clipboard, and headed to the bridge, two ladders up.

The young lieutenant knew his captain's prickly demeanor. That was bad enough, but during the ship's last home port call, Heinlein had met one of the captain's six daughters at a navy ball. They had started dating.

"Permission to enter the bridge!" Heinlein announced.

Captain King lowered his binoculars and nodded.

King was tall, much taller than his lieutenant. He looked down his nose and growled, "At ease, lieutenant. What do you have for me, Mr. Heinlein?"

Heinlein's hand shot out, holding the clipboard.

King read the message slowly.

"Get the navigator for me, Mr. Heinlein. And the air boss. We're going to be busy."

"Yes, sir." And with that, Heinlein spun on his heel and left the bridge.[31]

Over the course of the following several days, *Lexington* launched dozens of aircraft, delivering food and medical personnel to the beleaguered city. *Lexington*'s stores, medical supplies, and manpower kept a desperate situation from becoming dire. It was the first time a navy ship of this type was used in disaster relief, setting a precedent that has continued down through the decades since.

MARCH 1932

FLEET PROBLEM XIII, EASTERN PACIFIC

As Captain King's command tour was drawing to a close, he and *Lexington* would participate in Fleet Problem XIII. For this exercise, the air assets would be more equitably divided, as they had been in Fleet Problems IX, X, and XI. Unlike previous war games, the playing field was immense: it covered the eastern Pacific from Lahaina Roads, Hawaii, east to San Diego, north to San Francisco, and beyond to Puget Sound.

Blue, with *Saratoga* at its center, would sortie from Hawaii and attempt to strike a strategic blow on Black, which was defending the West Coast with *Lexington* and *Langley*. As soon as Blue sortied, it was confronted with a screen of five Black submarines, all lying in ambush and tasked with reporting the Blue's movements. Using its aircraft, Blue quickly scouted out and eliminated four of the five submarines, thus providing another early and important lesson on the use of aircraft to counteract submarine forces.

It took only a few days for the opposing forces to find one another, yet neither force could gain a clear advantage. In the remaining days of the exercise, one force would attack the other in rolling, far-ranging battles across the seaways of the eastern Pacific, but the territory was too large for one force to dominate. It proved, however, (a) the viability of carrier airpower to project itself into the combat scenario and (b) the need for more of it.

The majority of the discoveries of opposing ships were made by aircraft, and the damage inflicted was delivered primarily by air. This finding was crucial, for it showed without question that defending US possessions in the Pacific from a determined aggressor (such as Japan) would require six to eight carrier battle groups.

Fleet Problem XIII gave urgency to the need for additional aircraft carriers, but with limited funds and the Great Depression hovering over

---

31. Lieutenant Junior Grade Heinlein was, indeed, the very same Robert Heinlein who went on to become one of the most famous science fiction writers of the twentieth century. After promotion to lieutenant and another tour in destroyers, Heinlein was forced to medically retire in 1934 after contracting tuberculosis. Fortunately, he later recovered.

federal appropriations, these would not arrive quickly. The Hoover administration grudgingly approved funding for only one new carrier: USS *Ranger*,
CV-4, half as heavy as *Lexington*, a hundred feet shorter, five knots slower,
but capable of carrying just as many aircraft (seventy-six to eighty-six). She
would join the fleet in 1934.

APRIL 29–JUNE 10, 1935
FLEET PROBLEM XVI, NORTH CENTRAL PACIFIC OCEAN
Of all the Fleet Problems, XVI was the largest. More than 320 vessels and
upwards of seventy thousand officers and men participated in this six-week
production. Its scope also reflected a higher-profile navy, which the new
president, Franklin Roosevelt, a former assistant secretary of the navy, took
on as a pet project.

Once again, the enemy was the Imperial Japanese Navy, disguised as
Black. The "good guys," White, would sortie from San Diego and San Pedro,
ultimately confronting their enemies at Midway Island. Along the route, various exercises would involve the Aleutian Islands, Hawaii, and the West Coast.
The premise of Fleet Problem XVI was that victory in the Pacific could be
decided by one climactic set-piece naval confrontation.

In Fleet Problem XVI, the navy gained some valuable insights on a
potential war with Japan: First, despite all the resources thrown into the
game, the navy was once again forced to consider the enormity of the Pacific
Ocean and how hard it would be to defend such an expanse. Second, success
would depend on more than two fleet carriers and an aging semi-flattop,
USS *Langley*. Fortunately, the navy had a fourth aircraft carrier to throw
into the mix—USS *Ranger* had completed her sea trials and officially joined
the fleet.

Third, the level of competence of the auxiliaries, primarily the fleet oilers, had reached a point where at-sea refueling could include the aircraft
carriers. The ability to refuel at sea freed the flattops to act as independent
battle forces. This capability was critical.

Finally, the last phases of the exercise involved Pearl Harbor, including a test of the fleet's ability to conduct a mass emergency sortie from
Pearl under combat conditions. This showed the navy that Pearl Harbor
had important limitations in terms of adequate docking and resupply,
deficiencies that would have to be corrected.

NOVEMBER 1936
PUGET SOUND NAVAL SHIPYARD, BREMERTON, WASHINGTON
The stately Lady Lex pulled into the navy's massive Puget Sound works. She
would be tied up there four months while she underwent her most extensive

upgrade. By late 1936, she had completed nearly ten years of active service and was in the midrange of her projected service life. Constant maintenance, right down to the wax on her linoleum passageways, had kept her in tiptop shape. She had never suffered any major mechanical breakdowns and her powerplant had performed beyond expectations. She did have one major deficiency, as far as air operations was concerned, and it was time to correct it.

Starting as a battle cruiser and nearly one-quarter complete by the time of her conversion, she had retained her original tapered bow. In the initial years of her service, this had not presented too many challenges; however, *Lexington*'s flight deck was proving too slim at the bow to accommodate the newer, bigger aircraft. Unique among the ships of their day, *Lexington* and *Saratoga*, with their reversible turboelectric propulsion design, could move almost as fast in reverse as they could forward. This gave the skipper and the air boss the opportunity to launch planes from either end of the ship. With more planes, requiring more runway, it was important to make both ends of the ship capable of launch and recovery. The bow end of the flight deck would be widened and arrestor cables added. This configuration would also allow *Lexington* to continue to conduct flight operations in combat if one end of the flight deck became compromised.

JULY 1937

THE SEARCH FOR AMELIA EARHART

The electrifying news that famed aviatrix Amelia Earhart had gone missing broke on July 4, 1937. Earhart was among the most famous women on the planet, and coverage of her disappearance was widespread.

She and her navigator, Fred Noonan, had been negotiating a particularly risky leg of their round-the-world flight. They were journeying entirely over water, and success depended on Noonan pinpointing tiny Howland Island, 2,556 miles from their last takeoff point, Lae, New Guinea. Clouds, rain squalls, and poor atmospheric conditions for radio transmission dogged them from the outset. The US Coast Guard cutter *Itasca* had been pre-positioned near Howland Island in an effort to help guide the flight by radio.

Earhart's specially built Lockheed Electra had taken off from New Guinea at midnight on July 2. At 0843 (local) the following morning, *Itasca* received the last message that could be confirmed as positively coming from Earhart's ship. It was a voice message that said, simply, "We are running on line north and south." This meant that Earhart and Noonan were flying up and down a bearing line of 157/337, a position they had previously reported. They believed they were over Howland Island. Their last known altitude was 1,000 feet, and they were running low on fuel. *Itasca*, which was very close to Howland Island, never heard or saw the plane. Something was obviously amiss.

An hour after Earhart's last radio transmission, *Itasca* began an immediate search in the vicinity of the island and called for help. The US Navy was contacted by radio at the closest naval base, which happened to be the 14th Naval District Headquarters at Pearl Harbor, 1,898 miles away.

The navy was well aware of Earhart's mission and had been unofficially tasked with assisting. Had Earhart made it to Howland Island, her next objective would have been Hawaii. To help her along the Howland-Honolulu leg, the navy had stationed the aging seaplane tender USS *Swan* (AVP-7) halfway between the two points. As the need for additional search and rescue assets developed, *Swan* was redirected to Howland Island. That would take her two days. Unfortunately, *Swan*, even though a seaplane-support ship, had no aircraft with her at the time. For immediate airborne assistance, the navy dispatched a large flying boat to Howland; but three hundred miles out, the PBY ran into such nasty weather that it was forced to return to base.

Back in Washington, DC, the Navy Department was getting public and private pressure to "do more." The public adored Earhart and wanted to see her saved. Her husband, George Putnam, was a wealthy and well-connected publisher. Although the navy would not normally divert its resources toward a purely civilian matter, Putnam, along with some of his powerful friends in Washington, let it be known they would like assistance. Secretary of the Navy Claude Swanson was against any substantial commitment of navy resources, but his boss, the president, was not; so, the chief of naval operations at the time, Adm. William D. Leahy, dialed up the commander of the 14th Naval District in Hawaii, Adm. Orin G. Murfin, and told him to "make it happen."

There were no aircraft carriers stationed in Hawaii at the time, but the battleship USS *Colorado* had just steamed into Pearl Harbor on a training cruise from the West Coast. *Colorado* had three float planes, so Murfin pressed her into service. *Colorado*'s crew, ashore on leave, were hurriedly rounded up and sent back to the ship. Making matters more difficult, the *Colorado*'s aircraft were undergoing maintenance at a hangar on nearby Ford Island. They had been completely disassembled. The maintenance crews were told to put the pieces back together and get the planes back aboard—overnight.

A perturbed Admiral Murfin shot a message back to Washington that said, "If more extensive search operations are contemplated, dispatch of aircraft carrier most practicable, efficient method." Clearly, Murfin was eager to pass the buck back to Admiral Leahy. CNO was also restive, but Leahy knew he couldn't ignore the situation. He, in turn, cabled the commander in chief, US Fleet (CINCUS), in San Pedro: "Request aircraft carrier be fueled and prepared for search Amelia Earhart, if so directed by Navy Department."

Lexington made an emergency sortie from San Pedro the next day, accompanied by four of the navy's newest, fastest destroyers: USS *Perkins*, USS *Lamson*, USS *Drayton*, and USS *Cushing*—all capable of doing better than thirty-five knots, *Lexington*'s top speed. By July 7, the small fleet was approaching Hawaii.

Lexington radioed ahead for fuel. To date, no carrier had actually made a port call in Pearl Harbor, and no one knew if the nearly nine-hundred-foot ship could find a mooring that would accommodate her hull. As a consequence, she dropped anchor in Lahaina Roads. The destroyers went into Pearl to refuel, and the oiler *Ramapo* came out to replenish *Lexington* with fuel oil. USS *Avocet*, AVP-4, came alongside to deliver aviation gas and ship's stores.

Lexington and the refueled destroyers departed Hawaii on July 10 for Howland Island. By this time, of course, Earhart and Noonan had been missing for a week, and nothing further had been heard from them. There were three possibilities: The first option was that the Electra had crashed at sea and had gone down with its crew. The second was that Earhart had conducted a successful ditching of the aircraft and that she and Noonan had somehow launched the plane's single life raft, in which case, factoring local currents, they were drifting back out to sea at about two knots, getting farther and farther from land. The third possibility was that they had made landfall—somewhere. If they were on land, no one seemed to know where except that it was certainly not Howland Island.

If the pair had crashed and sunk, there was nothing more to do but conduct a decent search for any possible sign of wreckage and then go home. That appeared not to be the case, however. Tantalizing, faint clues continued to appear. Mysterious, weak, generally untraceable signals and "voices" materialized out of the mists. Morse code dashes were detected. It was enough to keep up the hopes of all who desperately wanted the world's greatest aviatrix to be alive.

The rescuers parsed out a logical division of labor: the surface ships *Itasca* and *Swan* would comb the nearby islands and atolls for any sign of survivors while *Lexington* and *Colorado*, with their air assets, would search at sea. On July 13, *Lexington* activated its first sea search, launching sixty of its sixty-two available aircraft. The aviators would fly a series of parallel tracks covering hundreds of square miles. After several hours, all the planes returned safely having not sighted a single scrap of wreckage, an oil slick, or the bright yellow survival raft.

Lexington launched sorties day after day, forty to sixty planes at a time, until July 19, when the futility of further searching and the ship's dwindling fuel supplies dictated that it was time to conclude the operation. The navy spent what was considered an astronomical sum for the time—$4 million—on the search. It was the first real experience that the navy had had in these types of operations and, truthfully, the techniques were rudimentary.

MARCH 9–APRIL 30, 1938

FLEET PROBLEM XIX

The entire Pacific basin was the playing field for Fleet Problem XIX. It was more than clear in 1938 whom the US Navy was battling in these war games. The Japanese even filed a diplomatic protest as Phase II of the problem came just a little too close to their territory in the Kurile Islands off Alaska. They also shadowed the exercises with keen interest, employing many naval and fishing vessels.

The commander of the Black (US) forces was Adm. Edward C. Kalbfus, known as "Old Dutch" from his Pennsylvania Dutch background. He was a cruiser and battleship sailor, tried and true. He was also a former president of the Naval War College (1934–1936) and had published the book *Sound Military Decision* (1936), which became the leading naval publication on the direction, control, and purpose of the profession (and was used as such until 1984). He was not, however, conversant with all of the newest and most effective aspects of naval aviation doctrine. For that, he would have, on his COMBATFOR staff, Rear Adm. Ernie King, who was at the time commander of the navy's carrier forces. The two men had served together in their younger days and were friends.

Friendship aside, King could not persuade Kalbfus to untie his carrier forces from the main battle fleet during Fleet Problem XIX. In truth, Kalbfus probably had his eye on the post of CINCUS, then held by Admiral Bloch, who had adopted the same strategy in the previous Fleet Problem. Kalbfus knew that Bloch was watching.

The White Fleet (Japan) was under the command of Adm. William T. Tarrant, commander of the Scouting Force. Kalbfus had *Lexington* and *Saratoga*, with Tarrant taking *Ranger*. Tarrant had enjoyed success in Fleet Problem XVIII by allowing his carriers some independence, and he elected to use that strategy again. It worked smashingly.

On March 17, Tarrant sent *Ranger* flying after *Lexington* along with thirty-six PBY long-range patrol bombers. Locked into the battleship formation and unable to exercise her speed advantage or launch her planes in a timely manner, *Lexington* was bombed out of the problem and sunk before Admiral Kalbfus could drink his coffee. It was another humiliating lesson on how not to use one's aircraft carriers.

In Phase V of the problem (March 25–30), a humbled Kalbfus turned to Admiral King. In this phase, King would have *Lexington*, *Saratoga*, *Ranger*, and *Langley*, by then redesignated as a seaplane tender. He decided to unleash a coordinated attack against the enemy, which was anchored in and around Pearl Harbor.

Remembering that this was March 1938, not December 1941, here is the shocking but prescient description of the events of Phase V as related by Alfred Nofi:

> King decided to effect a surprise air raid on Pearl Harbor. He directed *Saratoga* to the northwest of Hawaii. Using a convenient weather front, at 0450 on March 29, King launched an attack from a hundred miles that hit the Army's Hickam and Wheeler air fields and the Pearl Harbor Naval Air Station with devastating effect. While the air attacks were underway, *Saratoga* ran in close to shore, to facilitate recovery of the aircraft. All of the attackers were back aboard by 0835. Quickly refueling and rearming his fighters, King managed to have enough of them airborne in time to beat off a counterattack by PBYs operating from Oahu, many of which were "shot down." Although heightened security resulted in King's "surprise attack" on Pearl Harbor receiving no press coverage at the time, word soon leaked out. In January 1939, an article on the operation even appeared in the *Saturday Evening Post*.[32]

During this Fleet Problem, *Saratoga* was commanded by Capt. John Henry "Jack" Towers, Naval Aviator No. 3 (so designated in 1911), who would go on to become a four-star admiral and command all naval air forces late in World War II. Towers had dinner in Tokyo in the early 1950s with a former Imperial Japanese Navy vice admiral who had helped plan the Pearl Harbor raid and asked the former admiral how they had come up with the idea. Astonishingly, the admiral replied, "We studied your Fleet Problem XIX and took a page out of your own book."[33]

FEBRUARY 20-27, 1939

FLEET PROBLEM XX, CARIBBEAN SEA

One of the most important lessons learned from Fleet Problem XX was that the aircraft carriers were woefully short of fighter aircraft. At this time, the typical configuration of a carrier air wing was seventy-two aircraft: eighteen

32. Nofi, 231.
33. Reynolds, 139.

each of fighters, bombers, torpedo planes, and scout planes (one squadron of each type). Eighteen fighter aircraft were not sufficient to perform the dual roles of defending the ship from enemy planes and escorting strike forces to the enemy's ships. The navy decided to assign fighter duties, on occasion, to the scouting squadrons, but the scout planes were essentially bombers performing scout duties. They were slower, less maneuverable, and not well enough armed to perform the anti-air function. This situation would remain until early 1942 and would have a profound impact, as we shall see, on the fate of *Lexington*.

The navy also learned, from Fleet Problem XX, that horizontal bombing (the type of bombing performed by the big, lumbering PBYs and Army Air Corps bombers) was completely ineffective in anti-ship operations. The bombsights in use were very inaccurate. This finding was acted upon immediately, and the navy pushed ahead with the development of better torpedoes, new torpedo planes, and more capable dive bombers and dive-bombing tactics (most of which, unfortunately, would not materialize in time for the Battles of Coral Sea or Midway).

APRIL 1–MAY 17, 1940

FLEET PROBLEM XXI, PACIFIC BASIN

War broke out in Europe in the fall of 1939. By the spring of 1940, USS *Ranger*, three battleships, twenty cruisers, and fifty destroyers were on President Roosevelt's Neutrality Patrol in the North Atlantic. They would not have time to participate in any exercises—they were facing the real thing. Many of the rest of the units based in the Atlantic would also stay in place, but the Pacific Fleet would go ahead with the 1940 Fleet Problem, as revised.

The planners came up with a series of challenges that the navy in the Pacific would likely face sooner rather than later. These were rapid mobilization, extended base operations, underway refueling for all types of ships, fleet tactics for defending against carrier air attacks, conducting carrier air attacks, and moving from island to island across a wide area. All in all, it was a prescient picture of what World War II in the Pacific would be.

In the tactical problem scheduled for the end of April, the Maroon forces (the United States), who controlled the Hawaiian Islands, Midway, the Aleutians, Wake Island, and Panama, opposed Purple (Japan), which had captured Wake and Samoa and had established an advance base on Guam. Purple was to invade Hawaii. All of this eerily foretold what Japan would try to do in the early phases of the coming war, and it is therefore somewhat shocking that the US Navy, having practiced these very scenarios in Fleet Problems XIX and XXI, was so unprepared.

During Fleet Problem XXI, Maroon and Purple ranged across the mid-Pacific trying to outmaneuver one another, and while both sides scored points, the Problem was more notable for the critical lessons learned.

Underway refueling was—and still is—an exacting, labor-intensive task without much glamour. It requires the utmost precision, from the bridges of the ships performing the maneuver to the sailors tossing the lines between the ships and manning the fuel hoses. Fleet Problem XXI practiced underway refueling diligently. Considering that the navy started World War II at a disadvantage in terms of advanced base facilities, it would be a distinct plus to be able to refuel efficiently, effectively, and frequently at sea.

The navy also found out that it was woefully inept at conducting night operations. Even though radar was now being introduced, it was still so unreliable that it was not yet considered a significant operational advantage. The Imperial Japanese Navy, on the other hand, trained extensively at night, and they would soon be able to prove their skills to an underprepared US Navy.

Finally, Fleet Problem XXI proved again that independent carrier operations, where flattops could range at will, were the best use for these ships. An attempt was made to tie *Yorktown*'s anti-air defense to her accompanying battleships, with *Lexington* as her free-ranging opponent. The battleships proved to be too slow to keep up with *Lexington* and her air group, and as a result *Yorktown* was constructively sunk. The lessons were finally sinking in, too.

JUNE 13, 1940
BATTLE FLEET HEADQUARTERS, SAN PEDRO, CALIFORNIA
On June 13, 1940, *Lexington* welcomed aboard her last and arguably most dynamic commanding officer, Capt. Frederick Carl "Ted" Sherman, US Naval Academy Class of 1910. Sherman was definitely exceptional among Navy officers of his day. After graduating from Annapolis, he served for two years aboard battleships as a post-graduated midshipman. This was common practice in that era: all Academy graduates were required to complete an internship of two years in the Fleet before receiving their commissions as ensigns. Sherman received his commission in 1912, backdated, as was also customary, to his graduation year of 1910.

From 1914 through the end of the First World War, Sherman was assigned to submarine duty. As commanding officer of USS *O-7*, he and his men patrolled the waters of the western Atlantic. For his stalwart dedication and superior performance, Sherman would be awarded the Navy Cross (the first of three he would receive during his career).

After the war, Sherman commanded a submarine squadron before switching to surface ships. He was commanding officer of the cruiser USS

Detroit, then led two destroyer squadrons in the early 1930s. He petitioned, in 1935, to train as a naval aviator. He was forty-seven years old at the time, almost too old to qualify, but he wanted, like other ambitious naval officers, to gain access to what many of his contemporaries perceived as the navy's future. He successfully finished flight training in 1936, was designated as a pilot, and immediately was assigned to USS *Saratoga*, CV-3, as executive officer. A year later, he was commanding Patrol Wing 3 in Panama. In 1940, he completed the navy's Senior Officer Course at the Naval War College in Newport, Rhode Island.

Immediately after Newport, battleship sailor-destroyerman-submariner-aviator "Ted" Sherman reported aboard USS *Lexington* as commanding officer. As he trotted up the gangplank for the first time, he was accompanied by an ever-present companion, a black cocker spaniel named Admiral Wags.

The short, stocky, chain-smoking Sherman was a tough taskmaster. He once chewed out a senior enlisted sailor aboard *Lexington* for saluting him first before Sherman could salute the sailor. This seeming reversal in protocol was actually correct: the sailor, although much lower in rank, was a Medal of Honor awardee and was by regulation entitled to receive salutes from all ranks in advance of saluting a superior. The commanding officer's tour of a capital ship, like *Lexington*, had been shortened in the mid-1930s to one year's duration. With war, the navy asked Sherman to take *Lexington* for two years. They wanted their best captains at the helms of their most valuable ships. Sherman agreed. It would be a fateful decision for him—and *Lexington*.

Backing up Sherman, as executive officer (after January 18, 1942), was the affable, well-liked Cmdr. Morton T. Seligman. He, too, was an Annapolis grad (Class of 1919), a Navy Cross awardee, and a late-blooming aviator, but the comparisons between Sherman and Seligman stopped there. Seligman loved a good time, was a "hale fellow, well met," and came aboard *Lexington* with his fishing pole and golf clubs. He sported a mustache, wore his cap at a jaunty angle, and actively spread bonhomie. Sherman and Seligman were yin and yang, but they made a good team. In the final death dance of their ship, both men would perform with distinction and valor; post-battle, one man's star would rise while the other's would fall, dimmed by dark hints of treason.

JULY 28, 1940

BETHESDA, MARYLAND

Seventy-six-year-old retired Rear Adm. David W. Taylor, who helped save USS *Lexington* from the scrapper's blowtorches and turned a shunned battle cruiser into the "Queen of the Flattops," died at the Naval Hospital in Bethesda after an eight-year-long battle with crippling paralysis. A photograph of *Lexington* stood near his bedside.

FLEET PROBLEM XXII, SCHEDULED FOR JANUARY 1941

In the first months of 1941, one-quarter of the US Navy was already committed to maintaining the neutrality of the North Atlantic and was on patrol there. On April 10, USS *Niblack*, DD-424, would fire the first US Navy shots of World War II when it attacked a German U-boat off the coast of Newfoundland.

Despite the drums and rumors of war, extensive plans were drawn up for Fleet Problem XXII, and had it been held it would have taken place in the Pacific. On December 3, 1940, CNO Adm. Harold R. Stark wrote to the army chief of staff, Gen. George C. Marshall, saying, "In view of the international situation, plans for Fleet Problem XXII have been cancelled." So visible had the fleet problems been that the cancellation made the front page of the *New York Times*.[34]

～

During the dozen years between her commissioning and the advent of World War II, Lady Lex sailed tens of thousands of miles, launched thousands of sorties, and was "sunk" more than a dozen times during the various Fleet Problems in which she participated. She had also kept one large American city out of the dark, succored the homeless and needy of an allied nation after a devastating earthquake, and participated in one of the most famous search-and-rescue operations of all time. Several of the captains who commanded her would rise to prominence and glory during the coming world war, having practiced their craft while at her helm.

While men like Ernest King, Aubrey Fitch, and Sherman were holding down the higher positions aboard *Lexington*, hundreds of other younger officers were coming up through the ranks in her various departments. Executive officers, gunnery officers, chief engineers, air bosses, aviation intelligence types, and supply and medical officers were all learning how a carrier functions at sea and at war. Their knowledge and experiences were spread throughout the fleet as newer aircraft carriers began sliding down the ways.

Aviators whose names and deeds would become legend flew off of her flattop all through the prewar period, among them John S. "Jimmie" Thach, C. Wade McClusky, Max Leslie, Edward M. "Butch" O'Hare, and the ill-starred but valiant John Waldron. It was during the Fleet Problems that

---

34. Nofi, 268.

these men discovered the tactics that would lead the US Navy to ultimate victory in the Pacific. Aboard *Lexington* was where these pioneers learned that punching holes in an enemy carrier's flight deck was just as good as sinking the ship itself.

Former World War II dive-bomber pilot George J. Walsh said in July 2011:

> During the Fleet Problems each year the pilots faced danger every time they climbed into the cockpit. They faced casualties from carrier operational accidents, mechanical failures, and pilot error. They also had to fly missions that tested the limits of aircraft and pilot capabilities. Admirals experimented with night and bad weather flight operations as well as the limits of aircraft range, and the speed of carrier launchings and recoveries. . . . Finally, the Fleet Problems perfected more than aircraft carrier operations. At the same time the Navy was working out problems in logistics, intelligence, staff structure, communications, cryptology, and radar.[35]

35. Walsh.

CHAPTER 3

NARROW ESCAPE AT PEARL HARBOR

0816 LOCAL TIME, DECEMBER 7, 1941

450 MILES SOUTHEAST OF MIDWAY ISLAND

The electrifying news was already racing around the ship, even though the dispatch had been placed in Captain Sherman's hands just moments earlier:

AIR RAID ON PEARL HARBOR XXX THIS IS NO DRIPP!

The hyperventilating radio operator had meant to type "DRILL," but there was no mistaking the content of the message.

∼

Two days earlier, Lady Lex had slipped her mooring lines and eased away from the western side of Ford Island, opposite Battleship Row. *Lexington* was the centerpiece that day of Task Force 12, ordered to sea by Commander in Chief of the Pacific Fleet Adm. Husband Kimmel (CINPAC) to deliver eighteen Vindicator SB2U-3 scout bombers assigned to Marine Corps Scouting Squadron 231 to Midway Island. The heavy cruisers USS *Chicago* (CA-29), USS *Portland* (CA-33), and USS *Astoria* (CA-34) and five destroyers accompanied her. Rear Adm. John H. Newton commanded the task force, flying his flag aboard *Chicago*.

Admiral Kimmel had grown increasingly nervous in the days prior to Pearl Harbor and began defending his remote outposts after receiving a message from CNO Adm. Harold Stark on November 26 that war could be "imminent." Stark was particularly concerned about the bases at Wake and Midway islands, both gateways to the central Pacific and Hawaii.

Kimmel met with Vice Adm. William F. "Bull" Halsey on November 27, and the two men agreed on a plan to reinforce both islands. Halsey would take USS *Enterprise* and his Task Force 2, with Marine Fighter Squadron 211 embarked, to Wake Island. *Lexington* and Task Force 12 would head to Midway. Halsey departed Pearl Harbor the next day, and her complete air wing flew out to the ship from Ford Island a few hours later.

A week later, "Ted" Sherman directed *Lexington* away from the island. The sun was out, but typical for this time of year on Oahu, rain squalls skidded across the Pali and drove down over the harbor— the same route the first wave of Japanese attackers would follow two days hence.

On the western side of Ford Island, the "carrier side," ships were not tied to a pier but cinched up to enormous mooring buoys embedded in the floor of the harbor. Although tugs were standing by, Sherman, renowned for being able to dock the mammoth *Lexington* without their aid, simply pulled the ship away from the bollards and ordered all ahead slow.

Once out to sea, Sherman headed west and asked for twenty knots. By 1100, *Lexington*'s "birds" were coming aboard. The guest Vindicators landed first, followed by the Brewster Buffalo fighters of VF-2.[36]

Once all the birds were parked, it was a very crowded nest. *Lexington*'s intrinsic aircraft numbered sixty-five. Eighteen Marine Corps guests placed eighty-three planes on deck. VF-2 flew in seventeen F2A-3 Brewster Buffalo fighters; VT-2 brought aboard sixteen TBD-1 Devastator torpedo bombers; and VS-2 and VB-2 added fifteen and seventeen SBD Dauntless scouts (dive bombers), respectively. All the aircraft aboard were monoplane design, but not all of the single-wing aircraft were up to date.

The Buffaloes of Fighting Two had relatively new airframes but were already obsolete as effective fighting machines. They had excellent range, at almost a thousand miles, but they were slower and heavier compared to the Japanese Zeros. The Buffaloes could take punishment and carried a great deal of fuel and ammunition, but the added weight made them less maneuverable and more prone to landing-gear collapses on the carrier decks. The Buffalo sported four .50-caliber machine guns but could carry only two puny hundred-pound bombs, one under each wing.

The TBD-1 Devastator wasn't much better. First introduced to the fleet in 1937, the Devastator, by the outbreak of World War II, had been

---

36. At this juncture, carrier squadrons that were assigned to a specific carrier were given the ship's hull number. That is, *Lexington*'s fighter squadron would be VF-2 after CV-2; *Saratoga*'s bombing squadron would be VB-3 after CV-3, etc.

completely overtaken by the rapid pace of airframe development. It had a top speed in the range of two hundred miles per hour but could only drop its outmoded Mk 13 aerial torpedo at less than 115 miles per hour. This made the Devastator an easy target. Also lessening its survivability was its relatively thin armor and the lightweight defensive weapons: one .30-caliber machine gun in the hands of a rear gunner and another .30-caliber or .50-caliber mounted in the starboard side of the cowling. It was no wonder that its pilots derisively called their flying death traps "Torpeckers."

The Marine Corps SB2U Vindicators were another sad story. Their first flights had occurred in 1936; by 1941 these dive bombers were outclassed by the newer Dauntless models coming into the fleet. The Vindicator was slow (max speed of 250 miles per hour) and under-defended (two .30-caliber machine guns), and it suffered from two unfortunate nicknames: the "Vibrator" and the "Wind Indicator." It did, at least, carry a respectable thousand-pound bomb, and Marine Corps pilots had some success with them in land-based actions early in the war.

The best news for *Lexington*'s air wing came in the form of its Douglas Aircraft Corporation SBD Dauntless planes. Introduced in 1940, the Dauntless performed two roles aboard the fleet's carriers at that time: scouting and bombing. The plane was not fast (255 miles per hour), but it had an excellent cruising range (1,115 miles), carried four .50-caliber machine guns (two for the rear gunner and two for the pilot), and could haul more than two thousand pounds of bombs. It was the best dive bomber of its day.

TF-12 plied the waters between Hawaii and Midway at an unhurried pace. Although Admiral Newton and Captain Sherman knew that hostilities could erupt at any moment, war loomed only in the abstract. Their job was to deliver the Vindicator dive bombers to Midway and then turn around and steam back to Pearl Harbor, conducting training exercises along the way. December 7 changed everything.

As the last strains of the unnerving "GQ" claxon echoed away, *Lexington* grew strangely quiet. She had not yet changed her speed, an easy eighteen knots, because no one immediately knew where she was supposed to go. Sailors who had conducted general quarters drills a hundred times stood quietly at their stations, broiling in the sun or sweating in the tropical heat of the engine rooms. Hands rested lightly on switches, levers, dials, or triggers. Real bullets nestled in the chambers of the machine guns, and the anti-aircraft crews were carefully stacking the gleaming, brass-jacketed, five-inch rounds in neat piles near their weapons. Fighter pilots had scrambled to their planes. Ready rooms full of torpedo, scout, and bomber pilots nervously chain smoked while awaiting the signal.

High up on the bridge, Admiral Wags skittered under the navigation table. The bridge crew turned to their captain.

"Gentlemen, this is it," he intoned. A finger of ash from his last cigarette flecked his khaki shirt with a small smudge of gray. Sherman casually brushed the ashes from his chest.

Lexington leapt into action, silent no longer.

"All ahead two-thirds, make your speed twenty-five knots!"

"Signal the admiral. I'm changing speed, turning into the wind."

"Air boss! Start re-spotting the deck! We have to get those birds untangled so we can launch the fighters. I need a fighter CAP, ASAP!"

"Navigator! Range, bearing, and distance to Midway!"

"Radio! I want updates the instant you receive them!"

"Ops! Where's Halsey? I need to know where Halsey is! What's he up to?"

"Radar! I need a plot! What's in the area?"

"Get a supply officer up here! I need to know our fuel state—pronto! Ship's fuel and av gas."

"Somebody get the senior chaplain up here!"

Sherman picked up the sound-powered phone and spun the dial for ENGINEERING.

"Bridge, Engine Room!" a voice boomed back, half drowned out by the roar of machinery. It was Cmdr. Alexander F. "Heine" Junkers, the chief engineer.

"Heine, it's the captain. You've heard?"

"I have, sir. Is it the Japs?"

"No doubt. What's your state?"

"All's good here, Captain. I can give you whatever you need."

"Excellent. I'm going to go to all head full and launch the fighter CAP as soon as I can."

"I'll be ready. Engineer out."

Sherman's next call was to Cmdr. Herbert S. "Ducky" Duckworth, his air boss.

"Ducky!"

"Yes, Captain!"

"You gotta get those fighters untangled on the flight deck and get some of them up. I need a CAP."

"Yes, sir. I'm working on it."

"Work faster. Sherman out."

A nervous young petty officer of the watch ran over to the captain and snapped to attention, saluting.

"'Scuse me, Captain, sir!"

A distracted Sherman snapped, "Yes, petty officer, what is it."

"The chaplain's here, sir. He's askin' for permission to come on the bridge."

"Yes, yes, I called for him. Bring him over."

The young man ran over to the far side of the bridge and motioned for Cmdr. George L. Markle, the fifty-six-year-old senior chaplain, to step onto the bridge.

"You sent for me, sir?"

Sherman glanced up from the message he was reading. "Ah, yes, Padre. Listen—I'm going to be a little busy here. I need you to do something."

"Anything, sir. What can I do?"

"I want you to stay up here a while. Keep up with the message traffic, with me. The men like you, Padre. You'd be a calming influence. When we get something the men should know, I want you to get on the loudspeaker and tell 'em. It'll reassure them, I think."

"Yes, sir. I'll be glad to do that."

"Good. It'll be just like preaching on Sunday, Padre. Only keep the sermons short and to the point, OK?" Sherman chuckled at his own humor.

The deck plates began to vibrate as Lady Lex picked up speed. The waters were calm but Lex began to sway, as she always did, when she got to twenty knots or more. Her slender battle cruiser hull was good at slicing through the water, but her narrow beam sometimes wanted to act like a destroyer more than the giant flattop she had become. She was, of course, somewhat top heavy anyway with the huge hangar and flight decks high above the waterline. Sherman couldn't see the "bone in her teeth," but he knew it was there.[37]

Out of the corner of his eye, Sherman could see *Chicago*'s blinker light flashing furiously. Admiral Newton was signaling. Sherman was not Newton's biggest fan: the latter was a staunch member of the Gun Club and not a believer in the viability of independent aircraft carrier operations. He had little background in carriers and no experience in aviation. Sherman had even privately wondered why Newton had been placed in charge of this Task Force.

Executive Officer Cmdr. Wallace M. "Gotch" Dillon was standing nearby—waiting for his orders. Sherman grabbed him by the elbow and said, "Come with me."

At the rear of the bridge was the captain's day cabin, a small, enclosed compartment containing not much more than a desk, a lamp, two

---

37. In October 1941, when in dry dock at Hunter's Point (San Francisco), *Lexington*'s paint scheme was changed. A fake bow wave was painted on each side of her bow, which was intended to give the impression she was moving fast even if she were going slow or standing still.

comfortable chairs, a coffee table, and a bed for Admiral Wags. It was where the captain could step away from the frenetic activity of the bridge yet still be close by. Sherman went there to read his messages or take his meals when he was on the bridge.

Sherman motioned for Dillon to sit. Removing his fore-and-aft cap and then wiping his brow, Sherman sank down in the other chair.

"Gotch, things are going to get crazy very quickly now," he cautioned.

Dillon nodded in agreement.

"I think the men are well trained. We've done the best we could to get them ready. It's a good crew, but things have changed. They will be nervous, edgy, some will be overeager, some even frightened. This is where you can help."

"How so, Captain?"

"We'll have to leave the air wing to Bill Ault and his squadron commanders. He's in charge there, and I think he's a good man. I'm talking about our crew, the ship's company. They like you—certainly more than me . . ."

"I wouldn't say that, Captain . . ."

"Please, I have eyes—and ears. I'm the 'old man.' They have to respect me, and I hope they do, but I'm not going to coddle them. I have to have their unquestioned obedience, now more than ever. That's where you come in. I'm going to be busy up here until we figure out what the hell we're going to do next. I can't be all over the ship. You can. I want you to be my other eyes and ears, the ones that watch the crew, take their temperatures, tell me what they're thinking, how they're feeling, what they need to know. That's your primary job until further notice, get me?"

"Yes, Captain, I understand."

"Good."

There was a loud knock on the cabin door.

Sherman shouted, "Enter!"

Ensign Weber poked his head in the hatch and said, "Pardon the interruption, skipper, but there's flash traffic from Pearl and a signal from Admiral Newton."

"OK," Sherman replied, "On the way."

Sherman got up, Dillon followed, and both men stepped back onto the bridge.

"Captain's on the bridge!"

"Let's see the message from Pearl," Sherman demanded. Weber handed it over. It read: *Hostilities with Japan commenced with air raid on Pearl. Commence zigzagging on standard plan. Stand by for further orders—Kimmel.*

"OK, now what does Newton have to say?"

Weber cleared his throat somewhat nervously and read from his notepad the signal Newton had semaphored to *Lexington*: "Suggest you ready combat air patrol and launch soonest."

Weber saw the frown form on Sherman's face and watched as his jaw muscles clenched. Everyone on the bridge knew it was a needless order. Sherman had already set in motion the tasks to do exactly that.

Evenly, Sherman dictated, "Tell him 'Wilco' and I will signal when ready to launch."

0855

CLAG READY ROOM, HANGAR DECK LEVEL

The commander of *Lexington*'s air group (CLAG), Cmdr. William B. Ault, was holding an emergency meeting of his squadron commanders. At forty-three, Ault was the old man of his air group, a veteran pilot and thoroughly respected. He had joined the navy as an enlisted sailor at the outbreak of World War I but soon had an opportunity to attend the Naval Academy. He graduated from Annapolis in 1922. After two years of battleship duty, he requested a switch to naval aviation, which was granted in 1924. For the next dozen years, he served in a variety of scout, patrol, and torpedo squadrons, plus helped commission USS *Yorktown*, CV-5. His first command had been VT-6 aboard USS *Enterprise* in 1939, after which he commanded the Naval Reserve Base in Kansas City. In July 1941, he reported aboard *Lexington* as CLAG.

In the cramped CLAG Ready Room, he surveyed the men and the squadrons they commanded as they sat around his desk: Fighting Two (VF-2), led by Lt. Cmdr. Paul H. Ramsey, Annapolis 1927; Bombing Two (VB-2), Lt. Cmdr. Harry D. Felt, Annapolis, 1923; Scouting Two (VS-2), Lt. Cmdr. Robert E. Dixon; and Torpedo Two (VT-2), led by Lt. Cmdr. Claire L. Miller.

"Gentlemen, we've got a shooting war on our hands," Ault said. "I don't need to tell you what's at stake. This is what we've trained for, and now it's time to show 'em we're ready. I don't know what the plan is, as yet, but I suspect the skipper's going to want a combat air patrol all around the ship at least during daylight. We can't keep your fighters in the air constantly, Ramsey; so, Felt and Dixon, you should plan on having some of your aircraft join the mix. Make sure your people are up to speed on their procedures and get your mechs and ordnance people moving. As soon as I have any more dope, I'll pass it along. So, get to your ready rooms and brief your men. Dismissed."

〜

0923, USS *Chicago* to USS *Lexington*: *May be advisable to dispatch marine squadron Midway ahead of schedule—Newton*

"Dammit!" Sherman shouted. The marine fighters had just been sent to the hangar deck to get them out of the way so *Lexington*'s fighters could be launched. "Tell Duckworth to get the Vindicators back up as soon as we get the fighters launched."

0931, USS *Lexington* to USS *Chicago*: *Launching CAP—Sherman*

Six Buffaloes from VF-2 roared into the sky to circle high above *Lexington*, providing fighter cover from . . . no one knew exactly what.

1012, USS *Chicago* to USS *Lexington*: *Launch all remaining fighters for CAP—Newton*

Sherman, as the bridge crew could readily observe, was getting truly angry. First, he took umbrage that Newton, a non-aviator, would interfere in his scheme for protecting his ship. Second, it made no sense to Sherman to push all his fighters aloft unless there was some specific threat, and there seemed to be nothing imminent. He would obey, certainly, but the fighter cover would evaporate as soon as all seventeen of the fighters buzzing overhead ran low on fuel.

1021, USS *Lexington* to USS *Chicago*: *All fighters airborne-marine aircraft re-spotted on deck—Sherman*

1030, bridge, USS *Lexington*. Sherman rang up his air boss, Commander Duckworth: "Ducky, I want sixteen SBDs ready to launch."

"No problem, Captain. They'll be ready."

1038, USS *Lexington* to USS *Chicago*: *Suggest launch sixteen SBDs, full circle search, range to 165 NM. Unless enemy aircraft are positively identified in vicinity, consider undesirable have all fighters in air at same time—Sherman*

1042, USS *Chicago* to USS *Lexington*: *Plan approved—proceed. Permission granted reduce CAP by half—Newton*

1105, CINCPAC, Pearl Harbor, to commanding officer, TF-12: *Proceed immediately to rendezvous with Halsey, TF-8, vicinity western Hawaiian Islands. Believe enemy raiding force in same area. Intercept and engage—Kimmel*

1108, USS *Chicago* to USS *Lexington*: *Cancel plans to offload marine fighters to Midway. Form up on me. TF directed to rendezvous TF-8, find enemy and engage—Newton*

Chaplain Markle passed on the electrifying news via the ship's intercom that the task force was in hot pursuit of the enemy.

1230, USS *Lexington* Radar Shack: "Bridge, radar! Bogey bearing 269 degrees, forty-three nautical miles!"

In October 1941, radar had been installed during *Lexington*'s last yard period at Hunter's Point. The large, flat, square grid of interconnected wires, resembling a giant fly swatter, was mounted on the top, forward edge of *Lexington*'s huge funnel. A radar unit housing, or "shack," big enough for a couple of operators to squeeze into, was added to the front of the stack, at the same level as the bridge, and a narrow catwalk between the radar shack and the bridge was installed to facilitate foot traffic between the two spaces.

The radar set, from RCA, the CXAM-1, was rudimentary by today's standards but was revolutionary in its day. It was able to detect aircraft to fifty miles and ships to fifteen. The reliability factor in late 1941 was still generally low, but better than many had expected. The believability factor was even lower, but the early radars would soon have many converts.

Sherman directed that several of the CAP fighters run out the designated bearing and investigate the contact. It was a navy PBY flying boat. The radar worked.

1353, Bridge, USS *Lexington*. Sherman had a problem: the fighters aloft were running low on fuel and his deck was crowded. Rearranging the aircraft or striking some of them below to the hangar deck would take too much time.

"Engineering! This is the captain!"

"Go ahead, Captain," Commander Junkers shouted back on the phone.

"Heine, come to a full stop, then reverse polarity, then full ahead. As soon as you can, please."

"Aye, aye, Captain. Full stop, then reverse polarity, then full ahead."

"Commander Duckworth!"

"Aye, Captain."

"Prepare to launch your fighters."

Duckworth was flustered. "But . . . but, Captain, the fighters are on the stern! There's fifty aircraft in front of them!"

"I know that," Sherman snapped. "Turn them around. I'll give you wind over the stern."

It took less than five minutes for the ship to come to a complete stop and begin spinning the propellers the other way. Fifteen minutes later, with twenty-one knots of wind over the stern, the remaining Buffaloes could launch. As soon as those fighters were airborne, Sherman ordered his engineer to reverse the process. Within minutes, a sufficient breeze over the bow allowed the thirsty fighters to land.

1403, USS *Chicago* to USS *Lexington*: *CINCPAC believes Jap carriers south of Oahu. Likely withdrawal to coincide our track—Newton*

No one associated with the US Navy, least of all CINCPAC, actually knew where the Imperial Japanese task force was—or how many ships it contained. Everyone was chasing shadows. Vice Admiral Chūichi

Nagumo, commander of the carrier task force that had attacked Pearl Harbor, withdrew his carriers to the north and then sailed east of Midway Island to skirt any US Navy units that might be in the area. He was not within a thousand miles of the areas Halsey and Newton searched. Nagumo's caution (for which he was later criticized) probably benefitted the American forces immensely: had they run into one another it would have been, at most, two US Navy carriers against six frontline Japanese flattops. The outcome would not likely have been favorable for the US Navy.

1650, Flight Deck, USS *Lexington*. Captain Sherman continued to launch scout and fighter patrols all afternoon. At 1650, he sent out two SBDs as his last patrol for the day. Night would fall in two hours. After that, air patrols would be useless. They would rely on the radar for nighttime defensive operations.

1710, VS-2 SBDU-2, on patrol, 65 nautical miles southeast, USS *Lexington*: "I've got something out here . . . I think it's a Jap carrier!"

The excited pilot of Bombing Two radioed back to *Lexington* that he was in contact with the enemy's fleet. Sherman's crew, at General Quarters for most of the day, had relaxed their guard just a little. The mess boys had brought up sandwiches, fruit, hot coffee, and fresh water to all the fighting stations on the ship. Now everyone went back to full alert, dog-tired.

Commander Ault directed the other SBD in the vicinity to join up and investigate. In the waning light, both scout bombers bore down on the target. It seemed to be cutting through the water at a great rate of speed.

As the duo of Dauntlesses zoomed over the "carrier," it morphed into a partly submerged reef near French Frigate Shoals. The "bow wave" was simply the surf lapping over the outer lip of the shore. The two chagrinned pilots reported their findings back to *Lexington*. For the moment, everyone could breathe again.

But the returning scouts, ready to take their ribbing, couldn't find the ship. The relative bearings between ship and aircraft had become tangled in the excitement. The two scouts were flying blind, in total darkness, with no moon and a false horizon.

Earlier that year, before the radar had been installed, *Lexington* had had a new YE homing beacon mounted at the top of her very prominent tripod mast. This system sent out a short, simple Morse code signal from the ship for each thirty-degree radial of the compass. All the pilot had to do was intersect a radial, figure out which one it was, and fly the reverse radial back to the ship. Not all the *Lexington* aircraft were equipped with the receivers, but these scout planes had them. However, possibly because the pilots inadvertently scrambled without the correct code for that day, they could not decipher the homing beacon. Sherman faced two pilots in the drink with little prospect for rescue. He called the navigator, Commander Dudley, to his side.

"Commander Dudley, turn on the searchlights."

Dudley was stunned. Illuminating the powerful Aldis lamps would pinpoint the carrier's position. If there were any enemy ships in the vicinity, this would be a dead giveaway.

"But, Captain!" Dudley sputtered.

"Do it *now*, Mr. Dudley," Sherman growled.

Lexington was equipped with four powerful searchlights that could be seen for miles. The two errant aircraft used them to land safely at 1841.

USS *Lexington*'s first day at war had been one of confusion, conflicting signals, panic, excitement, questionable judgment calls, and minor accidents, combined with lessons learned, adrenaline, steady hands, a couple of lucky breaks, and some good calls. This would become the routine and the mechanics of war.

$\sim$

Much ink has been spilled since December 7, 1941, about the state of readiness of the navy and army at Pearl Harbor. Conspiracy theorists have gone so far as to allege that President Roosevelt and others in Washington, DC, knew about the Japanese plans and chose to let events unfold. The final proof for or against these arguments has yet to be uncovered—if it ever will be.

What can be said is that communication between the Navy Department and Admiral Kimmel's headquarters was less than optimal, at least in regard to helping Kimmel prepare for the attack. Moreover, Washington did not share or forward all it did know—or all it suspected.

Admiral Kimmel paid a high price, professionally and personally, for the attack on Pearl Harbor. What seems to have been lost, however, is what Kimmel did in the few days before and after December 7 when he still had command of the Fleet.

There was no ambiguity about Admiral Stark's November 27, 1941, message to Kimmel stating that, should hostilities erupt, the bases at Wake and Midway islands had to be protected. Kimmel did not hesitate: Halsey departed for Wake Island the next day, November 28. *Lexington*, still restocking and refueling, drew the assignment of relieving the pressure on Midway and sailed a week later, on December 5, thus escaping Admiral Nagumo's striking force.

It was an escape by the narrowest of margins. The history of the war in the Pacific may have been different had *Enterprise* and *Lexington* still been anchored off Ford Island on the morning of December 7. Admiral Kimmel does not receive adequate recognition for issuing the orders that took the two big carriers out of harm's way. Likewise, he does not receive much credit for the positive steps he took immediately after Pearl Harbor.

CHAPTER 4

WAKE ISLAND ABANDONED

In the days immediately following the Pearl Harbor attack, a crippled Pacific command was preoccupied with the damage inflicted by the Imperial Japanese Navy. Sailors were still trapped in hulls beneath the water, smoke continued to uncoil from stubborn fires, medical facilities remained overwhelmed, and many of the dead lay unburied, awaiting identification. Nervous anti-aircraft gunners, fueled on rumors, caffeine, and little sleep, shot at anything that flew by, including several American planes. *Enterprise's* VF-6 lost four planes and three pilots on the second day of the war to friendly fire. Every last nerve in and around Pearl Harbor was on edge, angry, and trigger happy. In this atmosphere of uncertainty and confusion, good decisions were hard to come by.

Where were the Japanese? Even the code breakers were at a loss. The enemy had gone silent. The overriding fear was that the Japanese carriers still lurked nearby and would return to finish the job; after all, the attackers had completely missed the gigantic fuel storage tanks, the big cranes, and the dry-docks. These vital facilities were frantically resurrecting the ships that could be salvaged and fueling the warships that were still viable. If these support structures were lost, the Pacific Fleet could be out of the fight for months, if not years.

One bit of bad information followed another as the *Enterprise* and *Lexington* battle groups hunted for the Japanese. *Lexington*, on somebody's best guess, was sent southwest, toward Johnston Island, thinking that the Japanese would be withdrawing in that direction toward their newly established bases in the Gilbert Islands.

Halsey, needing supplies and fuel and, wanting a look at the damage, cautiously pulled into Pearl Harbor on the evening of December 8. He was appalled. He departed the next morning, worried that the Japanese would pounce if they knew that one of the carriers was back in port. Kimmel was insistent that only one carrier at a time dock at Pearl. He could not afford to lose one more ship, especially a carrier.

Twenty-six hundred miles away, at North Island Naval Air Station, Rear Adm. Aubrey Wray "Jake" Fitch was bending every effort to get his air wing aboard his flagship, USS *Saratoga*. The officers and men of the "Sara" had received the news of the attack as they were sitting down to a leisurely Sunday lunch.

For the rest of that day and into the wee hours of the morning, the ship's company, her air wing personnel, and all military and civilian workers at North Island strove to get the ship armed, loaded, and ready to leave the dock. *Saratoga* pulled away from the pier early on December 8, accompanied by three destroyers. Since the entire Pacific had immediately become a dangerous place, she went to full wartime alert as soon as her bow slid past Pt. Loma.

DECEMBER 8–13
JOHNSTON ISLAND OPERATING AREA, 825 MILES SOUTHWEST
OF PEARL HARBOR

On the morning of December 8, 1941, Rear Admiral Newton, Captain Sherman, and Task Force 12 were still chasing rumors of war near Johnston Island. Like a punch-drunk boxer, the task force danced all over the sea, hoping to make contact but hitting nothing but air. The anger and frustration were palpable.

Shortly before noon, better direction arrived in the form of an additional task force led by one of the more underappreciated and now nearly forgotten senior naval leaders of the war: Vice Adm. Wilson Brown.

Brown was an old sea dog, four months shy of his sixtieth birthday. Having graduated from the Naval Academy in 1902, he had had plenty of experience afloat and had commanded both destroyers and battleships. He had also been a senior naval aide in London during World War I, had been superintendent of the Naval Academy, and had served as naval aide to presidents Coolidge and Hoover.[38] He was smooth, amiable, intelligent, diplomatic, and calm in a crisis.

With his flag in the heavy cruiser USS *Indianapolis*, accompanied by the heavy cruiser *Portland* and several destroyers, Brown steamed up to TF-12 and smoothly assumed command. His directions from Halsey were clear and simple: "Form up on me. We'll take one more sweep of the area to see

---

38. He would later return to Washington, DC, and serve in the same post to presidents Roosevelt and Truman.

if we can locate the enemy and if so, we will engage them. If no enemy ships are found by the end of this day, we will proceed to Pearl Harbor."

Even with Brown's reassuring presence, the next twelve hours would prove just how jittery and as yet unaccustomed to combat the US Navy was in the early days of the war. The cruiser *Portland* and the destroyer USS *Porter* were detached from the task force at 1300 to look for a missing scout plane that had not returned from the morning mission. The two ships fell back and searched near Johnston Island while the remainder of TF-12 made their sweeps ahead.

Separately, a PBY from VP-21, on a flight from Johnston Island to Pearl, excitedly reported seeing an enemy cruiser and destroyer. He had spotted *Portland* and *Porter*.

At about the same time, USS *Chicago*'s radar operator picked up contact on his screen that he interpreted as "many enemy aircraft," circling southwest, on a course toward the task force. The signal was, in fact, the radar return presented by the VP-21 PBY's chubby airframe.

Portland spotted the VP-21 PBY, thought it was a Nakajima Japanese flying boat, and reported herself "under imminent attack by enemy aircraft."

Sherman launched two sections of fighters and scout planes to aid *Portland* and *Porter*. They were soon overhead of the PBY, and the Catalina pilot then reported he was under attack by enemy fighters. *Portland* thought *Lexington*'s Buffaloes were Japanese Zeros and fired a few anti-aircraft rounds in their direction, fortunately hitting none of them. The PBY flew away from the area but soon saw an "enemy carrier" (*Lexington*) and made another excited report. The PBY turned to attack the enemy carrier and actually conducted a bombing run, but the ordnance failed to drop. As the PBY flew by, the crew on *Lexington*'s deck waved at the friendly aircraft.

Lexington's aircraft, meanwhile, found no enemy planes in the target area and returned to the ship.

To complete this comedy of errors, the tiny garrison on Johnston Island reported that they were facing imminent attack. Admiral Brown broke off *Indianapolis* and *Chicago* and charged to the rescue. When he arrived in the vicinity of Johnston Island, he discovered the enemy ships were none other than *Portland* and *Porter*.

The only good news of the afternoon turned out to be that the errant scout plane finally found its bearings and made it home.

Having had enough of these follies, Brown set his course for Pearl the next morning. The task force arrived later the same day and spent until the evening of December 13 patrolling the southwestern approaches to Oahu. *Lexington* slipped into Pearl Harbor that evening. She would not be there long.

~

Wake Island is a tiny speck of land of less than three square miles. Its highest elevation is twenty feet. It is really three separate atolls that encircle a broad, turquoise lagoon. It is literally in the middle of nowhere. Today, it is an active landing strip and radar station jointly administered by the US Air Force and the Department of the Interior. In 1941, it presented an opportunity for the American military to build a forward operating base to keep an eye on the Japanese. Construction of the facilities started in January. The military moved a small garrison of naval personnel and marines aboard in August, and on December 8 (December 7 in Honolulu) the Japanese bombed the island.

The Japanese felt that taking Wake Island would not be difficult. They failed to take into account the determination of the US Marine Corps and the punch of its long-range guns.

The attack began with an air raid: thirty-six land-based, twin-engine "Nell" bombers swooped in over Wake early on December 8. They had flown from the Marshall Islands to drop their ordnance, hoping to soften up the island in advance of the invasion force that was already on its way.

The men of Marine Air Squadron 211 (VMF-211) had already received the first radio messages from Pearl Harbor. The squadron CO, Maj. Paul Putnam, launched four of his F4F-3 Wildcat fighters to act as air cover, but visibility was poor over the island and they missed the first Japanese bombers to descend on the airstrip.

Tragically, the Japanese bombers devastated the VMF-211 forces still on the ground. They destroyed all eight remaining Wildcats and killed twenty-three of the fifty-five support personnel, including most of the mechanics. This was a devastating blow to the island's defenses, but there was worse to come.

The island's forces were led by Navy Cmdr. Winfield Scott Cunningham, Annapolis Class of 1920. A naval aviator, Cunningham had recently been CO of VF-5 before being ordered to take command of Wake Island, including supervision of all construction activities. He arrived at his new post on November 28, just ten days before the first bombs fell. He commanded 68 navy personnel, 1,221 civilian construction workers, and 449 men of the 1st Marine Defense Battalion led by Maj. James P. S. Devereux.

One of Cunningham's objectives was to set up the island's long-range radar facility. Fortunately, the radar equipment had not yet been delivered by the time the Japanese attacked and thus did not fall into Japanese hands. What Cunningham and Devereux did have, which they used to excellent effect, were six five-inch guns (from the old battleship USS *Texas*); twelve three-inch anti-aircraft guns; eighteen .50-caliber heavy machine guns; and thirty .30-caliber medium machine guns.

It was this powerful array of field pieces that the initial Japanese invasion force ran into on December 11. The four remaining Wildcats attacked the Japanese surface ships and managed to drop one bomb right on top of the stern-mounted depth-charge rack of the destroyer *Kisaragi*. The ship was blasted out of the water by the explosion and sank in minutes with the loss of all hands. The big coastal guns hammered another Japanese destroyer, *Hayate*, plunging at least two shells into the ship's magazines. That ship was blown in two, also sinking quickly with the loss of all hands. The commanding admiral's cruiser was hit by five-inch shells at least eleven times before he elected to withdraw and consider his options.

$\sim$

As soon as Lady Lex anchored at Pearl late in the day on December 13, Sherman and Brown received new orders from Kimmel: *Lexington* would be the nucleus of Task Force 11, sailing the next day. She would be accompanied by three heavy cruisers, nine destroyers, and the swift new fleet oiler, USS *Neosho*, AO-23 (named for the Neosho River that runs through Kansas and Oklahoma). Their objective was to conduct a raid on the new Japanese Naval Base at Jaluit in the Marshall Islands, an atoll that was 937 miles due south of Wake Island. The thrust was to divert the Japanese away from Wake. If successful, the ploy would give USS *Saratoga* enough time to get to Pearl, refuel, load up extra planes and troops, and charge toward the relief of Wake Island.

Admiral Halsey and USS *Enterprise* would remain near the Hawaiian Islands for home defense and stalking the Japanese submarines known to be lurking in the area. If all went according to plan, Admiral Brown would attack Jaluit on December 21, and the *Saratoga* task force would arrive to relieve Wake on December 22.

Admiral Brown knew he could be sailing into a trap. Intelligence, though sketchy, indicated he might face two Japanese carriers to his one. Kimmel gave Brown the discretion to pick another target or to cancel the operation completely if he received information that the mission could be compromised by unfavorable odds. Late on the 14th *Lexington* sailed, making straight for the Marshall Islands.

0758, DECEMBER 16, 1941
SBD 2 AND 3, BOMBING SQUADRON 2, 95 NAUTICAL MILES AHEAD
OF USS *LEXINGTON*

The startling message crackled over *Lexington*'s command radio, jolting everyone to attention:

"Japanese carrier! Bearing 210, ninety-five nautical miles your position! Commencing attack!"

Two pilots from Bombing Two, out on patrol ahead of the task force, had apparently stumbled onto a lone Japanese carrier.

Brown and Sherman leapt into action. Brown radioed *Neosho* to peel away, to get over the horizon and out of immediate danger. Sherman directed that ten fighters from Fighting Two get airborne as a combat air patrol and circle overhead.

The two scouts went silent. Sherman presumed they had been shot down. He scrambled a strike force of sixteen dive bombers, thirteen torpedo planes, and seven fighters and sent them winging toward the target.

No sooner had this strike force dashed away than the two scout planes arrived back at *Lexington*. The two pilots, Ensigns Mark Whittier and Clem Connally, tumbled out of their cockpits, dashed across the flight deck, and shot up the ladders to the signal bridge. Out of breath with the excitement and a scramble up three levels, they nervously came to attention in front of the ship's steely-eyed captain, gulping lungfuls of air.

"At ease, gentlemen," Sherman intoned as he stared down the young pilots. "Now tell me what you saw."

The two men glanced at one another, not knowing who was going to speak first.

"Well," Sherman boomed, his voice rising with impatience, "one of you speak up! I just sent three dozen aircraft out there chasing your contact! I sure as hell hope they're not on a wild goose chase!"

Ensign Connally eagerly shouted back, "No, sir! We definitely saw a Jap carrier . . ."

Whittier jumped in and backed up his squadron mate: "No question, sir. Big Jap carrier . . ."

"We conducted bomb runs on the target, sir—both of us!" Connally added. "Not sure if we scored any hits, though . . ."

The two animated aviators were talking over one another in a desperate tumble of words.

"Two bombs, Captain. We dropped both our bombs . . ."

"Was kinda strange, though . . ."

Sherman's gaze narrowed, "What was strange, Mister . . . uh . . ."

"Whittier, sir. Ensign Mark Whittier."

"Mister Whittier. . . . What was strange?

"We didn't take any fire, sir. Not one gun on that carrier took a shot at either one of us."

"No evasive action either, sir," Connally added. "Ship didn't seem to move. Dead in the water."

"Sir . . ." It was Commander Dudley, the navigation officer, leaning close to the captain's right ear and quietly asking, "Might I have a word?"

Sherman stood glaring at the novice pilots for a few more moments and then turned to step away, retreating to the starboard side of the bridge, Commander Dudley in trail.

"What is it, Commander?"

"Well, sir, perhaps you remember . . . just after the attack on Pearl, one of the navy's big oceangoing tugs was pulling a very large dynamite barge from Pearl to the naval air station on Palmyra Island? The tug was told to cut the barge loose and get back to Pearl, where she was needed to help rescue ships?"

Sherman winced. "You're not telling me . . ."

"Sorry, sir, but I think it could be. I've been keeping a rough plot on that barge as a potential contact of interest, just in case."

"Thank you, Mister Dudley. Carry on."

"Yes, sir."

Sherman walked slowly to where the two fliers remained riveted to the deck.

"Gentleman." Sherman drilled them with his stare. "You don't, perhaps, think that maybe what you saw and reported as a 'carrier' might, in fact, have been a large, drifting barge, do you?"

Both men replied in wide-eyed unison, "Oh, no sir! We're very sure . . . quite positive."

"Did you see any other aircraft in the vicinity? You know, the kind that might be on an enemy carrier?"

"No, sir," both men agreed.

"And the 'carrier' made no aggressive moves, fired no guns in your direction—or any direction?"

"No, sir."

"And when you conducted your bombing runs, I presume you were right over the 'carrier' and that you dropped at, what? One thousand feet or so?"

"Yes, sir, that's correct."

"And you didn't see, through your windscreens, any sharp, distinguishing features of the 'carrier' as you bore down on the ship?"

Again, the two men exchanged nervous glances, with Connally answering on behalf of them both, "Well, no, sir. We were concentrating on our bombsights, sir, and they were, sorry to say, a little obscured, with condensation, just like the cockpit glass, too, sir. All fogged up."

"I see," Sherman sighed. "Very well, I'll speak to your commanding officer. Dismissed."

"It was a carrier, sir, surely," Whittier added desperately.

"Get off my bridge!" Sherman roared.

NOON LOCAL TIME, DECEMBER 17, 1941

CINCPAC, PEARL HARBOR

"So, that's it," Admiral Kimmel exhaled slowly as he read the telegram in his hands.

"What is, sir?" his chief of staff inquired.

"I've been relieved, by Executive Order of the President, via Admiral Stark, pending a Board of Inquiry."

The room was entirely silent.

"Admiral Pye will take over command until my permanent relief, Admiral Nimitz, can get here. Be sure to give him a complete briefing. I'll be in my quarters—packing."

Without another word, Kimmel left the room and walked away.

Vice Admiral William S. Pye, immediate past commander of the Battle Force (suddenly short several battleships), assumed temporary command of the Pacific Fleet on the afternoon of December 17, 1941. Annapolis, Class of 1901, Pye had spent his prewar career in a variety of battleship and staff positions. He was a staunch member of the Gun Club and was a rare officer who had been awarded a Navy Cross for the quality of his paperwork in World War I, before requirements for the award were changed to require exceptional heroism in combat. He was cautious, old-school, obedient, and fully aware that he was only a caretaker. He received the post because the Navy Department wanted to relieve Kimmel immediately—someone had to pay the consequences for Pearl—and Pye was the next senior admiral on hand. His task was to shepherd the Wake Island relief operation, already in progress. His successor, Adm. Chester W. Nimitz, would arrive by December 31.

During his first full day on the job, Pye received news that would color his decision-making process for the short duration of his command. Radio intercepts, decrypted at Pearl, indicated that the Japanese Fourth Fleet, in charge of the invasion of Wake, was unexpectedly coordinating with the Japanese 2nd Carrier Division. The 2nd Division had been part of the Pearl Harbor Invasion Force and had at least two carriers, *Hiryū* and *Sōryū*, assigned to it. Pye deduced that two Japanese carriers, maybe more, were being dispatched to Wake Island to finish off its stubborn defenders. The cryptanalysts were also able to confirm that the Japanese had set up a seaplane base on Makin Atoll and had invaded and occupied the island of Tarawa. Both of these bases lay along the path that Admiral Brown and *Lexington* were taking on the way to Jaluit.

This situation would expose Brown's task force to land-based bombers in addition to any carriers lurking in the area.

DECEMBER 19–21, 1941

AT SEA

A perfect storm of potentially bad choices and possible doomsday scenarios swirled about the US Navy forces at sea on December 19, 1941. The Wake Island garrison was barely hanging on. Without relief, they would be forced to surrender within a week at the most. They were running out of bullets, bombs, food, water, and manpower.

Rear Admiral Frank "Jack" Fletcher's Task Force 14, with USS *Saratoga* at its center, was pushing toward Wake, but at an agonizingly slow speed. The ancient oiler accompanying the task force, USS *Neches* (launched 1919), was only able to make 12½ knots. The *Neches* fuel was critical to the task force, and therefore they could only proceed as fast as she could go. Still, if all went smoothly Fletcher might be able to arrive at his target on December 22, in time to relieve Wake.

Task Force 11—Admiral Brown and *Lexington*—were on track for Jaluit with a December 21 target date, but Brown was fretting about Makin and Tarawa.

Task Force 8, Vice Admiral Halsey, and the *Enterprise* battle group had successfully refueled and restocked at Pearl and were headed toward Midway Island to act as a reserve force, able to jump in whatever direction they were most needed: Wake, Jaluit, or Pearl.

Hanging over all was the question of the whereabouts of the Japanese carriers. There were at least six of them out there somewhere. The US Navy had only three. The Japanese Navy had at least a two-to-one advantage. Admiral Pye did not like the odds and he did not want to be the caretaker who lost more capital ships, especially the precious carriers. By December 19, he had decided that Wake was the most critical assignment and could not be left to a single carrier.

While Admiral Pye contemplated his next move, Admiral Brown, exercising his pre-sailing discretion, decided to call off the Jaluit raid and attack the bases at Makin and Tarawa instead. No sooner had he issued instructions to his task force about the change in plans, he received a message from Admiral Pye: "Cancel the raid on Jaluit and head to Wake."

The Japanese threw a curveball at the Americans in the early morning hours of December 21: forty-nine aircraft, all carrier based, swooped down on the Wake defenders. Lacking a working radar set, the island's garrison was completely surprised. The Japanese bombed and strafed with devastating effect. The aftershocks of this raid sent reverberations throughout the fleet and CINCPAC. After this, the navy hierarchy knew for certain that the Wake invasion force had been supplemented by carriers.

This put Pye between the pinchers of a nutcracker. The attacking planes were clearly marked as coming from the carriers *Hiryū* and *Sōryū*. This meant that *Saratoga* was rushing toward a possible confrontation with two fleet carriers and twice as many aircraft as she could put in the air. *Lexington* could even the odds, but she wouldn't get there in time. Pye's choice was rapidly becoming one of risking the loss of one-third or more of his flattops or abandoning Wake to its fate.

0753, DECEMBER 23, 1941
RADIO ROOM, USS *ASTORIA*, ADMIRAL FLETCHER'S FLAGSHIP

On December 11, immediately after the first Japanese invasion attempt at Wake Island had been rebuffed, CINCPAC had radioed Commander Cunningham, the garrison commander, asking if he needed anything. It sounded like unbridled machismo, but Commander Cunningham's reply was historic: after detailing a laundry list of ammunition, aircraft, personnel, and supply needs, he appended this phrase to his message: "Send more Japs." The presses around the globe seized on this bit of drollery and held Cunningham up as a shining example of combat sangfroid. In reality, the phrase was most likely "padding," an extra set of words that radio operators deliberately added to messages to throw off enemy translators. Nonetheless, it struck a nerve.

At 0753 on the morning of December 23, however, there was no ambiguity in the message Commander Cunningham sent to Admiral Fletcher. The Japanese were bombing the island again, and the Imperial Japanese Marines were storming ashore. Cunningham radioed: "The issue is in doubt." No padding was needed.

Task Force 14 was 450 miles from Wake at that moment. Admiral Fletcher's operational orders directed him to launch his planes as soon as he hit an arc that was two hundred miles from the island. He'd be able to hit that mark and send in USS *Tangier* (a brand-new cargo ship loaded with supplies, spare parts, men, and food) by the end of the day, no later than dawn on the 24th. The airmen aboard the *Saratoga* were in a high state of readiness and anxiety, champing at the bit to get airborne and dash in to mix it up with the Japanese.

The fate of Wake Island was decided two minutes later when USS *Astoria*'s duty radio operator logged the following: "CINCPAC to Commander TF 14, break off attack Wake Island. Return to Pearl best possible speed after refueling."

When Admiral Fletcher read the message, he took off his gold braided cap and slammed it to the deck in rage and frustration. Admiral Fitch, aboard *Saratoga*, was stunned. *Saratoga*'s skipper, Capt. Archibald H.

Douglas, begged Fitch to call up Admiral Fletcher and at least allow *Saratoga* to launch a punitive air raid against the Japanese ships. Fitch was sympathetic but had to leave *Saratoga*'s bridge "because of the 'mutinous' nature of the conversation."[39] The pilots were outraged. Someone wrote in VF-6's diary, "Everyone seems to feel that it's a war between the *two* yellow races."[40]

The *Lexington* task force received a recall order as well. Admiral Brown and Captain Sherman reluctantly turned their ships around and headed back to Pearl, too. It was a bitter disappointment, but there was no room for interpretation of the orders. Wake Island would be abandoned. The garrison fought heroically, but by Christmas Eve Commander Cunningham could clearly see that each additional life sacrificed would make no difference to the battle's outcome.

For the US Navy, Wake Island had become both a liability and an embarrassment. Making matters even worse, the command structure in the Pacific was in disarray. Admiral Pye was not willing to make command decisions that would tie the hands of his successor.

Pye was forever tarred with the brush of abandoning the gallant defenders of Wake Island, yet that judgment may have been too harsh. The casualties at Wake (120 killed, 49 wounded, 2 MIA) were tragic, and the subsequent harsh treatment of the survivors was barbaric, but on January 1, 1942, Admiral Nimitz assumed command of a Pacific Fleet that still had all three of its aircraft carriers. Those three ships would be the ones to take the war to the Japanese and start the long, tough sail to victory.

39. Lundstrom, 52.
40. Lundstrom, 53.

CHAPTER 5

THE SLEEPING GIANT AWAKES

"A military man can scarcely pride himself on having 'smitten a sleeping enemy'; it is more a matter of shame, simply, for the one smitten. I would rather you made your appraisal after seeing what the enemy does, since it is certain that, angered and outraged, he will soon launch a determined counterattack."
— Admiral Isoroku Yamamoto, January 9, 1942, concerning the attack on Pearl Harbor

Admiral Chester W. Nimitz took over as CINCPAC on January 1, 1942, during what was the Pacific Fleet's darkest hour. A 1905 graduate of the Naval Academy, Nimitz was extraordinarily fortunate to have gotten so far. As a young ensign, assigned to the destroyer USS *Decatur*, he had been court-martialed and given a letter of reprimand. He had accidentally grounded *Decatur* on an uncharted sandbar off the Philippines in 1907 while conning the ship. Normally, these sorts of incidents were career killers, but during the same incident he saved one of his crew from drowning, an act for which he was awarded the navy's Silver Lifesaving Medal. Nimitz kept his commission, and two years later he was sent to Submarine School, from which he graduated with distinction. He was immediately promoted to full lieutenant, skipping over the rank of lieutenant, junior grade.

Nimitz spent many of the years from 1910 to 1933 in submarines, commanding several, becoming a submarine division commander, and serving on important submarine staffs. Promoted to captain in 1927, he was the founder of the Navy ROTC Unit at the University of California, Berkeley. In 1933, he was given command of the cruiser USS *Augusta*, followed two years later by a posting as assistant chief of the Bureau of Navigation in Washington, DC. He then moved up to commander of a cruiser division, soon followed by promotion to rear admiral in 1938. The gamble his superiors had taken on him had paid off handsomely.

In 1939, he was back in Washington, this time as chief of the Bureau of Navigation. While in DC, the smart and savvy Nimitz made many friends in the highest political circles of the capital and gained exposure to and respect from many of the top brass at the Navy Department.

Because of his sterling reputation, connections, and intellect, Nimitz catapulted over many more senior admirals and was given command of the Pacific Fleet. He was even promoted directly to four-star admiral, skipping the grade of vice admiral entirely.

JANUARY 1942
CINCPAC AREA OF OPERATIONS
What Admiral Nimitz was able to accomplish during his first months in command of the Pacific Fleet was impressive. Officers who could not, or would not, adapt to Nimitz's organizational style and strategic methods were pushed aside or reassigned. The most promising midgrade officers, many trained in the latest techniques for coordination, control, and supply, were elevated to positions of great responsibility. New aircraft were requisitioned, especially for the fighter squadrons, and all pilots, mechanics, and aircraft handlers were trained, retrained, and trained again. Admiral Fitch, the officer in the navy with the most experience in aircraft carrier operations, was pulled ashore—with great reluctance on Fitch's part—to help in some of the administrative overhauls that were, in Nimitz's view, absolutely necessary.

The staggering improvements in efficiency and morale that Nimitz engineered during this short period were aided by American ingenuity and drive, but they were also propelled by a sense of urgency and a smoldering thirst for vengeance that was palpable. Admiral Yamamoto's worries about that "sleeping enemy" were becoming very justified.

While skilled fleet officers, the intelligence operation, and shore-establishment managers at Pearl all functioned at a high level, the picture afloat was different. No one knew where the Imperial Japanese Navy was or what their intentions were. Although three American carrier task forces searched assiduously for their enemies, it was probably a good thing they didn't find the Japanese. At sea, the navy still struggled with unresolved organizational, materiel, and tactical issues.

The most nagging materiel deficiencies within the carrier air wings existed in the fighter and torpedo squadrons. While most fighter units were equipped with the inadequate Brewster Buffalos, the newer, superior Wildcats were finally getting out to the fleet squadrons, albeit more slowly than unit commanders would have wished. As for the aging and ineffective Devastators, the replacement Avengers were just beginning to roll off the assembly lines back in the States. They were still several months from arrival.

In January 1942 Task Force 11 was still commanded by Admiral Brown, and Task Force 8 was under Admiral Halsey. Task Force 14, however, underwent a major shakeup: Admiral Fitch had been brought ashore to assist Admiral Nimitz, and Admiral Fletcher was sent to San Diego to speed up the deployment of the new USS *Yorktown* and her carrier air group. Rear Admiral Herbert F. Leary, a 1905 Annapolis classmate of Admiral Nimitz, replaced Fletcher. He had no carrier or aviation experience.

During this reorganization, the three carrier groups continued to shuttle in and out of Pearl Harbor, following Admiral Kimmel's dictum that not more than one carrier should be in port at a time. Visions of another air strike vaulting over the Pali Range were still uppermost in the minds of the Pacific Fleet staffers.

In reality, the IJN flattops had been detailed to cover the invasion activities taking place far to the west, primarily in the Marshall and Gilbert islands. The prime threat to the American carriers was Japan's considerable submarine force. A number of the large, far-ranging Japanese I-boats had been sent to the vicinity of the Hawaiian Islands to find and destroy the American carriers. Since at least two carriers were at sea at all times, it was likely that at least one Japanese skipper was going to get his periscope on a valuable target.

That's exactly what happened on January 11, 1942, at 1915. *Saratoga* was zigzagging at a leisurely twelve knots, 420 miles southwest of Pearl Harbor. Flight operations had been secured for the day and most of the crew were sitting down to dinner.

From 4,700 yards away, the Japanese submarine I-6 fired three torpedoes at three-second intervals. One of the torpedoes slammed into Sara, port side, amidships. The big carrier wobbled, heeled sideways, and began listing to port. Three fire rooms were blown open and flooded, and six firemen were killed. The I-6 turned away and dove to 330 feet. A short time later, the sonar operator of the I-6 heard two loud explosions followed by several smaller ones. The excited submarine captain interpreted those noises as the sounds of the carrier breaking up and sinking. In actuality, the booms were depth charges from destroyers on a frantic search for the enemy sub. The I-6 boasted to her command authority in Guam that she had sunk a "*Lexington*-type" carrier.

Saratoga was wounded, badly, but swift damage-control measures and appropriate counter-flooding saved the ship. She limped back to Pearl but could not be fully repaired there. She headed to Puget Sound, where she was dry-docked and out of action for six months. The Pacific Fleet carrier force was instantly reduced by one-third. *Lexington* also endured a frustrating January 1942 but survived intact. At the beginning of the month, she suffered a major electrical malfunction in one of her four turboelectric drives. If it could not have been fixed locally, Lady Lex, like Sara, would have headed to the West Coast. Fortunately, repair crews at Pearl were able to make the proper adjustments.

The weather was an unwelcome factor. The Pacific was not kind to ship traffic during this month, generally, with heavy ocean swells boiling out of the northwest. On January 11, the same day *Saratoga* was torpedoed, two gigantic waves slammed into *Lexington*, bow on. Tons of water cascaded over the flight deck and poured down the open shaft of the forward elevator. Both elevators short-circuited and many aircraft on the hangar deck were damaged. *Lexington* returned to Pearl on the 16th for repairs and aircraft replacements.

On January 22, Task Force 11 left Pearl, bent on harassing the Japanese at Wake Island. *Lexington* was accompanied by four heavy cruisers, a destroyer squadron, and the pokey fleet oiler *Neches*. The next day, Japanese submarine I-72 popped to the surface, 135 miles west of Oahu, and took aim at the nearest enemy vessel, which happened to be *Neches*. The first torpedo smacked the oiler portside amidships, but failed to detonate. The second torpedo, which buried itself in the oiler's engine room, blew away the entire space. I-72 sent a third and final torpedo into *Neches*'s port side, then surfaced to finish off the crippled oiler with her three-inch deck gun. The valiant crew of the mortally wounded *Neches* did not go down without a fight, however. They blasted away with their two, five-inch guns, to no avail, as the I-72 escaped by submerging. The *Neches* slowly settled by the bow and plunged into the deep with the loss of fifty-seven brave sailors.

The task force's fuel supply was gone. A frustrated Admiral Brown reluctantly ordered all ships back to Pearl.

For the Pacific Fleet carrier groups, the month closed with a whimper. No hits of any kind had been made on the Japanese fleet, with the exception of a few attacks against enemy submarines. The US Navy, on the other hand, had been bloodied by the temporary crippling of the *Saratoga* and the loss of the *Neches*. The airedales had also lost an alarming number of aircraft to accidents, equipment malfunctions, friendly-fire incidents, and poor piloting. Most of the bullets fired and bombs dropped by the navy were on shadows—mistaken targets or drifting barges. At-sea commanders made questionable calls, and confusion was too often the order of the day.

There were pluses, however. Admiral Nimitz had instituted changes that would have profound effects. Admiral Fletcher was soon to arrive with a new carrier battle group, anchored by USS *Yorktown*. Wildcat fighters were shipping out to the fleet. The bombers were carrying bigger and better ordnance. Pilots were getting combat experience, and the best of them were rising to leadership positions throughout the air wings. Back on the mainland, a formerly moribund economy was strengthening with the demands of wartime production as it cranked out mountains of bombs, bullets, equipment, and new technologies. Things were about to change.

FEBRUARY 1942
CINCPAC AREA OF OPERATIONS

By the first two weeks in February, the navy was beginning to replace caution with aggression, even though CINCPAC had only half the frontline carriers of the Imperial Japanese Navy.

On February 1, *Lexington*, still the anchor of Task Force 11, was steaming away from Pearl Harbor to rendezvous with Halsey's Task Force 8. The assignment was to deliver the new fleet oiler, *Neosho*, to Halsey's thirsty ships. Once *Neosho* was safely handed off, Admiral Brown was directed to turn south and escort a convoy of troop transports reinforcing Christmas Island, Canton Island, and New Caledonia.

Aboard USS *Lexington* was VF-3, Fighting Three, commanded by Lt. Cmdr. "Jimmy" Thach. VF-3 was *Saratoga*'s fighter squadron, but because Sara was under repair, Thach and his pilots were out of a ship. Thach's men had the new Wildcat fighters, whereas Lady Lex's VF-2 still had the old Brewster Buffaloes. A swap was negotiated: *Lexington* would off-load VF-2 to Oahu's Ewa Field, which would receive the next batch of Wildcats. When that occurred, Lt. Cmdr. Paul Ramsay's VF-2 would transfer their Buffaloes to the marines, train in the new Wildcats, then rejoin *Lexington* when she returned from her current patrol.

John S. "Jimmy" Thach, an Arkansas native, graduated from the Naval Academy in 1927, spent two years in battleships, then requested a transfer to aviation. He received his pilot's wings in 1930 and spent most of the 1930s as a test pilot, and flight instructor, while growing his expertise in aerial gunnery and fighter tactics. Thach, from the start of his aviation career, impressed everyone with his easygoing manner, natural leadership abilities, and uncanny skills as a pilot. He took command of Fighting Three in December 1940, after serving a year as VF-3's executive officer. He took every new pilot that came to the squadron on a personal "check ride" to test his abilities. Most of the cocky newbies believed they had already learned all they needed to know about flying. Thach disabused each of them of that notion quickly. He was famous for flying circles around his "nugget" pilots while either munching on an apple or calmly reading a newspaper.[41]

One of the young pilots who joined Thach's "Felix the Cat" squadron in 1940 was Edward H. "Butch" O'Hare, Naval Academy Class of 1937. O'Hare's parents divorced when he was thirteen. His father, a lawyer, moved to Chicago, where he became a confidante of Al Capone. The elder O'Hare later turned state's evidence against his boss, helping the government convict Capone of tax evasion. After Butch graduated, he served two years aboard the battleship USS *New Mexico* before being accepted into flight training. Sadly, late in 1939, O'Hare's father was shot to death in Chicago. Although never proven, it was likely an act of revenge orchestrated by Capone.

Butch O'Hare received his wings in May 1940 and was sent to VF-3 aboard USS *Saratoga*. Like the others, he received the "Thach Treatment" almost immediately, but Lieutenant Commander Thach was impressed with O'Hare and began mentoring him in tactics and aerial gunnery. O'Hare quickly began to excel in both, particularly gunnery.

Thach, O'Hare, and the rest of VF-3 were warmly welcomed aboard Lady Lex by Captain Sherman, Air Wing Cmdr. Bill Ault, and the rest of the squadrons. Thach observed:

> There was a different and better spirit aboard the Lex. The work on the flight deck went on with less noise and delay. The port holes were opened in the day time so that fresh air entered the ship and the evening meal was eaten in whites (a dress uniform). It was a good start, filled with promise for a happy cruise.[42]

Apparently, Captain Sherman set a tone that the true professionals, like Thach, could admire and appreciate. That ship spirit was in full force on February 5, when *Lexington* and the other ships in the task force crossed the equator.

The US Navy has held line-crossing rituals from its earliest days. The basic purpose is to turn "slimy Polliwogs" (those sailors who have never sailed across the equator before) into "Golden Shellbacks," worthy denizens of King Neptune's domain. Each captain handles the ceremony differently, and the rules are open to interpretation. The basic custom is for the senior "Shellback" aboard the vessel (the officer or sailor with the earliest line-crossing date) to hold "court" as King Neptune, initiating the "Polliwogs" into his realm by demanding answers to ludicrous questions while forcing the initiates to perform ridiculous tasks or stunts. Outlandish costumes

41. Lundstrom, 34.
42. Lundstrom, 104.

made up of garish accoutrement are the norm. A favorite torture for Polliwogs was running a gauntlet of Shellbacks armed with paddles, rotten fruit, paint, Jell-O, fire hoses, or whatever implements and objects might be at hand. Polliwogs were taken to "court," grilled, castigated, embarrassed, and "fined" all sorts of small amounts of money to buy "smokes and Cokes" for the Shellbacks.

Lexington, especially under Captain Sherman, had a proclivity toward the merriment and traditions of a line crossing. The ceremonies aboard Lady Lex were legendary. On this particular date, it was even more monumentally historic because the ship had a plethora of new sailors and airmen, most of them new to the navy as well. Two who were held up to particular scrutiny were the young bomber pilots—Whittier and Connally—who had identified the drifting dynamite barge as a Japanese carrier and had proceeded to conduct bombing runs upon the "enemy ship."

Line crossings, back in the day, could be ordeals for Polliwogs, and some even produced serious injuries, but like most incidents of hazing, the intent was to bond a ship and her crew. After the ceremonies, each new Shellback received a certificate, often elaborately designed and printed aboard the ship. Almost every sailor who has ever gone through a line-crossing ceremony will speak of it with nostalgia, and display his or her Shellback certificate with pride.

NOON, FEBRUARY 6, 1942
NEAR THE EQUATOR
Admiral Brown received new orders, directly from Admiral King, to steam for the South Pacific. He was to team up with a surface task force under the command of Royal Australian Navy Rear Adm. John G. "Jack" Crace. King was creating an ANZAC (Australia–New Zealand Army Corps) Command. Rear Admiral Leary was sent ashore to coordinate the American side of the equation, and Brown would stay at sea in command of the task force. Brown's first assignment under this new structure was to set his sights on the town of Rabaul, in the Australian Territory of New Guinea, in an attempt to disrupt the Japanese plans for development of a strategic base on that island. A tentative strike date against Rabaul was set for February 21.

1000, FEBRUARY 20, 1942
NORTHEAST OF BOUGAINVILLE ISLAND
After a dozen years of Fleet Problems, thousands of training sorties, and hundreds of mock attacks, real enemy bombs and bullets were hurled at an American aircraft carrier for the first time. The action began with an unidentified blip on *Lexington*'s CXAM radar at precisely 1000 hours.

Six Wildcats from Lt. Cmdr. Jimmie Thach's VF-3 had been pre-spotted on the flight deck, warming up, anticipating they would soon replace the six Dauntless SBDs already out ahead of the carrier, on patrol.

Sherman was not at all sure the CAP, or combat air patrol, was going to be necessary: just because the radar had identified a flight of bogeys inbound, it didn't mean they were enemy planes. The mysterious planes could be their own SBDs from VB-2 on their return leg. Sherman was not going to take any chances, however.

The big blip was, in reality, a Kawanishi H6K flying boat under the command of IJN pilot Lt. j.g. Noboru Sakai. It would be easy for the CXAM operator to confuse this very large, four-engine, long-range patrol plane with a group of smaller aircraft. Designated by the code name "Mavis" by the Allies, this aircraft normally carried a crew of nine or ten and enough fuel to stretch out on twenty-four-hour patrols that could cover four thousand miles. Lieutenant Junior Grade Sakai and his crew had started their day at the seaplane basin on Rabaul, 450 miles away from Task Force 11. Sakai's aircraft was one of three that had been sent out to scout for the enemy, with each Mavis covering a different fifteen-degree arc. *Lexington* was squarely in Sakai's 075 to 090 sector, and at 1015 he and his crew laid eyes on Lady Lex. He immediately reported back to headquarters on Rabaul that he was looking at "an enemy striking force, including one carrier."

Sakai inched in closer, using the scattered clouds in the area to mask his position. He darted from cloud to cloud, hoping to escape detection. He was not counting on *Lexington*'s radar, as the IJN did not have this secret weapon.

$$\sim$$

Back aboard *Lexington*, the ship's fighter direction officer, or FDO, Lt. Frank F. "Red" Gill, was carefully plotting the progress of Sakai's blip. Gill, a ten-year veteran pilot with a prominent shock of red hair, had the tough task of acting as the choreographer for all fighter aircraft aloft. Using methods that were still under development, his status board crammed into a tiny corner of Air Plot, Gill's primary job was educated guesswork. Computerized screens or CRT displays did not yet exist. Gill worked with paper charts, plastic plotting boards, a standard navigational ruler, and a compass. His raw data were the contacts, ranges, and bearings he could hear over the radios from his pilots and the information supplied by the radar operators. Using this limited data, plus his own flying experience, the FDO needed to quickly calculate where his own aircraft were and where the enemy planes might be, and to maneuver his forces to effect an intersection of the combatants. Given that all of his charges were flying at different altitudes and speeds while using evasive maneuvers under general radio silence, it was a nearly impossible task. Red Gill's call sign was "Romeo."

"Green section [Thach and his wingman], Romeo [FDO Gill]: vector 205 [fly 205 degrees], angels two [2,000 feet altitude], distance three-five [thirty-five nautical miles], buster [fly as fast as you can]."

Lieutenant Commander Thach and his wingman, Ensign Edward Sellstrom, flew out to Gill's coordinates and ran smack into a wall of clouds. Thach elected to break radio silence; it was a risky move, but Thach felt it necessary under the circumstances:

"Romeo, Green: large rain squall dead ahead. Is target in there?"

"Green, Romeo: affirmative."

"Roger, going in."

Thach ordered Sellstrom, a new and inexperienced pilot, to stick close to Thach's left wing. Pushing the throttle to the max, he plunged into the clouds. The two aircraft were immediately pelted by driving rain and buffeted by strong winds. There were breaks throughout the puffy, gray mass, however, and almost immediately Thach spied the gigantic, lumbering Kawanishi right below him. Gill had put them right on top of the target. Luck or skill, Thach didn't care.

Thach and Sellstrom peeled off to the right, out of the cloud, to line up a run on the Mavis. They were flying faster than their quarry and needed to pull back around to get behind the target. As soon as they commenced their turn, Gill reported that the Mavis had disappeared from radar. To Thach, this could mean only one thing: the big ship was diving for the deck. One of the crew must have spotted the Americans and alerted Lieutenant Junior Grade Sakai to drop down and run like hell, which was precisely what Sakai was doing.

The navy pilots punched back into the cloud to press home their attack, but the Japanese plane had disappeared. The Americans went into a dive, and as they plowed out of the lowest layer of clouds they regained a visual on the Mavis, heading away from them at the fastest speed it could make, which was slightly over two hundred miles per hour. This was no match for the Wildcats, and they soon caught up. Ordering Sellstrom off to port to conduct an attack of the left side of the big patrol plane, Thach dove in from the right, high above. The Mavis was not well armed. It was, after all, a patrol plane, not an attack aircraft, but it did have one impressive "stinger": a powerful 20-millimeter cannon in the tail. To avoid the tail gunner, the American aviators needed to swoop in from the obliques and as high as possible.

Thach opened fire with his Browning .50-calibers and stitched the high parasol wing[43] on the starboard side. Gasoline started to stream from the wing tanks and smoke billowed from the two right-side engines. Sellstrom, exuberant, came in too low and level and was immediately targeted by the tail gunner. Only some high-speed "juking" took him out of the stream of red tracer bullets racing toward him. Sellstrom distracted the gunner, however, allowing Thach to line up for another run unmolested. This time, Thach's bullets tore into the entire wing, setting the gasoline-filled horizontal sail on fire. The Mavis dipped sharply and plowed into the water at full speed, bursting into an enormous ball of fire and wreckage. The tower of black smoke could be seen from *Lexington*'s deck, over twenty miles away. It was an exhilarating moment for the Lady Lex and her air wing; it was their first "kill."

What this meant, however, was that Task Force 11 had been discovered. Lieutenant Junior Grade Sakai and his crew had paid with their lives, but they had alerted their base to the existence of an enemy carrier task force headed their way. Admiral Brown had a tough decision: he could press ahead with his plans to attack Rabaul the next day, as scheduled, but he knew the Japanese, with twenty-four hours warning, could sortie their ships, escape his attack, and get the jump on him by sending land-based aircraft out to attack his ships. The ever-aggressive Sherman urged Brown to stay the course, to attack as planned. But Brown was plagued by another nagging problem: he had no spare fuel. The only available oiler was five hundred miles behind him, sailing with Admiral Halsey. If he got into a running gun battle with the Japanese, he could be out of gas before it was over. The fuel consideration was the overriding factor, and he broke off the attack. He did agree, however, to a feint in the direction of Rabaul to distract the Japanese. Perhaps the threat of an American task force in the vicinity would take some of the pressure off the forces battling the Japanese in the East Indies. He directed the task force to turn southwest and bear down. They would steam in to about two hundred miles from Rabaul, then break for home.

～

The Japanese commanders on Rabaul were not about to take any chances. Rear Admiral Eiji Gotō was in charge of the 24th Air Flotilla on Rabaul, and he drew the assignment of dealing with the US Navy threat. The 24th was a composite unit consisting of land-based bombers, seaplanes, and fighters, all assigned to the IJN Fourth Fleet. It was Gotō's bombers that had savaged Wake Island during the first days of that campaign.

The fighters in the 24th did not have the range or the external drop tanks to get out to *Lexington*'s position, conduct attacks, and return safely

---

43. A "parasol wing" was the main wing, but it was not part of the fuselage; rather, it was above the fuselage and attached to it only by a series of struts.

before running out of fuel. The Mavis seaplanes, already out on patrol, were not useful for conducting anti-ship attacks anyway. Gotō's bombers were the only aircraft he had that could deal with the Americans. They were the new Mitsubishi GM4 types, christened "Betty" by the Allies, and Gotō had eighteen of them at his disposal.

Gotō's staff urged him to hold back until the Americans got closer so that the fighters could escort the bombers to their targets. Gotō was unwilling to wait. The opportunity to strike was immediate, and he felt that surprise would be on his side. He had taken some stinging criticism for the losses his flotilla had absorbed at Wake and also against Admiral Halsey's raids on February 1.[44] Gotō, perhaps impatiently, also wanted to test the abilities of his new bombers against seaborne targets.

The Betty bomber was a twin-engine aircraft with a crew of seven—two pilots, a radioman, an engineer, and three gunners. It had superior range and could carry up to a ton of bombs or torpedoes. It was light, versatile, and fast for a bomber, with a max speed of 265 miles per hour. Yet it had two critical negatives: protective armor and self-sealing gas tanks had been sacrificed for its increased speed, range, and loading capacity. The crews of the Bettys derisively called their flammable rides the "Type One Lighter." The Americans called them "Flying Zippos."

Admiral Gotō elected to launch all of his Bettys against Task Force 11. They were armed with two 250-pound bombs each. Gotō would rather have sent them on their mission with a mix of ordnance, but the deadly Japanese "Long Lance" torpedoes had not yet been delivered to Rabaul. Two sections of nine planes each were readied, but one of the Bettys developed engine problems and could not be launched. Another Mavis went ahead of the bombers to point the way.

1600, 20 FEBRUARY, 1942

USS *LEXINGTON*

After the morning's initial flurry of action, the radar screen remained blank until 1542, when the array picked up another bogey, range seventy-six miles. The mysterious contact quickly dropped away and did not reappear. It was enough of a concern that Lieutenant Gill recalled the CAP then aloft, which had been in the air for several hours. He wanted a fresh set of Wildcats off the deck and on station. Six fighters, under the lead of Lt. Noel Gayler, were spotted and launched beginning at 1606. It proved to be a wise move.

At 1611, another large contact popped up on the radar, bearing 255, seventy-five miles. Gill plotted the bogey, but at 1622 the contact disappeared.

44. Task Force 8 had attacked Japanese bases on Kwajalein, Wotje, and Taroa on February 1, 1942, and done some minor damage. Gotō had lost fifteen of his aircraft to the US Navy's seven losses.

The Air Department decided to go ahead with recovering the thirsty air-craft aloft, but three minutes later the contact reappeared, this time at bearing 276 and only forty-seven miles. Five minutes later, at 1630, the con-tact was only twenty-four miles out; whatever it was, it was moving fast and directly at the formation. Gill vectored Gayler's patrol toward the target while Captain Sherman rang up flank speed (thirty knots). The air boss, Commander Duckworth, told the airborne pilots to wave off. Duckworth had four more Wildcats and twelve bombers fully gassed and armed on the deck, and if the ship was attacked while they were still on board, it could be a disaster. The first priority was to get those sitting ducks in the air. The ominous contact that the radar had picked up was the first section of nine Betty bombers bearing down on *Lexington.*

The leader of this *chūtai* (squadron) was Lt. Masayoshi Nakagawa, a solid pilot and skilled bombardier. The other pilots were also combat veterans. Each Betty had defensive machine guns in the nose, in both waists, and in a top turret. The tail gunner had a powerful 20-millimeter cannon that was specifically designed to counter threats from the rear of the aircraft, a favorite focus for American planes. Nakagawa had every reason to believe that he could get to the American carrier and attack it successfully: he had skilled crews, new aircraft, capable bombs, good defensive weapons, and the element of surprise. Lacking knowledge of *Lexington's* radar, he would be fatally incorrect. Lieutenant Gayler and his wingman, Ensign Dale W. Petersen, barely got to their desired altitude (13,000 feet) before spotting the onrushing Japanese 1,500 feet below them. The enemies were flying like angry, armored geese, in three "Vs" of three planes each. Slightly nose down and dashing along at over 170 knots, they did not see the Americans buzzing above them. Gayler and Petersen were in a perfect position to drop down and plunge into the Japanese formation from a steep, high-side angle. Gayler's second section, Lt. j.g. Rolla S. Lemmon and Lt. j.g. Howard F. "Spud" Clark, were right behind their leader. Gayler's third section, Lt. j.g. Willard E. Eder and Ensign John W. Wilson, were tardy. Wilson's engine was struggling, not developing sufficient horsepower to keep up with his wingman. Eder ended up below the Japanese formation, looking up at the enemy bombers. Wilson couldn't make the altitude and dropped away.

"Romeo, Red Leader [Gayler]. Contact. Commencing run. Haven't seen these babies before."

Gayler was looking at planes of a type he had not found in his aircraft recognition books. These were green-and-gray, single-tailed, cigar-shaped craft of unknown design, but the big, red "meatballs" painted on each wing left no doubt as to their fealty. The bright, twinkling flashes and searing red tracers suddenly erupting in his windscreen told Gayler that he was no longer unrecognized, either.

Gayler and Petersen conducted a textbook pass on the last plane in the formation and tattooed the bomber's wings right behind both engine nacelles. Both airman were surprised when the Japanese bomber burst into flame from stem to stern and corkscrewed wildly away. There was no time for analysis, however, and the two Americans pulled up and turned back for a second pass.

Lemmon and Clark followed their leader and bore down on the next Betty. It, too, blew up spectacularly and fell away, a flaming wreck. The "E" for Excellence in gunnery recently awarded to VF-3 was paying big dividends quickly.

Eder, slightly below the Japanese formation, pulled up sharply and fired a burst into the belly of the next Betty, and immediately a third enemy bomber was dropping away from the formation and into a death spiral. Simultaneously, from above, Gayler was pumping another burst into the same bomber, hastening its demise.

The remaining six Bettys pressed ahead, tightening up their dwindling formation. Lieutenant Nakagawa could see the big American carrier ahead by then, and even though he was under fierce attack, he did not waver. Several ships in the task force could see the Japanese formation by that time and would later report their astonishment, as well as some grudging admiration, over the fortitude of the Japanese flyers. Nakagawa's bombers were not dive bombers: their ordnance, in order to be successfully delivered, had to be dropped horizontally, which required straight and level flying. Although the Japanese attack might have seemed suicidal, it was actually the correct bombing tactic.

Gayler and his men continued to bear down, picking off a fourth bomber (by Lieutenant Junior Grade Lemmon), then a fifth (by Ensign Petersen). At about the same time, the deck guns from the cruisers began banging away, filling the sky with flak. They were wildly inaccurate, which was fortunate since the ship's gunners did not distinguish friend from foe.

Meanwhile, aboard Lady Lex, the deck gang was scrambling to launch the remaining Wildcats and the refueled bombers, another fifteen planes altogether. Lieutenant Commander Thach was back in the air, along with Doc Sellstrom, Butch O'Hare, and Lt. j.g. Marion "Duff" Dufilho, O'Hare's wingman.

Four of nine Bettys remained, one crippled and completely missing its port engine. It had been shot out of its nacelle. The Bettys were finally close enough to be a real threat to Lexington—and too close for further pursuit by the fighters. These bombers represented eight bombs that could do considerable damage to the carrier.

From the bridge, Ted Sherman, the master ship handler, could see the Japanese planes swinging around to line up a stern attack, straight down his flight deck. He would not give them an easy target. With Lady Lex at thirty-plus knots, Sherman watched carefully and as soon as the Bettys lined up, he swung the stern away, forcing the bombers to realign their formation. As soon as they did, Sherman pushed the helm away again. When the planes finally got to their drop point, their bomb bay doors opened. This was Sherman's final cue. To the growing panic of his bridge crew, Sherman waited until the last possible second before finally shouting, "Hard a-port!"

The giant ship slowly slewed to the left just as the dark shapes of the enemy bombs trickled out of their bomb bays. As Lady Lex furiously churned water astern, and the four enemy bombers flew by in a hail of anti-aircraft fire, every single Japanese bomb missed its mark. The closest bomb carved out a meaningless crater in the sea three thousand feet away.

Everyone on the bridge breathed a sigh of relief, but danger still loomed. The mangled bomber with the missing engine broke formation from its fleeing mates and made an agonizing turn toward *Lexington*. No one knows for sure, but this Betty might have been the command ship of Lieutenant Nakagawa. Most, if not all, of its crew were wounded and many were dead, including at least one pilot, given that a large black hole gaped on the left side of the cockpit. All her guns were silent. The *chūtai* had failed and the wounded plane would not make it home. The unknown pilot would make one last, desperate attempt to avenge his friends and the honor of his squadron.

In the days before the kamikaze, Japanese pilots had adopted a tactic they called *taiatari*, or "body strike." Captain Sherman knew that the Betty's pilot could cause a great deal of damage, maybe even take *Lexington* out of the war, at least temporarily. All he would have to do was line up on the carrier's stern and plunge his crippled bomber into the deck and all the parked aircraft. This appeared to be his intent.

Sherman ordered the stern-based five-inch guns and all rear-facing 1.1-inch anti-aircraft mounts and .50-cal machine guns to blast the Betty out of the sky. As the guns roared, the bomber began to shudder. Smoke poured out of its fuselage. The Betty fluttered momentarily before its nose lowered and it splashed into *Lexington*'s wake, a scant seventy-five yards from its goal.

The American pilots took off after the three surviving Bettys, two of them already damaged. Fortunately for *Lexington*'s fate, Red Gill reined in two of the airborne Wildcats. While Lieutenant Commander Thach and the rest pursued the fleeing enemy planes, Gill ordered Lieutenant Junior Grade Dufilho and Lieutenant O'Hare to stand by. Both men chafed at Gill's decision, but Gill wanted a CAP over the ship in case there were more enemy aircraft in the area.

~

When the original formation of seventeen Bettys had taken off from Rabaul, they had split into two *chūtai*, each on a different search vector. The Japanese were not certain where, exactly, the *Lexington* task force might be, so Admiral Gotō directed the two squadrons to split up and then rendez-vous once the enemy was found. Lieutenant Nakagawa flew out on a heading of roughly 075, and the second *chūtai*, under Lt. Cmdr. Takuzo Itō, flew along a bearing that would eventually take them north of Task Force 11.

In the middle of the first tangle with the Japanese bombers, the CXAM had actually spotted Lieutenant Commander Itō's eight-plane formation, but in all the confusion, with multiple targets scattered all over the screen, the second enemy formation did not stand out from the clutter. By 1656, as more Bettys dropped into the sea, the second formation became obvious.

At 1700, Lieutenant Commander Itō was still searching for his partner, Lieutenant Nakagawa, who was by then dead. Itō decided to turn south, back toward his own base. This fortuitous course correction lined him up squarely on *Lexington*'s stern, which Itō spotted, glimmering in the distance, from his perch of 15,000 feet. He directed his *chūtai* to descend immediately, to 11,000 feet, picking up speed to 190 knots. With Lieutenant Commander Thach and the rest of his fighters wave-hopping, chasing down the three remaining Bettys from Nakagawa's decimated unit, the field was wide open for Itō to execute a full-throttle, stern-on attack. He could not have diagrammed it better. The only opposition standing in his way were the two lonely Wildcats that Red Gill had held in reserve: O'Hare and Dufilho.

Lieutenant Gill radioed Lieutenant Commander Thach that he and his fighters were needed back at *Lexington*—a new and unexpected threat drew close. Thach had a devil of a time rounding up his scattered planes.

Lieutenant Don Lovelace and Lt. j.g. Howard Johnson were chasing one of the remaining Bettys, Lovelace from below and Johnson from behind. The tail gunner in the Betty opened up on Johnson's Wildcat and hammered several shells into Johnson's engine, which shuddered and promptly seized. Shrapnel from the blast sliced into both of Johnson's legs. At about the same moment, Lovelace opened up on the tail of the Betty, filling it with slugs and silencing the cannon. Johnson's plane rolled over on its back and started to spiral downward. In pain and losing a lot of blood, Johnson still managed to bail out. Lovelace radioed *Lexington*, and Sherman ordered the destroyer USS *Patterson* (DD-392) to chase down Johnson and rescue him, which *Patterson* did within thirty minutes.

Thach and Sellstrom, still trying to locate their squadron mates, came upon Ensign Jack Wilson, piloting the Wildcat with the underperforming powerplant. Shockingly, Thach saw Wilson boring in on a wounded Betty from directly astern. This was the worst possible position for Wilson, but with a balky engine, he didn't have the power to execute a safer, high-side run. Thach radioed the young pilot to break away, but Wilson either ignored his commander or didn't hear him. The tail gunner in the Betty blasted 20-millimeter cannon shells directly into Wilson's face. One of the rounds hit the Wildcat squarely on the windscreen and plowed through the cockpit, likely killing Wilson instantly. The fighter rolled over and spiraled directly into the ocean. The Japanese had their first revenge on the day.

Thach turned and executed a perfect strafing run on the Betty that had downed Wilson. He pumped a long burst into the bomber's right engine and wing root. The plane blew apart and fell into the sea.

Seconds later, one of the last two Bettys flew directly underneath Thach, hellbent on escape. Thach nosed over, throttled ahead, and came down on top of the enemy bomber. He stitched the entire top of the fuselage with bullets, but the plane did not waver. Realizing that its engines and wings were most vulnerable, Thach pulled up under the Betty and zoomed back up to execute another high-side run. He aimed carefully for the right nacelle and fired. The engine burst into flames and tore off nearly all the right wing as it fell away.

That left only one Betty out of the entire *chūtai* still in the air. Thach saw it pulling away and was tempted to follow, but Gill's urgent pleas to get back to the ship persuaded him he was needed elsewhere. Thach and his pilots banked away and sped back to *Lexington*. The last surviving Betty from Lieutenant Masayoshi's doomed squadron had the bad luck to fly straight into Lt. Walter F. Henry, XO of VB-2. Bombing Two was on its way back to *Lexington* from its afternoon search out ahead of the task force. As the Betty zoomed by, all Henry had to do was turn and follow. It took a few miles for Henry's superior speed to finally catch up and overtake the enemy bomber. Henry could see crew members moving around in the fuselage, but strangely, no one was firing at him. He lined up and fired a burst from his twin .50 cals directly into the port engine and cockpit. The entire plane immediately caught fire, and like a dying comet it plunged straight into the water below. An entire squadron had been obliterated.

A few miles back toward *Lexington*, Henry spotted the carcass of one of the previously downed Bettys floating on the surface of the sea. Several crew members were scrambling over the wreck. Henry dove on the sinking bomber and fired. The plane blew apart in a ball of fiery gas, flying metal, and body parts. All Henry saw were enemy airmen when he fired; but, in retrospect, it was not the US Navy's most humane moment.

1705

ASTERN OF USS *LEXINGTON*

O'Hare and Dufilho were loitering five miles astern of the carrier at 11,000 feet. At 1705, they both spotted the formation of Lieutenant Commander Itō's bombers below them, descending rapidly from about 7,000 feet, bore-sighted on the stern of their ship. From their height advantage, it was easy enough to turn and dive on the enemy aircraft; still, it was an eight-against-two scramble. O'Hare, as senior, took the lead. Coming in from behind and above, he took careful aim at the rear-most Betty on the right side of the *chūtai*.

Under Lieutenant Commander Thach's tutelage, O'Hare had not only become one of the best pilots in VF-3, he was also its best marksman. He picked off the first Betty with a short burst that blew apart the starboard engine. Streaming smoke, oil, and fuel, the bomber spiraled downward. The destruction was so quick and accurate that O'Hare didn't have to do anything but jink out of the way to continue, on the same pass.

O'Hare fired another short and deadly burst. A second Betty began streaming a trail of milky fuel. The bomber dropped down, and out of formation. The pilot opened his bomb bay doors, jettisoned his useless ordnance, and ran toward Rabaul as fast as one engine would allow.

O'Hare's and Dufilho's momentum had by then carried them to the far side of the Japanese formation, which, according to Lieutenant Commander Itō's plan, steadily pressed ahead. It was Dufilho's turn, but his guns were jammed. He peeled away to try and clear them, but to no avail. O'Hare was the only airborne defense against the six remaining bombers, who were almost on top of *Lexington*.

O'Hare turned back in, this time on the left side of the *chūtai*, and, as before, started with the trailing bomber and worked his way forward. He hit his first target in the left engine, which promptly caught fire. The Betty, piloted by Petty Officer 1st Class Koji Maeda, dove away to the left and descended. Maeda hit the fire extinguisher button. The port engine was ruined, but the fire went out. Maeda gamely added full power to his remaining engine, pulled up, and tried to get back in formation.

O'Hare's next victim was the Betty immediately to Itō's left. O'Hare riddled its left wing and engine and it, too, dropped away to the left, on fire and spinning uncontrollably. As that Betty fell away, Itō, the intrepid commander of the squadron, was squarely in O'Hare's gun sight. On the other hand, O'Hare was centered in the gun sights of every remaining

Betty machine gun that could slew around and fire at him. O'Hare ignored the blasts aimed at him and fired directly into Itō's port engine, which exploded. The blast tore the entire engine out of the nacelle, and it fell away. Itō's craft dropped away, maimed and smoking.

Three remaining Bettys were directly over *Lexington*. Incredibly, the wounded Betty flown by Petty Officer Maeda had caught up and it, too, was ready to disgorge its payload. O'Hare swung back around and took careful aim at his sixth target of the afternoon. He pressed the trigger and each machine gun fired about ten rounds, then quit. He was out of ammunition. He pulled up and away and watched helplessly as the four remaining Bettys opened their bomb bay doors.

Down below, Captain Sherman was not yet out of tricks. As before, he threw the ship at top speed, one way and then another, making it hard for the bombers to align their strikes. As the enemy bombs finally came tumbling out, none of them landed closer to *Lexington* than a hundred yards.

One of the crippled Bettys came roaring across the wave tops, aiming straight for the carrier. A gaping black hole where the port engine should have been indicated that it was Itō, possibly wounded and enraged, struggling to remain airborne as *Lexington*'s guns zeroed in on him. Skimming the water, Itō's plane absorbed round after round of anti-aircraft fire. At the last moment Sherman turned again, and the Betty dipped and smashed into the water off *Lexington*'s port bow.

The four remaining Bettys gathered together and lumbered away toward Rabaul. Only two of them would get there. Ensign Sellstrom, who had refueled and relaunched, as had Lieutenant Gayler, chased the formation halfway back. Each of them picked off a Betty before their fuel supply demanded a return. Two Bettys from the original seventeen planes limped back home. Shot full of holes, both carried dead and wounded crewmen. One was so badly crippled, it ditched in the lagoon.

With the immediate threat neutralized, Sherman swung *Lexington* into the wind again to recover the gas and bullet-starved fighters that were about to fall into the sea.

Lexington's air wing had lost two Wildcats and one pilot, Ensign Wilson. Lieutenant Butch O'Hare had been credited with six kills on the day by Air Plot and Lieutenant Gill, but he himself could claim only five for sure.[45] Five was enough, however, to make him the navy's first ace of World War II. He was an instant celebrity, and his actions cheered an American public that had absorbed a lot of bad news since December 7.[46]

---

45. In actuality, the total was four: he had definitely shot three Bettys out of the sky in the battle, as witnessed and sworn to by others. He had hit and badly crippled two more, one of which was ultimately finished off by LT Gayler as it tried to make it back to Rabaul. The fifth plane was so badly damaged it would not fly again, but it did make it home, as later records would substantiate. Nonetheless, it was a magnificent performance in both aerial skill and gunnery.

46. Lieutenant O'Hare would soon be pulled from his flight duties and transferred back to the United States. As a national hero, he would spend April 21, 1942, at the White House, where his wife, Rita, would place a Medal of Honor around her husband's neck, with a beaming President Franklin Roosevelt looking on.

FEBRUARY 21, 1942

WARDROOM, USS *LEXINGTON*

In the wee hours of the morning on February 21, Thach and O'Hare, still pumped up on adrenaline, sat in the wardroom rehashing the previous day's events. They wanted to pull together a set of lessons learned to share with the rest of the pilots. At 0800, Thach gathered all of his men in the squadron ready room for a briefing.

Of chief concern to Thach was the need for group discipline and staying in radio contact with him. When Thach's pilots had scattered and chased after the survivors of the first wave of attackers, they had left their ship vulnerable. It was only by sheer chance that O'Hare was able to break apart the second wave of bombers before they could damage the ship. This critical lesson became air wing doctrine, and the squadron and wing commanders spread it from carrier to carrier.

Thach also stressed the need to avoid the "cone of destruction" behind the new Betty bombers. Both Wildcats lost, and the squadron's only fatality had come from attacks made on planes flying directly behind the Bettys. Within this cone, the Betty's tail gunner had a clear shot with a powerful cannon.

Dufilho's jammed guns were also a hot topic. It wasn't the first time it had happened, but it turned out there was an easy fix. The armorers needed to be more diligent about loading the belts of ammo into the pods. Loose packing allowed the belts to shift in flight, making it easy for them to get out of alignment with the breeches of the guns.

Thach also talked about basic gunnery and the importance of gunnery practice. It wasn't just luck that had brought down fifteen Bettys and two Mavis patrol planes: nine out of twelve of VF-3's pilots had earned the navy "E" for "expert" in gunnery before they even took off on their first combat flights. O'Hare, in particular, had demonstrated that it wasn't how many bullets you fired but where you placed them that really counted.

Sherman's adroit ship handling was another tactical tidbit for broad consumption, especially the maneuvers he had used to keep his ship out of the zones of highest danger.

Gunnery officers had discovered quickly that their shipboard shooters needed more practice and better firing discipline. Commanders also realized that they had underestimated the skill, determination, and commitment of their foes. IJN pilots had shown that they could maintain combat discipline under stressful conditions. They were fearless and apparently willing to sacrifice their lives to achieve their combat objectives. These lessons were a far cry from the conclusions of Fleet Problem XV (1934), which had determined: "It is by no means probable that an Asiatic power could wage such an efficient war of attrition. . . ."

~

After the successful repulse of the IJN attack on Task Force 11 and the conclusion of the feint toward Rabaul, Admiral Brown turned east to hook up with the fleet oiler USS *Platte* (AO-24) for a much needed drink. The Japanese, stung by the failure of February 20, sent out several probes, including a full-blown torpedo plane raid (with the newly arrived Long Lances), to find and destroy the American carrier. *Lexington*, by then, was long gone.

Back in Washington, the impatient Admiral King yearned for even more action out of his carrier forces in the Pacific. He leaned on Admiral Nimitz, who, in turn, pressed Admiral Brown: Nimitz wanted Brown to strike back at the Japanese on Rabaul before the IJN could build up and fortify the base more than they already had. Brown, a cautious officer, began a torrent of messages and memos back to CINCPAC arguing that a renewed attack against Rabaul could not be conducted without a buildup of his Task Force or without at least two carrier air groups.

To Brown's surprise, Nimitz agreed and ordered Rear Adm. Frank "Jack" Fletcher and the new *Yorktown* carrier group to link up with Brown as fast as possible. Surprised by the order, Brown backpedaled. He speculated on the tenuous nature of logistically supporting two entire carrier battle groups so far from home base and wondered if even two carriers would be enough. Nimitz's response was, in essence, "I don't necessarily disagree with you, but do it anyway. Fletcher's already on his way."

Steaming toward Brown's task force, Fletcher had raised his flag aboard USS *Yorktown*, Capt. Elliott Buckmaster in command. *Yorktown*, CV-5, launched in 1937, was in the Atlantic when war broke out. She was immediately hustled to the West Coast in late December 1941. By early January 1942, *Yorktown* had been in and out of Pearl Harbor and had participated, with Admiral Halsey, in the Marshall and Gilbert islands raids of February 1. After these early operations, *Yorktown* split away from Halsey's Task Force 8 and continued on her own as Task Force 17 as USS *Saratoga* was still under repair in Bremerton.

USS *Yorktown* was considerably younger than Lady Lex. She was faster by three-plus knots and more maneuverable due to an easier helm, and even though she was a hundred feet shorter, she could carry more aircraft (ninety, as opposed to seventy-eight). She had the advantage of three elevators over *Lexington*'s two, which gave her the ability to shift aircraft and re-spot her flight deck more agilely. *Yorktown* was also air conditioned, which made a great deal of difference in crew comfort and equipment maintenance in the tropical heat of the South Pacific. On steamy *Lexington*, condensation cascaded down the passageways. New technologies and recent marine engineering advances outpaced the innate capabilities of Lady Lex.

0900, MARCH 6, 1942
USS *LEXINGTON*, CORAL SEA

Admiral Fletcher's task forced steamed into view and rendezvoused with Admiral Brown on the morning of March 6, as well as the ANZAC Squadron sent by Admiral Leary from Australia. The ANZAC contingent consisted of the heavy cruisers USS *Chicago* and HMAS *Australia*, the light cruiser HMAS *Hobart*, and the US Navy destroyers *Perkins* and *Whipple*, all under the command of Rear Adm. John Gregory "Jack" Crace, RAN. This would give Admiral Brown two carriers, eight cruisers, fourteen destroyers, and 168 aircraft (several of which were not operable).

Admiral Brown convened his leadership team aboard *Lexington*. Since none of the admirals present was a naval aviator, Captain Sherman received the singular honor of being the designated air group commander for both carriers. After considering projected weather, fuel states, and the still-achievable element of surprise, the group picked March 10 for the attack—or actually two attacks: the *Lexington* air group would strike Rabaul and the *Yorktown* pilots would go after the newly constructed Japanese airstrip at Gasmata, on the western side of the island of New Britain. Then everything changed.

The next day, a lone Australian patrol plane, reconnoitering up the New Guinea coastline, spotted a large convoy of Japanese transports and support ships sailing off the eastern shore. They were in a hurry, possibly toward a landing somewhere along the northeast coast. Separate reconnaissance over Rabaul revealed another Japanese armada, twenty-three ships in all, gathering steam. Sure enough, on March 8 they were gone.

The harbor that Admiral Brown wanted to attack was empty; moreover, there was absolutely no activity, nor any aircraft, at Gasmata. The Japanese seemed to have stolen a march on the Allies, even though they didn't know American forces were in the vicinity. Sooner than anticipated, the Japanese had begun the invasion of New Guinea. If successful, they would be scant miles from Australia, a critical and vulnerable American ally.

1800, MARCH 8, 1942
ADMIRAL'S QUARTERS, USS *LEXINGTON*

A blue haze clung to the overhead as Ted Sherman and a dozen officers filled Admiral Brown's work space with cigarette smoke. They bent over Brown's large conference table, staring at the charts of New Guinea and the northern Coral Sea.

Australian coast watchers had reported that the Japanese had begun landing forces at Lae and Salamaua. The two coastal towns were only a few miles apart, both tucked into the end of a sheltered bay. It was a good anchorage with a flat, coastal plain immediately behind the beaches. The terrain offered the opportunity for a strategic airstrip, which was no doubt why the Japanese had selected the location. A long, mountainous peninsula plunged southeast from behind the coastal plain. Port Moresby lay around the tip of the peninsula, which many strategists believed was the next objective for the Japanese. If they could capture Port Moresby, it was a short step across the Coral Sea to the Queensland Coast of Australia.

Admiral Brown's combined task force was two hundred miles from the apex of the peninsula. It would be easy enough to sprint up the eastern coast of New Guinea via the Solomon Sea and land on the backs of the Japanese. The problem was that just as the Allies could be at the rear of the Japanese on New Guinea, the IJN forces and land-based bombers at Rabaul would then be at Brown's back.

"Admiral, how about we sail up the western side of the peninsula, past Port Moresby, and move right up to about here?" Sherman pointed to the upper Papua Gulf. "We could attack Lae and Salamaua from the backside."

Brown stared at the chart. "But, Ted, if we did that we'd have to get our aircraft across these mountains," Brown frowned, indicating the intimidating Owen Stanley Range that slid, like a giant spine, down the peninsula. "Some of these peaks are, what, over 12,000 feet? I don't think our fully loaded fighters could get up that high, never mind the torpedo planes."

"Yes, sir, that's correct, but look here." Sherman indicated a slash on the chart marked *Kokoda Track*. "This is a pass through the mountains, right at our objective's backdoor. It's only 7,500 feet high. I believe we could get everyone through there, even the Devastators."

"What about weather? What if that pass is full of clouds or rain?"

"The Aussies have told my staff that the pass is generally clear in the mornings, from about 0700 to 1100. If we launched at 0800, we could get through there easily."

The cabin fell quiet as Brown contemplated the options.

"OK, Ted, let's do it. Get the orders worked up. Let's get moving. Nimitz is on my ass, and King's on his. Let's get this done."

0749, MARCH 10, 1942

PAPUA GULF

Lexington's fighters took off shortly before Sherman's 0800 objective. The Wildcats circled overhead, waiting for the bombers and torpedo planes to follow. As soon as those aircraft were up, the fighters immediately trapped back aboard. The fighters, being more nimble and requiring less takeoff roll, flew off first. The heavier, bomb- and torpedo-laden Dauntless and

Devastator aircraft needed more deck space to get airborne. They also took more than half an hour to get aloft, and the fuel burned by the Wildcats during this interlude concerned Thach, so he had all his fighters slip back aboard to top off their tanks. With their faster speed, they'd quickly catch up with the rest of the strike group. *Yorktown* did not have the same challenge. Her three elevators made it easier to re-spot and juggle all her birds.

Commander Bill Ault, *Lexington*'s air wing commander, was already circling over the Kokoda Track pass in his personal Dauntless. His bird was unburdened by bombs to give him maximum speed and loitering time. It was Ault's job to guard the pass, so to speak. He checked the weather for the strikes going in—perfect that morning—and he would stay at the same spot to guide the returning aircraft back through, should the clouds close in.

Thach's fighters quickly caught up with the bombers and struggling torpedo planes and roared through the cut. It would be their job to "plow the field" of any enemy aircraft that might be up. The bombers flew through the pass right behind the Wildcats. The torpedo planes could not climb high enough or fast enough, with their massive weapons slung beneath. Then the CO of VT-2, Lt. Cmdr. "Jimmy" Brett, noticed a wide, flat plain at the foot of the pass and "remembered his glider training. He got his ships over the area and found an updraft of about twelve hundred feet a minute. This just washed him up over the top and got him started down the other side."[47]

A thousand pounds lighter after dropping their torpedoes, as well as the fuel consumed after the mission, the Devastators would have no trouble going back through the mountains. The Americans were learning to think quickly and creatively.

As soon as *Lexington*'s planes were hurtling down the eastern side of the mountains, *Yorktown*'s came dashing through. *Yorktown*'s bombers and torpedo planes would head to Salamaua, where their fighters would seek targets of opportunity. The *Lexington* group flew toward Lae, but all pilots had been briefed to be alert, ready to jump either way, depending on combat circumstances.

As Lieutenant Commander Thach streamed out over the brilliant blue waters of the Gulf of Huon, he could tell instantly that the Japanese had been caught off guard. There were no Zeros in the air; in fact, there were no enemy aircraft of any type in the air. A quick peek at the new airstrip at Lae showed that it was ready to use but there were no planes parked on the tarmac. Apparently, the navy flyers had gotten there in advance of the deployment of the Japanese *chūtai*.

However, three large troop transports were at Lae, one dockside and two swinging at anchor in the company of two IJN destroyers. Two

47. Lundstrom, 157.

Japanese army transports were just off Salamaua. A little farther out was the IJN light cruiser *Yūbari*, flagship of the convoy commander. Near the cruiser were a large mine-laying ship, three more destroyers, and two minesweepers. Furthest offshore, about twenty-five miles, lay a large sea-plane tender and another destroyer.

The melee that followed was one-sided. The Japanese managed to get a couple of anti-aircraft guns unlimbered, and they launched one pesky floatplane, an antiquated biplane code named "Dave" that sported two minimally effective 7.7-millimeter machine guns. The brave two-man crew tackled the fighters that were harassing the cruiser. Lieutenant Gayler finished off the floatplane with one short burst. The Japanese anti-aircraft crews downed one of VS-2's Dauntlesses, flown by Ensign Joseph P. Johnson. Flying at just 200 feet, Johnson smashed into the sea just off-shore. He was the only fatality of the raid.

By shortly after 1000, the battle was over. All the aircraft from both carriers—minus Ensign Johnson—made it back through the mountains to their ships. By noon, Admiral Brown's task force was steaming away at twenty knots, heading to the southeast.

The day's tally included three transports sunk, one moderately damaged; the seaplane tender was also damaged; the cruiser had more than a few holes poked in it; and there was moderate damage to the mine layer and two destroyers. Shore facilities were strafed and gun emplacements had been shot up. The Japanese lost 130 killed and 245 wounded.

In the grand scheme of things, it was a minor dust-up, but a big morale booster. American carrier operations were evolving, and, significantly, it was the beginning of inter-carrier operations coordination, which would become critical in the weeks and months ahead. The raid also demonstrated that Ted Sherman was more than a brilliant ship driver—he was also a fine tactical thinker. Though he did not yet know it, his name had already been submitted to Admiral King for promotion to rear admiral.

Admiral Brown's star, on the other hand, was waning. Admiral King was already fuming about his cautiousness. Admiral Nimitz, who had a free hand to pick his admirals, was not ready to pull Brown out just yet, but he, too, was concerned. Moreover, Brown's health was no longer robust: he was having difficulty getting up and down *Lexington*'s many ladders, probably due to early-onset heart failure.

MARCH 16, 1942
TASK FORCE 11, BOUND FOR PEARL HARBOR
Lieutenant Commander Thach heard an insistent knock on his stateroom door. Continuing to tackle his pile of paperwork, he barked, "Enter!"

Lieutenant "Butch" O'Hare stepped through. Even though Thach was a senior officer and squadron commander, his own personal space was not that large—barely enough for these two friends to have a chat without being nose to nose. Thach motioned for O'Hare to take the single extra chair next to his desk.

"What's up, Butch?" Thach inquired as he continued to scribble away at his reports.

"Skipper, is it true you're putting me in for the Medal?"[48]

Thach was suddenly paying attention. He put down his pen and stared at O'Hare.

"Yes, Butch, I am."

O'Hare twisted in his seat, fitfully.

"Jimmie . . . sir . . . I really wish you wouldn't."

Thach gave O'Hare an incredulous look.

"Why? You sure as hell deserve it, for what you did, defending the ship like that, probably saving lots of lives. Why in God's name wouldn't you want it?"

"It's just that, well, it'll mess everything up, that's all."

"What do you mean 'mess everything up'?"

"We've got no use for medals out here. I only did my job. Hell, you shot down four Nips yourself that day. I don't want to be recommended for any medal."

They sat in silence. Both men knew what it would mean. Thach had been nominated for a Navy Cross for the same action, but it would not have the same impact as a Medal of Honor would have on O'Hare. The nation was desperate for heroes, yearning for positive news about the war. If O'Hare were nominated for the Medal, and if he were to be approved for it—which was more than likely—he'd be yanked out of his beloved squadron, pulled off the ship, sent back stateside, and paraded around for the public to adore. Worse, in O'Hare's view, he'd be out of the war, deprived of the action he had started to crave.

"Look, Butch," Thach sighed. "You know as well as I do what's at stake here. These are very bad times. The outlook is far from certain. I know you did what you did because it's what you were trained to do, but it was a hell of a thing, Butch. People need to hear about it. We're in for a long, bloody haul, and if we can't let the folks back home see and hear and touch what we're doing out here, they'll lose hope. If they lose hope, we don't get the planes and bombs and bullets we need to do this job."

"But, sir . . ."

"Nope. No 'buts.' I'm putting you in for the Medal and that's final. It's bigger than both of us, Butch."

---

48. The Medal of Honor.

O'Hare knew he was boxed in. He brooded silently.

"Butch, do this for us, please. You'll catch a break, you'll get to see Rita, they'll parade you around for a while, they'll make you sell some war bonds, but, sooner or later, they'll have to let you back in it. You're too damn good to leave ashore."

Thach proved to be correct, but it would take almost a year.

MARCH 26, 1942

OUTSIDE PEARL HARBOR

Fighting Squadron 3 flew off the deck of *Lexington* for the last time on the morning of March 26, as Lady Lex neared Pearl Harbor. USS *Saratoga* was heading back to the Pacific, and it was time for VF-3 to rejoin its regular ship. *Lexington* had been at sea on combat operations for fifty-five days, which at the time was a record. She was in dire need of a port call, for morale as well as materiel. The engineers wanted to make improvements, which were to begin immediately. *Lexington* pulled into the Repair Basin later that morning.

As soon as the gangway was secured, Admiral Nimitz and members of his staff walked to the foot of it, waiting to congratulate the returning warriors. Admiral Brown came down the steep stairs slowly and with difficulty. When he finally stepped off onto the pier, he was greeted warmly. He suspected that it might be one of the last times he would set foot on this proud ship.

Lady Lex remained at Pearl for three weeks, undergoing major alterations to her armament and changes to her crew complement, air wing, command structure, and even paint scheme.

Lexington's eight-inch gun batteries had been an anachronism for over a decade. They had rarely been fired, and never in anger. Designed into the ship's configuration as paean to the officers who believed that aircraft carriers would somehow be required to engage in ship-to-ship combat, they had ended up as dead weight. They could not be fired across the flight deck, for obvious reasons; they couldn't be fired fast enough to engage in aerial duels; and they couldn't be elevated high enough to shoot down enemy aircraft flying higher than a few hundred feet. The navy's carriers were finally surrounded by ships large and small, all of which had more effective and sometimes larger guns, as was the case with the heavy cruisers.

About the only rationale anyone had come up with for utilizing the eight-inch guns was described by one of the last officers who commanded them, Thomas J. Nixon III, then a lieutenant, who wrote, "We had worked out a doctrine for using the main batteries [the eight-inch guns] against low-flying torpedo planes by shooting into the ocean and throwing up a splash of water in their path of approach." The huge slug of water caused by an eight-inch round slamming into the ocean was solid enough that a torpedo plane hitting it would be obliterated—at least that was the idea. There are no records to indicate that the tactic was ever successfully employed.

It was time for the big guns to go. The largest lifting device in Pearl Harbor, a 250-ton hammerhead crane stationed on a specially reinforced pier, was used to lift each of the jumbo gun mounts, each weighing approximately 170 tons, from the deck of *Lexington*. It took four days to complete the task. All the weight shed from *Lexington* had to be compensated for, which was done by installing multiple batteries of more effective anti-aircraft weaponry. A total of seven 1.1-inch, four-barrel anti-aircraft guns; twenty-two 20-millimeter cannons; and a dozen .50-caliber machine guns were added, scattered around the perimeter of the flight deck. It had been planned to add four additional five-inch, 38-caliber guns, but the mounts had not arrived at Pearl. Their installation was postponed until the next time *Lexington* came into harbor.

With the departure of VF-3, *Lexington* got her own fighter squadron back. VF-2, under the leadership of Lt. Cmdr. Paul Ramsey (of the same 1927 Naval Academy class as Jimmie Thach), had been ashore, exchanging its antiquated Buffaloes for new Wildcats. During the transition, ten of Ramsey's experienced enlisted naval pilots had been yanked away from him to join VF-6. Ramsey was going to have to hustle to get his squadron up to snuff to rejoin *Lexington*. Ramsey raided the recently returned VF-3 with acquiescence from Thach, who knew he was going to be on the beach for a while.

Horse-trading around Pearl, Ramsey picked up twelve experienced pilots from Thach and fifty-six of his support and ground personnel. Four new pilots came in from the training command. Thach gave Ramsey nineteen of his new Wildcats in exchange for seventeen of Ramsey's old ones, so that the new planes would be in combat. Thach also gave Ramsey one of his best personal "weapons" in the guise of Lt. Noel Gayler, who would assume the duties of VF-3 executive officer.

Wilson Brown cleaned out the admiral's cabin aboard *Lexington* on April 1. His new assignment, ashore, one designed to help him regain his health, was commander of the Pacific Fleet's amphibious forces: the supply, transport, ammunition, and fuel ships that were less glamorous but still critical to warship operations.

Rear Admiral "Jake" Fitch took Brown's place on *Lexington*. Thoroughly fed up with his two-month stint ashore, Fitch came aboard eagerly. He was home, in a sense, having commanded *Lexington* for a year back in 1936–1937. His time at Pearl did give him the lay of the land in many ways, and the experiences he had in helping Nimitz reorganize the shattered Pacific Fleet gave him an advantage in expediting supplies, repairs, and manpower for *Lexington*.

~

Losing the eight-inch guns, gaining the new anti-aircraft weapons, swapping out aircraft, exchanging squadrons, and experiencing normal crew rotations meant personnel changes for the Lady Lex during this hectic three-week period. Hundreds of men came and went. *Lexington*'s normal complement of 2,200 ballooned to 2,951. The vast majority were military, but there were a few civilian technicians and observers aboard, mainly to assist with integrating radar upgrades and training on the new guns. Among the civilians who ambled aboard was one particular individual who would have a profound impact on *Lexington*'s historical memory.

Stanley Johnston was a war correspondent for the *Chicago Tribune*. During his tenure aboard *Lexington*, he would become a friend to many, particularly among the officers and especially to the ship's XO, Cmdr. Mort Seligman. Generally well liked by all the crew, he was curious, industrious, and personally brave. He would also become, through his own machinations, the most significant threat to the navy's most carefully guarded secret. He would nearly single-handedly derail the Allied march back across the Pacific to the shores of Japan, absolutely ruin one officer's career, and nearly end up in prison, guilty of treason—but this is getting ahead of the story.

The fact that Johnston was even aboard *Lexington* was surprising. His employer, the publisher of the *Chicago Tribune*, Colonel Robert R. McCormick, was an opponent of FDR's New Deal and had lobbied against the war. He had also been a rival of Secretary of the Navy Frank Knox when Knox, before the war, had been the publisher of the *Chicago Daily News*. McCormick was not well liked at the Navy Department, to say the least. Nonetheless, his request to put a reporter aboard a navy ship was granted, perhaps as a gesture by Knox to change McCormick's negative stance. McCormick hustled Johnston off to Hawaii before Knox could change his mind.

Johnston landed in Pearl Harbor in April 1942. Since he had written pro-military stories about the Battle of Britain, which many of the aviators in the Pacific Theater had read, *Lexington* seemed a good choice for Johnston to begin his assignment. The final approval came from CINCPAC, and as luck would have it, directly from an officer on Nimitz's staff who had worked with the *Tribune* prior to the war. During the processing of all of Johnston's required paperwork, though, someone forgot to have him sign the standard agreement requiring all reporters to submit their dispatches to the navy's censors before they were filed. This oversight would become the crux of a monumental brouhaha.

Johnston was larger than life, and in more ways than one. Born in Australia in 1900, he was physically imposing, more than 6½ feet tall. He became a champion rower in his youth, then enlisted, at age seventeen, in an Australian artillery unit for service in World War I. At Gallipoli, his personal courage had earned him a nomination for the Victoria Cross, which was not awarded, for reasons unknown. After the war, he returned home and enrolled at the University of Sydney, but he attended for only a short time. For the next twenty years, he traveled and worked throughout Europe and the Far East doing many odd jobs, including itinerant reporting. He met a German showgirl in Paris in 1940 and fell in love; the two of them fled to London ahead of the Nazi takeover of France. In London, Johnston became one of the *Chicago Tribune*'s foreign correspondents and covered the Battle of Britain until late 1941. He also became an American citizen.

$\sim$

As *Lexington* was being reconfigured topside, yard workers and swabbies from *Lexington*'s Deck Division hung over the sides of the ship, from stem to stern, applying Measure Eleven 5-N navy blue paint to the hull of the ship. This particular shade of paint was crafted to match, as nearly as possible, the deep blue hues of the tropical South Pacific. This repainting gave the entire crew a more than subtle hint of where the "old girl" was headed next.

On April 14, *Lexington* took onboard, by hoist from cranes alongside, fourteen of the ship's discarded Brewster Buffaloes. This time, thankfully, they weren't coming aboard as "ship's company." These hand-me-downs had been inherited by Marine Fighter Squadron 211 (VMF-211), and *Lexington* was to ferry the aircraft and all her Marine Corps personnel to lonely Palmyra Island.

Lady Lex sailed out of Pearl on April 15, accompanied by the heavy cruisers *Minneapolis* and *New Orleans* plus seven destroyers. A scattering of family members, friends of crew members, a navy band, and representatives from CINCPAC staff stood on the pier waving aloha as the gigantic ship slid gracefully away. Several leis fell in her wake, tossed from the flight deck. The garlands honored an old Hawaiian tradition that said if the flowers tossed overboard floated back to shore, the ship and all those who sailed in her would return safely. The leis drifted out to sea.

CHAPTER 6

BLIND MAN'S BLUFF

*L*EXINGTON LEFT PEARL HARBOR on April 15, 1942, with no operational reason to think she wouldn't be back. This was supposed to be a short training and ferry mission, nothing more. Fitch and Sherman would exercise her air wing and continue to hone the fighting skills of the crew, especially the ship's anti-aircraft gunners. They also had to drop off VMF-211 and their aging Buffaloes at Palmyra Island, which they did on April 18.

Next on the agenda was hooking up with the battleships *Pennsylvania* and *Tennessee* and conducting more exercises until May 4, when *Lexington* was scheduled to return to Pearl. The assignment was simple and direct, except for one short clause buried in Fitch's mission profile. The Task Force was required to be "available to undertake any combat mission assigned."

2212, APRIL 18, 1942

OFF PALMYRA ISLAND

Fitch received a message from CINCPAC late in the evening of April 18 canceling his rendezvous with the battleships and suspending his training mission. He was ordered to proceed, at normal cruising speed, to coordinates that would place his task force two hundred miles north of Fiji. This would put *Lexington* within easy striking distance of the Solomon Islands, New Guinea, and the Coral Sea. This news sent a bolt of electricity through the entire ship; it meant, first, that combat was becoming more likely than training, and second, that the ship would be crossing the equator. It was time for one more Line Crossing Ceremony. The conditions aboard ship were also "equatorial." The correspondent Stanley Johnston, new to the rigors of service aboard a warship in tropical climes, penned vivid descriptions of life aboard *Lexington* during this voyage:

> The great man o' war—888 feet long—sweated like a man in a Turkish bath. Beads of moisture combined to form rivulets which forever coursed down floors, walls and roofs, the bulkheads, decks and side plates—of this great floating city. Aboard the Lex there was no relief from the heat and sweat. . . . She had none of the comforts of later carriers. . . . Air conditioning was not known when she was designed. . . . As a result, even the breath of the mechanical hurricane forever blowing though her bowels was hot and humid. While it changed the air within her, it did nothing to cool the interior or the crew. . . . The result was that the Lex's crew continually lived in sweat-soaked clothing and breathed and moved though a mist only slightly less moist than the element in which the mighty ship itself floated.[49]

Temperatures in the engine rooms were seldom below 120 degrees, causing the chief engineer, Commander "Heine" Junkers, to rotate his men in four-hour watches. Salt tablets were consumed by the fistful. Topside, gun barrels and breeches became so hot in the tropical sun that they would cause first-degree burns if touched without gloves. The crew quarters, located just below the hangar deck, were seldom below a hundred degrees even after the sun went down. Starched uniforms withered moments after they were donned. The entire ship was rank with body odor, the sharp pinch of gasoline fumes and fuel oil, cooking grease, hydraulic fluid, and acidic brass polish. Fortunately, the ship's large condensers were up to the challenge of de-salinizing enough saltwater to allow the men frequent showers. It also helped to clear the air when the ship turned into the wind for launching aircraft: a twenty- to thirty-knot breeze would flow through the ship, exchanging foul vapors for fresh, if warm, air.

1800, APRIL 20, 1942
"KING NEPTUNE'S COURT," USS *LEXINGTON*
The names of the five hundred or so Pollywogs to be initiated by the veteran Shellbacks were made known to King Neptune and his Court. There were so many potential initiates on this cruise, given the influx of new men, that separate inquisitions had to be set up throughout the ship. The kangaroo

49. Johnston, 1–3.

courts were divided by officers and enlisted, and by division and duty station. The Great Grand Inquisitor, the head Poo-Bah, was always the senior
man aboard in terms of age and tenure as a Shellback. On his trip, the honor
fell to Cmdr. Walter W. Gilmore, the senior supply officer. Now in his late
fifties, he had started his naval career as a supply officer in France in World
War I, then moved to posts on several ships and shore stations as a Supply
Corps specialist. He was a meticulous organizer, known for his attention to
even the minutest detail, right down to the proper number of napkin rings
in the officers' mess. Unfortunately, he had taken his profession too seriously and had packed away more than his fair share of the supplies. He was
grossly overweight, which became a challenge for him aboard *Lexington*
with its myriad decks and impossibly steep ladders. Nonetheless, he was
a jovial and popular officer. His Falstaffian physique and demeanor made
him a fitting King Neptune, especially when garbed in the oversized toga,
wig, and scepter that went with the role.

Since every 'Wog was guilty of something before he even came before
the King, each was first hauled before a Court and interrogated, after which
an appropriate punishment was inflicted. Stanley Johnston described one
poor novice who ended up in Commander Gilmore's clutches:

> The next victim [was] one of the young pilots. "Oh, ho! A pilot." The
> Commander's words dripped with scorn. "Why aren't you wearing your
> fur lined flight jacket? In fact it might be a good idea to put your entire
> winter suit on—pants, boots, jacket, helmet, gloves. Then come back and
> report to us." The poor victim would disappear then come back dressed
> as ordered, perspiration coursing down his face. . . . One young ensign
> made the tactical error of admitting before the bar that he was attached to
> Naval Intelligence. That was greeted with hoots, jeers and howls, for every
> Shellback knows there is no such thing.[50]

The intelligence officer was told to retrieve a box of colored pins, the
type of which he typically used to mark his charts. He was then required to
use the pins to craft an outline of Australia on his uniform jacket while still
wearing it. "We don't mind if you prick yourself occasionally," Gilmore told
the stunned officer.

The climax of the festivities occurred the next day. All the Pollywogs
were lined up at the stern end of the flight deck. One by one, they were
forced to run a gauntlet of all the Shellbacks, hundreds of them, stretching
the entire length of the flattop. The Shellbacks were allowed to lather the

50. Johnston, 13.

men up with various substances and whack them with rolled-up canvas tubes. By the end of the day, each new Shellback was anxious for a shower to rinse off the ceremonial filth and return to the serious business of war.

As *Lexington* moved toward her assigned coordinates, which included a hookup with the fleet oiler USS *Kaskaskia*, AO-27, another electrifying event occurred to the north: USS *Hornet* launched Lt. Col. Jimmy Doolittle's B-25 bombers for their raid on mainland Japan. As history would record, the bombers did little actual damage, but the attempt itself lifted American spirits. It was a much needed counterpoint to a whole raft of bad news during the weeks immediately preceding the raid. On land, Singapore had fallen, Bataan was gone, Corregidor was about to surrender, and the Allies were retreating from Burma. At sea, the Allies had lost an entire squadron at the Battle of the Java Sea: ten ships and almost 2,200 sailors. Java had been overrun, and the Allies retreated to Australia. The picture in the Pacific was grim.

More intercepts of Japanese messages indicated that an invasion of the Solomon Islands and New Guinea was imminent. Admirals King and Nimitz, still working with an under-strength allotment of four carriers, were trying to figure out how to slow the Japanese juggernaut. It appeared the best course of action was to intercept the IJN in the Coral Sea. To that end, Nimitz sent Rear Admiral Fletcher and Task Force 17 to New Caledonia with USS *Yorktown*. Rear Admiral Fitch was being moved to the Fiji area, placing Task Force 11 close to Fletcher. Vice Admiral Halsey and Task Force 16 were ordered back to Pearl Harbor to gas up and resupply. Halsey was further ordered to proceed, with carriers *Hornet* and *Enterprise*, to a rendezvous with Fletcher and Fitch and assume command of all operations in the Coral Sea.

The balance of the month of April, for *Lexington*, was spent refueling, loitering in radio silence around Fiji, and then stealthily approaching New Caledonia to make contact with Admiral Fletcher. *Lexington* maintained combat air patrols across her line of march all day, every day. The escorting destroyers continuously dashed around the task force looking for enemy submarines. On May 1, the two powerful carrier groups of Fletcher and Fitch made contact two hundred miles north of New Caledonia.

It was turning into a giant game of blind man's bluff in which the stakes were deadly serious. As the first week of May 1942 opened, the subtropical Coral Sea was quiescent. The annual cyclone season had tapered off as April ended, and the trade winds had shifted from southeast to southwest. The ocean spread its aqua hues over long and gentle rollers. Ships transiting the sea during the nighttime hours left wispy, bioluminescent wakes. Daylight lasted sixteen hours, and temperatures soared into the high nineties.

Against this steamy and stultifying backdrop, two naval battle groups of considerable might plunged into the same quadrant from opposite vectors, each ignorant of the other's exact location. The Japanese, having linked an invasion force from the homeland and a carrier group from Truk Island, were steaming southeasterly, skirting through the Solomons, heading for New Guinea. The US Navy, near the island of New Caledonia, had turned northeast. The two opponents were on a collision course. Whichever group located their opposite number first would have a clear advantage.

Any clash between these combatants would be a first in the history of naval warfare. Each formation contained a class of warship that had never squared off against its counterpart in combat.

Angling toward Port Moresby, the IJN task force consisted of two fleet aircraft carriers, one light aircraft carrier, nine cruisers, fifteen destroyers, twelve troop transports (with five thousand frontline army troops), and assorted support ships. The Japanese carriers had 127 warplanes, and flying these aircraft were numerous pilots with solid experience in recent battles. Many had participated in the strike on Pearl Harbor.

The US Navy's unified task force consisted of the fleet carriers *Yorktown* and *Lexington*, nine cruisers (including two from the Royal Australian Navy), thirteen destroyers, and three support ships. The two American carriers had 128 aircraft between them. Roughly half the pilots had participated in the operations conducted against Japanese forces at Lae and Salamaua. The balance of the pilots had yet to fire a shot in anger.

Neither side had any battleships. The Japanese navy considered their battle wagons of limited value in fast-strike, task-force invasions. They were saving these behemoths for the ship-to-ship confrontations that the IJN leaders felt were sure to come. Most of the US Navy's battleships were on the bottom of Pearl Harbor, or undergoing repair.

The Imperial Japanese Navy had become a well-oiled machine, storming island chains and Pacific nations unchecked, securing vital natural resources for the Empire. The British, Australian, New Zealand, and Dutch navies, and even the US Navy, had all recoiled against its advances, due to a lack of coordinated resources and experience. It was time to change that dynamic.

By May 2, the stage was set. The warm, placid waters of the Coral Sea were about to heat up, and for the first time in the history of naval warfare, two opposing fleets would attack each other without a single ship from either formation setting eyes on the other.

~

Lexington's Air Wing at Coral Sea consisted of four squadrons: VF-2, or Fighting Two, with twenty-one Wildcat fighters; VB-2, or Bombing Two, with eighteen Dauntless dive bombers; VS-2, or Scouting Two, with seventeen Dauntless dive bombers; and VT-2, or Torpedo Two, with twelve Devastator torpedo planes.

The Mk 13 torpedo was the Devastator's main weapon. It had been engineered in 1925, and although it packed a wallop, it was prone to misfires, failing to dive to target depth, or—worst of all—not running, period. It could not be launched from above 115 miles per hour, and it required a level, steady flight path toward the target. By 1942, the Devastator had become a flying death trap. The Dauntless was not fast, with a top speed of 255 miles per hour, but it was tough, was maneuverable, had "long legs" (range), and handled easily. It was the best dive bomber of its era.

The F4F Wildcat, with its top speed of just over three hundred miles per hour, was far slower than the Zero but more rugged. In the slugfests that would become typical of air-to-air combat over the Pacific, the Wildcat could take more punishment than the Zero, which made a big difference—especially combined with the superior US Navy fighter tactics being developed by leaders such as *Lexington*'s Lt. Cmdr. Jimmie Thach.

Rear Admiral Aubrey Wray "Jake" Fitch commanded Task Force 11, with *Lexington* as his flagship. An Annapolis grad, Class of 1906 (as were virtually all the Navy's senior officers pre-World War II), and an aviator, Fitch had commanded both USS *Langley*—CV-1, the Navy's very first aircraft carrier—and *Lexington* (1936–1937). Promoted to rear admiral in September 1941, his first flag assignment was as commander, Carrier Division 1, aboard USS *Saratoga*. When World War II broke out, Fitch had more carrier command experience than any other admiral in the navy. Rear Admiral Frank "Jack" Fletcher rounded out the leadership structure of the American side in the Coral Sea. Also a graduate of the Naval Academy Class of 1906, Fletcher was a surface warfare officer through and through. From graduation until the outbreak of World War II, he had served in and commanded a vast array of patrol craft, destroyers, cruisers, and battleships. He was also one of the most highly decorated senior naval officers of his day. As a young lieutenant, he had been awarded the Medal of Honor for bravery during the 1914 Vera Cruz campaign. He and his ship had rescued hundreds of refugees from the Mexican port, innocent civilians who had been caught in the crossfire between the US Marine Expeditionary Force and the Mexican army. In 1919, he was awarded the Navy Cross for outstanding service as commanding officer of the destroyer USS *Benham*, DD-49, in World War I. *Benham* had been assigned to escort crucial convoys through German U-boat wolf packs in the North Sea and, later, she helped clear German mines in the Irish Sea.

Fletcher was a favorite of the new Pacific commander, Admiral Nimitz. Although Fletcher had little experience in naval aviation and had never served on an aircraft carrier, Nimitz placed him in charge of a carrier strike force in February 1942. Nimitz was not about to stand on protocol when the navy was reeling under the direction of other, more timid officers who advised caution. He needed warriors and men who were decisive. He felt Fletcher was, like Bull Halsey, a tiger, so he let him loose in the Coral Sea.

Rear Admiral John Gregory "Jack" Crace, Royal Australian Navy, lent support to Fletcher and Fitch. Crace was a true British tar in the old style. Born in Australia, he was schooled there and in England. He joined the Royal Navy in 1902 and rose steadily through the officer ranks, specializing primarily in torpedoes and surface ships. Crace migrated back and forth between the Royal Navy and the Royal Australian Navy as his postings changed. He was made a rear admiral in the RAN in 1939, and in April 1942 he was placed in command of Task Force 44, a joint US-Australian surface warfare group that, at Coral Sea, would consist of the RAN cruisers *Australia* and *Hobart*, the cruiser USS *Chicago*, and the American destroyers USS *Perkins* and USS *Walke*. TF-44, along with the other surface vessels of TF-11 and TF-17, would actively seek the Japanese.

～

Rear Admiral Chūichi Hara was the commander of the fast carrier strike group ordered to protect the IJN Port Moresby invasion force. Stockier and taller than most of his contemporaries, he was nicknamed "King Kong" by his friends. The 1933 movie had been a wild hit in Japan as well as in America. Like his cinematic namesake, Hara was affable until roused to anger. The nickname stuck, and it was particularly apt during his career in World War II until he was forced to hand over his ancient family sword aboard USS *Portland* in September 1945.

Hara was an expert on artillery and torpedoes and had been steadily promoted through the officer ranks since his graduation from the Imperial Japanese Naval Academy in 1906. He commanded patrol craft, destroyers, and cruisers and had even held the prestigious post of naval attaché at the Japanese Embassy in Washington, DC, in 1934 and 1935. He was promoted to rear admiral in 1939 and assumed command of the 5th Carrier Division in 1941. The 5th contained two brand-new aircraft carriers, *Shōkaku* ("Flying Crane") and *Zuikaku* ("Happy

Crane"), and both ships, with Hara in charge, had participated in the attack on Pearl Harbor.

On May 1, 1942, Hara, with his flag aboard *Zuikaku*, sailed from Truk with orders to supply air cover for the invasion force about to strike Port Moresby and to intercept and eliminate any Allied naval forces that might oppose the operation. This would place him in direct opposition to admirals Fletcher and Fitch, but as Hara sallied forth, he had no idea both were already in the Coral Sea.

Hara was not an aviator, but he was a skilled, aggressive ship handler. He was a formidable opponent; after all, he had that nickname to live up to.

Hara's immediate superior, and the officer in charge of the Imperial Japanese Naval forces in the Coral Sea, was Rear Adm. Takeo Takagi. Takagi and Hara had been classmates at the Japanese Naval Academy and knew each other well. Takagi spent most of his early career in the submarine service. Like Hara, he had spent some time in the United States, in the 1930s. He had also been assigned attaché duties in Europe.

On the day that Takagi's Strike Force left Truk, along with Hara's carriers, Takagi received a message informing him of his promotion to vice admiral. He placed his new flag aboard the heavy cruiser *Myōkō* and set sail with an additional heavy cruiser and six destroyers.

On May 3, the Japanese descended on the island of Tulagi, setting up an airstrip and seaplane base. Their next step seemed likely to be an attack on Port Moresby, a prelude to a full-scale invasion of New Guinea. It was finally time to move. Fletcher and Fitch began searches to locate the Japanese invasion force. Radio intercepts indicated that at least two carriers, maybe three, were out ahead of them. Halsey struck out from Hawaii, but he would not arrive in time.

CHAPTER 7

THE BATTLE OF THE CORAL SEA
MAY 4 TO MAY 6, 1942

The Battle of the Coral Sea was what *Lexington* had been designed and built for twenty-five years earlier: the first carrier-versus-carrier confrontation in the history of naval warfare. Opposing warships would battle it out separated by distances so great that they would never set eyes upon one another. All of the strategy and tactics that had been honed by the Fleet Problems, the hundreds of exercises and thousands of aerial sorties, would finally be tested in combat.

Myriad individual crew members had trodden her decks, although there was at least one remarkable sailor who had been with Lady Lex from the beginning. John B. Brandt had come aboard *Lexington* on December 8, 1927, as an apprentice seaman. Fifteen years later, now a chief boatswain's mate, he was still part of the ship's company.

In the last edition of the ship's newspaper, which would be published shortly after her sinking, Chief Brandt wrote: "When I reported to the *Lexington* she was still not commissioned but we soon put out to sea from Quincy, Mass. At that time I was just a taxi man [one who assists pilots in taxiing their planes on the flight deck] but had the honor of pushing the first plane aboard the deck. I am still assigned to the V2 [deck] Division."[51]

Lexington had been the training ground for scores of aviators, some of whom were leading squadrons from her flattop that would fly into history in the days ahead. Her deck, engineering, and support personnel were the best in the fleet. Service aboard the "Queen of the Flattops" had become a

---

51. Johnston, 35.

mark of distinction. *Lexington* had won many navy awards under her ten different captains and had sported a large "E" for "efficiency" on her enormous stack (until the war broke out and camouflage paint wiped away these marks of distinction). Materially, *Lexington* was in as good a shape as a fourteen-year-old aircraft carrier could be. She had no structural defects of any importance. Her brass gleamed, her decks were waxed to a high gloss, and her flight deck's solid teak was in tiptop condition.

From all reports, she was also a happy ship. It may have been hotter than blazes for her crew, sailing in the tropics, but that didn't seem to interfere with their duties or their morale. Correspondent Johnston, new to the ship and looking for stories, remarked especially on the crew's "make-do" response to the adverse environmental conditions.

Captain Sherman was feared, idolized, and respected, all at once. Even his dog, Admiral Wags, always underfoot and fouling the deck, was adopted by the crew as their own. The wardroom had strict rules for dress at dinner, and they were not conducive to comfort, but even this bit of discipline added to the level of camaraderie.

From the reports, diaries, books, reminiscences, and personal recollections available in regard to Lady Lex's state of readiness, infrastructure, and morale of its crew as she sailed into the waters of the Coral Sea, there seemed to be no ship and crew in the Pacific Fleet—perhaps in the entire US Navy—better prepared mentally, materially, and tactically for combat. Yet lurking deep within her hull, forgotten and unnoticed, were the structural components of her own destruction.

∽

On May 3, Admiral Fletcher had decided to wreak some havoc upon the IJN base at Tulagi. He wanted to send a message: "You can no longer operate in this theater with impunity." Admiral Fitch was still refueling his ships, so Fletcher took *Yorktown* and the surface ships of what had been his old Task Force 17 and barreled north at twenty-seven knots to a point one hundred miles off the island of Guadalcanal. This area would be a good set of jumping-off coordinates for his aircraft. Overcast and stormy weather gave Fletcher a natural umbrella under which he could hide. Early in the morning on May 4, Fletcher pounced.

Since Japanese intelligence had expressed confidence that there were no Americans nearby, the IJN commander at Tulagi and his forces were taken totally by surprise. The overzealous Americans reported inflicting serious losses on the Japanese, but the actual figures were not quite so staggering: The *Yorktown* airmen sank one antiquated IJN destroyer and three minesweepers. A large minelayer and another destroyer were slightly damaged. The *Yorktown* air wing lost three SBDs.

Even though the Japanese losses were slight, the Americans got the enemy's attention. Admirals Takeo Takagi and Shigeyoshi Inoue had to stop their momentum and concentrate on the immediate threat. The pressure on Port Moresby eased off until the war at sea was decided. The IJN began a full-court press to find and destroy the Americans.

At the conclusion of the Tulagi strike, Fletcher moved back south to rejoin Fitch, which he did on May 5. Also rejoining the combined strike group was Admiral Crace's ANZAC squadron, renamed Task Force 44. On the same day, Admiral Takagi held the mistaken belief that the Americans were somewhere east of the Solomons and sent a scouting force in that direction in search of the carriers. Since the Americans were much farther south, the Japanese pilots found nothing.

After failing to locate the US Navy, Admiral Takagi turned west, placing his ships on a course that would put him within scant miles of his objective. At the same time, Fletcher received a message from a coded intercept that the invasion of New Guinea was scheduled for May 10 (which was true).

The combatants spent most of May 6 searching for each other and conducting refueling operations. Finally, late in the day, a Japanese scout plane spotted the *Lexington* task force. Takagi learned that his carriers were only seventy miles from the Americans. He told his staff that May 7 would be the day.

1800, MAY 6, 1942
ABOARD USS *NEOSHO* (AO-23)
Commander John S. Phillips, commanding officer:

> We finally finished refueling *Yorktown* at 1800. At this point, we were just about bone dry and riding pretty high in the water. I ordered the deck crew to stand-down and retrieve the refueling gear. We still had a couple of high-lines across, because we were still exchanging bags of mail and such. Admiral Fletcher didn't want to break radio silence, so he had one of his staff officers high-line a message over to me with one of the last sacks of crew's mail. It was then I learned that we had probably been spotted by a Japanese flying boat, so it was time to get the hell away from there. The admiral assigned the destroyer USS *Sims* as escort. My orders were to repair to the southeast, head toward the Australian coast, and await further instructions. Everyone knew a battle was imminent and the admiral didn't want his only oiler in the middle of it, and, frankly, neither did I.

The big canvas bags of correspondence, official requisitions, orders, and routine reports were hauled aboard and stowed safely below—bits of paper and letters home that would never reach their destinations.

Commander Phillips, a veteran ship handler and Annapolis graduate, class of 1917, had done a remarkable job of saving his less-than-one-year-old ship from the bombs at Pearl Harbor. *Neosho* had been tied up on Battleship Row on the morning of December 7. USS *Arizona* blew up behind her and USS *Oklahoma* almost capsized on top of her. Only quick thinking and swift action by Captain Phillips saved *Neosho*. He ordered the crew to chop away her mooring lines with axes so he could back away from the destruction and get her to safety. As he peeled away from Task Force 17, he would not be quite so lucky in the twenty-four hours ahead.

1805, MAY 6, 1942
USS *SIMS* (DD-409)
Lieutenant Commander Willford M. "Buster" Hyman, Commanding Officer:

> Just my luck. The whole task force is headed into the biggest battle of the war so far, and we're stuck babysitting "The Fat Lady."[52] "Make sure she gets to a safe place," the admiral tells me. Hartwig's going to owe me for this, that lucky bastard.

Willford Hyman picked up his scatological nickname at his alma mater, the US Naval Academy, where he graduated with the class of 1924. "Hartwig" refers to classmate Lt. Cmdr. G. "Roy" Hartwig, who at the time was commanding officer of *Sims*'s sister ship, USS *Russell*, DD-414. *Russell* had originally been detailed as escort for *Neosho*, but a leaking fuel feed pump necessitated that she stay close to the main body of ships in case that defect got worse. *Sims* was sent in *Russell*'s place. As *Sims* sailed away with *Neosho*, on what was supposed to be a routine trudge to safer waters, neither Commander Phillips nor Lieutenant Commander Hyman could imagine the savage battle that lay ahead.

2000, MAY 6, 1942
BRIDGE, USS *LEXINGTON*
Stanley Johnston, war correspondent, *Chicago Tribune*:

> One of the sleek little destroyers, I'm not sure which one, came alongside for a "drink" just after dark. The Lex had drained the big fleet oiler [USS *Neosho*] earlier in the day, and some of the smaller ships were taking turns tanking up from their "mother ship." The moon was up and full.

I wandered up to the signal bridge to view the refueling operation from that high perch. I found Captain Sherman there, leaning over the rail, watching his crew and the men on the destroyer go about their business. The two ships were tied securely together, fore and aft, becoming one for a while, even zigging and zagging together, as directed by the Lex's navigation plan. As the smaller ship filled her tanks, packages and sacks of all shapes and sizes flew back and forth over separate lines of rope and wire. There were mail bags, dispatches, orders, supply requests, packages and boxes. Captain Sherman related to me that his Supply Department was the best in the Fleet. A captain's pride, for sure, I told him, and he smiled. "We're expected," he said, "to have just about everything anyone could get ashore. For example, this destroyer alongside us now asked for a one-ounce block of resin for a violinist's bow. And we had it," he grinned. "We had a cruiser alongside last week. Some wise guy sent over a request for five-foot-two of blonde. Unfortunately, we didn't have one of those," Sherman laughed.

2015, MAY 6, 1942
AIR PLOT, USS *LEXINGTON*

Commander Bill Ault and Lt. Cmdr. Paul Ramsey stood staring at the aircraft status board. It showed the readiness of all aircraft among the four squadrons aboard the Lady Lex:

LEXINGTON AIR GROUP

Fighting Two	LCDR Ramsey	21 F4F-3 & 3 As	Ready: 19
Bombing Two	LCDR Hamilton	18 SBD-2s & 3s	Ready: 17
Scouting Two	LCDR Dixon	17 SBD-3s	Ready: 17
Torpedo Two	LCDR Brett	13 TBD-1s	Ready: 12
			Total Ready: 65

Both men, and plenty of the other pilots, were concerned about the Japanese "Zero" fighter.[53]

There was no question that the Zero was state of the art in fighter design. It was speedier, more maneuverable, and sleeker, and it could climb faster and fly farther distances than the Wildcat. It had two 7.7-millimeter machine guns synchronized to fire through the propeller and a powerful 20-millimeter cannon in each wing. The Zero had swept the Chinese air force out of the sky during the Second Sino-Japanese War and,

---

53. Lundstrom, 230.

more recently, had bowled over most of the land-based fighter opposition of the Allies.

What the Wildcat pilots might have lacked in speed and maneuverability they counter-balanced with armor protection for their pilots and self-sealing gas tanks. The Zero had neither.

2100, MAY 6, 1942
IJN CARRIER *SHŌHŌ*

Another of the many IJN ships sailing quietly under the moonlight was the Japanese light carrier *Shōhō*, Capt. Ishinosuke Izawa commanding. *Shōhō* was a former submarine tender that had been converted into a light carrier late in 1941. Captain Izawa was her first—and last—commander. The "Happy Phoenix" was smaller than the line carriers, slightly under 675 feet and under 11,500 tons. Lightly armed, her main purpose was to ferry aircraft or, as on that night, escort troop transports. Her entire complement of aircraft consisted of eight Zeros, four obsolete Type 96 "Claude" fighters, and six Type 97 "Kate" torpedo bombers. *Shōhō* could carry up to thirty aircraft, but she was under capacity on this mission due to shortages of aircraft throughout the fleet. LT Kenjiro Notomi, a senior lieutenant, an experienced aviator, and a graduate of the Japanese Naval Academy (Class of 1934), commanded the *Shōhō*'s air wing.

Like their counterparts aboard *Lexington*, Izawa and Notomi speculated about the battle that loomed. Unlike Sherman, Ault, and Ramsey, the two Japanese officers did not see themselves as central to any drama that might lie ahead. Both believed that the big carriers *Shōkaku* and *Zuikaku* would bear the brunt of any fighting. *Shōhō*'s job was to make sure that the troop convoy bearing down on Port Moresby got to its destination with a minimum of enemy interference. It was an important task, but neither officer believed they would be in the center of a bull's-eye. Both men would barely survive the next day.

2200, MAY 6, 1942
ADMIRAL'S QUARTERS, USS *LEXINGTON*

Fitch was alone with his thoughts. He idly wondered what his classmate "Jack" Fletcher was doing on board *Yorktown*, just three miles away. Although they were the same age and same class, Fletcher was senior to Fitch, a quirk of the old system of graduation lineal numbers: the higher your class standing, the more senior your number. Fitch had served well and steadily but hadn't yet earned any distinguished hardware (like Fletcher's Medal of Honor and Navy Cross). The two men were friends; still, Fitch worried about Fletcher, who was not known for his aggressiveness. And he didn't have anything close to Fitch's experience in carrier command and aircraft carrier operations.

MIDNIGHT, MAY 6
USS *LEXINGTON*

Under combat conditions at sea, with only the sound of the salt spray slapping the sides of *Lexington* as she sped along, Stanley Johnston recorded these pre-battle thoughts:

> All night long the flotilla knifed its way at twenty-five knots northward. There was moonlight, and brilliant starlight from the Milky Way, now and then obscured by big floating clouds of the sort never seen outside the tropics. I went up to the flight deck and looked out to see the fleet drawn in close together. It was a wonderful sight, one I'll never forget. Sliding along as we were, all ships holding the same fast clip and never varying for an instant their relative position, gave me a sudden realization of the immense forces exerted to drive all these ships through the black waters.[54]

54. Johnston, 139.

CHAPTER 8

THE BATTLE OF THE CORAL SEA
MAY 7, 1942

0625, MAY 7, 1942
TASK FORCE 17 (ADMIRAL FLETCHER) AND
TASK FORCE 44 (ADMIRAL CRACE)

Fletcher's entire combined task force and Admiral Crace's Task Force 44 were located 132 miles due south of Rossel Island (the easternmost of the Louisiades Group, southeast of New Guinea) at latitude 13°20' S, longitude 154°21' E. Fletcher, fearing that the Japanese invasion ships would use the Jomard Passage to sneak around the tip of New Guinea and get to Port Moresby quickly, sent Crace and his surface ships to the west to block it. This was an uncharacteristically bold move for Fletcher. He was splitting his forces, stripping away vital anti-air coverage from his carriers and simultaneously denying Crace air cover. It was a big gamble, but Fletcher justified it by realizing he needed to go after the big threat—Takagi's carriers—while Crace tried to hold off the lesser one—Rear Adm. Kōsō Abe's Invasion Force (which included the escort carrier Shōhō). At 0629, believing that Takagi's carriers were somewhere to the north, Fletcher launched ten SBDs on a scout in that direction. His intelligence was wrong.

0600

IJN CARRIER STRIKE FORCE (VICE ADMIRAL TAKAGI)

At 0600, the main IJN carrier strike force—carriers *Shōkaku* and *Zuikaku*, plus their supporting ships—were not north of Fletcher but at latitude 13°12' S, longitude 158°05' E—or, 350 miles east of Fletcher's position. Rear Adm. Chūichi Hara, commanding the carriers, convinced Takagi that the Americans were to their south. Takagi directed Hara to launch twelve Type 99 "Val" bombers on a scout for the US Navy carriers. They would not find their desired prey.

0640

IJN COVERING FORCE,

PART OF THE PORT MORESBY INVASION FORCE

At 0640 Rear Adm. Aritomo Gotō, commanding the Covering Force—including *Shōhō*, four heavy cruisers, and several destroyers—was steaming southwest, heading toward the Jomard Passage. Two of his heavy cruisers, *Kinugasa* and *Furutaka*, had type 94 "Alf" floatplanes, two each, which Gotō launched to scout for the Americans near the Louisiades. Due to the relative positions of the ships, these aircraft, if they flew far enough to the southwest, had a chance of finding their targets. Also in the air were four "Mavis" flying boats from Tulagi, three Type 1 "Betty" bombers from Rabaul, and four more "Alf" floatplanes from Deboyne Atoll.

0722

Radio silence was the order of the day; no one wanted to give away a position prematurely. The radio sets of the day were primitive by modern standards, subject to all sorts of atmospheric interference. With their low power outputs, they had limited range. The receivers on the other end were often plagued by static, poor reception, and operator misinterpretation. It was no wonder that reports were often confusing and copied inaccurately.

The first contact report of the day would be scored by the Japanese.

"Val" scout-bomber pilot Masao Yamaguchi excitedly barked into his microphone, relaying what he was seeing to his gunner in the back seat: "The admiral [Hara] was right! The Americans are here! Send this to *Shōkaku* immediately: American ships, bearing 182, range 163 miles, your position."

Yamaguchi's gunner broke radio silence: the Americans were right where Admiral Hara said they would be. Hara asked Takagi to let him unleash his air wing. Takagi was a bit more circumspect. He wanted additional reassurance that they weren't dealing with an over-eager pilot hoping to score points with his commander.

At 0745, a second Val in the same scouting flight reported: "The enemy carrier force consists of one carrier and one cruiser as main force and three destroyers, course 000, speed 16 knots."

Takagi gave the go-ahead. Seventy-eight Japanese aircraft leapt off the decks of *Zuikaku* and *Shōkaku*: thirty-six Val bombers, twenty-four Kate torpedo bombers, and eighteen Zeros as escort fighters.

0815
VS-5 DAUNTLESS

From 10,000 feet, balancing a plotting board on his lap and holding the stick between his knees, Ensign John L. Nielsen from *Yorktown's* Scouting Five made the first sighting of the Japanese that day. The pilot reported the enemy's position 260 miles to the northwest of Task Force 17 and typed "two carriers and four heavy cruisers." That didn't square with Fletcher's understanding of where the Japanese were supposed to be, but he wasn't going to argue with a pair of eyes that were looking at actual enemy ships. Fletcher readied a massive strike of his own.

0820
IJN CRUISER *FURUTAKA* FLOATPLANE

One of the Alf floatplanes from the IJN cruiser *Furutaka* spotted Task Force 17 at 0820. That was followed ten minutes later by a confirming report from one of the *Kinugasa* floatplanes. Neither plane reported the composition of the ships they had discovered. Admirals Takagi and Hara were puzzled by these sightings. The conclusion they drew, incorrectly, was that Fletcher had split his task force into two carrier battle groups. Takagi and Hara decided to press the attack they had already launched to the south against one of the suspected carriers; at the same time, they turned their task force northwest to close the gap between themselves and the second carrier group. As soon as the southward strike finished destroying whichever carrier was down there, these planes could be refueled, rearmed, and relaunched to go after the second carrier group.

0915
IJN 5TH CARRIER DIVISION STRIKE FORCE,
ABOVE USS *NEOSHO* AND USS *SIMS*

It didn't take Lt. Cmdr. Kakuichi Takahashi, leader of the 5th Carrier Division Strike Force, long to determine he had a problem. His seventy-eight aircraft were drilling circles in the sky at the point where Lieutenant Yamaguchi's Val had reported a US Navy "carrier and cruiser, plus three destroyers." All Takahashi had below him was one lonely destroyer (USS *Sims*) and a fleet oiler (USS *Neosho*).

Where is the carrier—and the other capital ships? Takahashi wondered. *They must be near their oiler,* he reasoned, and he directed several of his scout planes to fan out and look.

0925

FLAG PLOT, USS *LEXINGTON*

Based on Ensign Nielsen's 0815 sighting of "two Japanese carriers" to the north-west, Fletcher and Fitch, like their counterparts, Admirals Takagi and Hara, decided on an all-out strike. Beginning at 0925, *Lexington* started launching aircraft: ten Wildcats, twenty-eight Dauntless bombers (eight to stay close to CV-2 as an anti-torpedo patrol), and twelve Devastator torpedo planes. Commander Ault, *Lexington*'s air group commander, was in charge of the aircraft from Lady Lex. Shortly after, *Yorktown* would launch eight Wildcats, twenty-four Dauntless bombers, and ten torpedo planes, with Lt. Cmdr. Bill Burch in command of the bombers and scout planes and Lt. Cmdr. Jim Flatley leading the fighters. All in all, the attack group numbered ninety-two aircraft.

0929

BRIDGE, USS *SIMS*

Out of nowhere, a large geyser of water erupted a hundred yards off *Sims*'s port quarter.

"What in God's name was that?" Lieutenant Commander Hyman, the CO, shouted at no one in particular. He raced out onto the port bridge wing and stared up into the sky. Disappearing into the clouds, some 15,000 feet above, was a dark shape, too small and too fast to identify.

"Captain! Lookout reports that plane dropped a bomb!"

Sims was out in front of *Neosho* on submarine picket.

"Contact Commander Phillips. Tell him we're commencing a zigzag pattern. Have him follow us. Sound General Quarters! Increase speed to twenty-eight knots!"

"General Quarters, aye, speed two-eight knots," replied the officer of the deck as the GQ claxon began to resonate throughout the ship.

The Japanese strike aircraft continued to toy with *Sims* and *Neosho* until someone in higher authority could tell them what to do. At 0945, *Neosho* reported fifteen enemy aircraft flying, in formation off the port side at a high altitude. *Neosho* was equipped with four five-inch 38-calibers and four 20-millimeter anti-aircraft cannons. Both guns, when used by experienced gunners, could generate a decent defense. *Neosho*'s gunners took a few shots at the planes but scored no hits.

At approximately 1000, *Sims* fired on another formation of seven Japanese bombers flying off to port, also with negative results. At 1033, ten Val bombers crossed the sky above *Neosho* and *Sims.* Three of these Vals broke formation and attempted a coordinated horizontal attack on the ships. Each Val dropped one bomb from high altitude; all three bombs missed, but two came within twenty-five yards of *Neosho's* port bow.

1012

FLAG PLOT, USS *YORKTOWN*

"Another report, Admiral. This one is from MacArthur's boys. Three B-17s flying long range search from Freemantle."

"Let me see that," Fletcher demanded. The admiral read the message and then threw it down on the chart table.

"Damn it! The B-17s say they've found a Jap carrier, ten troop ships, and sixteen other surface vessels at . . . let's see . . . ten-thirty-five south and one-fifty-two east. Plot that. Quickly!"

An aide jumped to that chart and penciled in the position report.

"That's about thirty miles south of the first report from that SBD pilot. Is it the same group? No . . . wait, our pilot said he saw two carriers. Maybe this is another carrier group."

1019

FLIGHT DECK, USS *YORKTOWN*

Ensign Nielsen tramped aboard, taxied to the side, and jumped out of his Dauntless, glad to have his feet back on deck for a short time and excited about what he had seen. All he wanted to do was take a piss, get a cup of joe, and get his plane refueled as quickly as possible. He wanted to get back in the air and catch up with his buddies who were already winging toward the Japanese. Several other pilots, waiting for the next launch, ran over to Nielsen as he alit.

"John! Tell us about those carriers you saw!" one pilot asked excitedly.

"How big were they? Could you tell?" another shouted at him.

Nielsen was stopped cold. "Carriers? What carriers? I didn't see any carriers!"

"Your sit rep, John, it said you spotted two Jap carriers."

Nielsen's sweat turned cold. He dropped his gear to the flight deck and whipped out his notepad and coding book, frantically looking back at what he had copied and sent.

He had transposed two code letters. Two "cruisers" had become two "carriers." He broke and ran for the bridge.

1041

BRIDGE, USS *LEXINGTON*

With an entire strike force flying toward an uncertain target, Admiral Fletcher consulted with Fitch, his aviation expert, who in turn called in Sherman. Should the strike be recalled? If so, what if they arrived back at the carriers just as a Japanese strike was inbound? That would be disastrous.

"Captain!" the OOD interrupted. "Radar has a bogey, bearing zero-four-five, forty-one miles, inbound!"

Sherman feared the worst: the Japanese were already inbound, and there was only minimal cover over their heads. He got on the circuit with his FDO in Air Plot, Lt. Red Gill.

"I've got it, Captain. I'm sending two Wildcats now, sir," Gill reported calmly. "I'll update you as soon as they get out there. Shouldn't be long."

Gill had been designated FDO for the task force and was, thus, coordinating the flight activities of all fighters aloft from both carriers—an intimidating and almost impossibly complicated job.

1051

IJN 5TH CARRIER DIVISION STRIKE FORCE,

ABOVE USS *NEOSHO* AND USS *SIMS*

Lieutenant Commander Takahashi was, by 1051, certain that there was no American aircraft carrier beneath his circling planes.

How could his scout pilots have made such a huge mistake? He glanced down at the two US Navy ships below. This was no formation of "carrier, heavy cruiser, and three destroyers," though the large oiler—a new type he had not seen before—could have been mistaken for a carrier. She was long, without much superstructure, and certainly looked flat from a distance. She was also riding high in the water, which would make her look more carrier-like. That little destroyer escorting the oiler was no cruiser, by any means. And what about the "three other destroyers"? There were no other ships anywhere in the vicinity. They had been looking for over an hour. Dark clouds on the horizon? Fogged windscreens? Shadows on the water? It no longer mattered.

1052

IJN HEAVY CRUISER *MYŌKŌ*

Vice Admiral Takagi addressed his staff.

"Takahashi-san's report is very disturbing. Hara is wrong after all. The Americans are not to the south. That target is only one small destroyer and one of their refueling ships, nothing more. This means, gentlemen, that we have a very big problem. If the Americans are not here"—he stabbed at the chart before him, indicating the position of *Neosho* and *Sims*—"that means they are over here—somewhere." He waved his hand across the space between the airborne strike force and the open Coral Sea, to the west. "What it also means, and this is of utmost concern, is that the Americans are now between us and Admiral Abe's MO force.[55] We must react immediately!"

1053

FLAG PLOT, USS *YORKTOWN*

Ensign Nielsen's coding error did not sit well with Fletcher and his staff. The army bomber report only added to the confusion. Fletcher, reasoned, however, that something big was out there, and given that the two sightings were only thirty miles apart, he decided to keep the strike on task. He did, however, redirect the flyers to the position reported by the B-17s.

1059

EIGHT MILES FROM USS *LEXINGTON*

Lieutenant Red Gill's section of two Wildcats caught up with the bogey about eight miles from the ship. A large, lumbering plane popped out of the clouds seven miles ahead of Lt. j.g. Richard Crommelin and his wingman, Ensign Richard Wright of *Yorktown*'s VF-42. The snooper was a big, four-engine Mavis.

The Mavis saw her pursuers immediately and ducked back into the clouds before either fighter pilot could get a clean shot. The Wildcats began a deadly game of cat and mouse at dangerously low levels, below 1,000 feet. The clouds were not solid, however, and all three planes soon broke free. The Cats pounced. Wright came zooming in from above and behind and Crommelin delivered a high-side attack from the left. The .50-caliber slugs from both fighters tore into the Mavis's engines as the Wildcats blew by, circling for a second pass. All four engines on the parasol wing burst into flame and began streaming fuel down both sides of the fuselage. The free-flowing gas ignited and the entire aircraft blossomed into a meteor, plunging straight into the ocean below. Ten brave Japanese aviators were consumed in their own funeral pyre. Lookouts on *Lexington*, eight miles away, could see the impact easily.

1100

TASK FORCE 17 STRIKE GROUP, NEAR MISIMA ISLAND

It was not easy to manhandle a bulky pair of binoculars while bouncing along at 16,000 feet, but Lt. Cmdr. Weldon Hamilton, CO of VB-2, gave it

---

55. The Japanese had code named the Port Moresby Invasion "Operation MO."

his best shot. As the strike formation put tiny, volcanic Misima Island on its left, Hamilton, straining against images jumping around in the lenses, made out faint, white streaks on the water, roughly forty miles ahead: ship's wakes!

Hamilton was close enough to Lt. Cmdr. Bob Dixon, CO of VS-2, to signal him to look ahead. Dixon spotted the ship's trails immediately, then twisted his SBD closer to Cmdr. Bill Ault and motioned for him to look in the same direction. Ault signaled for the flight leaders to follow him, and he angled a bit more to the right, on an intercept course. The enemy was finally in sight. Flying below the bombers, Lt. Cmdr. Jim Brett, CO of VT-2, noticed the turn and waved his torpedo planes to follow along.

Within two minutes, one of the shapes ahead resolved into a ship with a long, flat deck. They had discovered one of the Japanese carriers.

The enemy carrier was in the center of a diamond formation with large cruisers at each of the four corners of the diamond. One, maybe two destroyers or smaller ships trailed astern.

Ault radioed the *Yorktown* air group, giving them the target position and indicating that they were going in first. The *Yorktown* planes, ten to fifteen minutes behind, were welcome to pile on as soon as they arrived.

1115

IJN 5TH CARRIER DIVISION STRIKE FORCE,

ABOVE USS *NEOSHO* AND USS *SIMS*

Lieutenant Commander Takahashi received a message from Admiral Takagi: "destroy the ships beneath you immediately, then return as fast as possible." Takahashi didn't hesitate. Without enemy fighter cover in the area, his fighters were not needed. He sent them back to their carriers. Likewise, he ordered the torpedo planes to return immediately without striking. They would be more useful in going after the real American carriers. Takahashi would finish off the two vessels below him with only his bombers.

THE ANNIHILATION OF *SHŌHŌ*

1100

IJN CARRIER *SHŌHŌ*

Just before 1100, lookouts aboard *Shōhō* spotted a large formation of planes circling several miles away at altitude, seemingly assembling themselves for attack. Captain Izawa had recovered his previous CAP of four Zeros and was in the process of launching a relief CAP, three Claud fighters and one Zero flown by Warrant Officer Shigemune Imamura, a highly experienced and capable pilot.

Shōhō was a remake of a submarine tender, reconfigured with a flattop. The hybridization made her an ungainly aircraft platform, with shortened flight deck space, small aircraft elevators, and limited capacity for aircraft, all of which affected flight operations. Many tasks required the physical manhandling of planes and juggling in insufficient spaces. Facing an imminent attack, *Shōhō* had only three fighters available for defense. The others were being refueled and rearmed and the balance of her complement was in the cramped hangar deck spaces being loaded with torpedoes. Izawa was in a tight spot. He would have to depend on his seamanship skills, the three fighters—two of which were old and problematic—and the gunnery from the accompanying cruisers.

Bill Ault wanted to be the first American aviator to take a crack at a Japanese carrier. Ault was in his personal CLAG SBD with a section of two other Dauntless pilots from VB-2. At an altitude of 10,000 feet, he pushed over and commenced his steep dive. His section followed.

"Hard left rudder!" Izawa shouted to his helmsman, who immediately spun the wheel frantically to port. Izawa was eying the three closest bombers with his binoculars, and as soon as he saw them start their dive, he turned his ship sideways to the threat. He knew that once a dive bomber started its plunge, it was committed. The only two things the bomber pilot could do in a dive would be to pull up and try again or continue on, hoping he could drop his bomb before his target spun away.

Up above, Ault and his section, screaming downward, popped their speed brakes. This committed them to the trajectory they were following.

"Damn it!" Ault shouted at his bombsight. The target was turning away. Ault chose to keep on the target, betting he could get to his release point before the ship was safely beyond his drop.

Izawa beat him. All three bomber pilots pickled their five-hundred-pound bombs at once, and all three missed.

Next up were the ten SBDs of Lieutenant Commander Dixon's VS-2. Dixon had watched Ault's attack from 16,000 feet. Right after Ault's section pulled up and away, Dixon took his Dauntlesses down to 12,500 and got them steadied up. Anti-aircraft fire began to climb toward the SBDs from *Shōhō* and the cruisers surrounding her. Dixon pushed the black puff balls out of his mind and told his men to commence their runs. Just as they nosed over, *Shōhō*'s two Claude fighters jumped Dixon's men, trying to break up their attack. It was too late. As soon as the SBDs popped their speed brakes, the fighters, who had no air brakes, haplessly blew by the Dauntlesses.

Dixon and his pilots had to stick to their bombsights and ignore both the fighters and the flak. The airmen did their jobs, but changes in altitude and temperature fogged up several of the optical sights as the SBDs went from cool, high-altitude air down into the warm, moist tropical air.

Izawa did his best to outfox Dixon, too. Once again, instead of steadying up out of his turn in order to launch more of his fighters, as Dixon had expected Izawa to do, the wily captain continued his turn, pushing to port even harder. Dixon and his men had lined up on the stem-to-stern axis of *Shōhō*, giving them the long flight deck to aim for. With Izawa still turning away, the narrow, side-to-side axis of the ship was all the bombers had to release on. Not one of Dixon's men scored a hit.

As water leapt up all around his ship from near misses, Izawa took a few precious minutes to steady up and launch three more Zeros into the air. This doubled his air cover, but proved to be a costly maneuver.

VB-2 was watching from above, waiting for its chance. The second Izawa steadied up his helm, Lieutenant Commander Hamilton ordered, "Dive! Dive! Go!" to all fifteen of his bombers. Hamilton's planes nosed over at 12,000 feet. With a seventy-degree dive angle and a velocity approaching the speed of sound, it would take only two minutes for Hamilton's pilots to get to their release points. It would not be enough time for Izawa to execute another turn.

At 2,500 feet, perfectly aligned on the *Shōhō*'s flight deck, Hamilton pulled his bomb release. As he pulled up, only 200 feet off the water, his bomb armed itself and sailed toward its target. The thousand-pounder plowed squarely into the center of the flight deck and erupted in a tremendous ball of fire, billowing smoke, and flying debris. Hamilton could not have executed a better run if the target had been standing still. Moments later, a second thousand-pound bomb plunged into the flight deck, farther forward. *Shōhō* was aflame fore and aft.

The twin explosions tossed everyone on *Shōhō*'s bridge to the deck, including Captain Izawa. Splinters of wood and razor-sharp pieces of shrapnel flew everywhere. Both bombs penetrated the lightly armored flight deck and plunged into the hangar deck, where chaos reigned. The fully fueled torpedo planes, and several of their torpedoes, started exploding. Huge balls of fire shot out of both sides of *Shōhō* and gigantic clouds of thick, black smoke began to tower over the ship. The Americans were not done, however. VT-2, Lieutenant Commander Brett's torpedo planes, were skimming across the wave tops toward the crippled carrier.

The wartime performance of the Devastators had been spotty at best, as they were slow and vulnerable, their torpedoes cranky and unreliable. Not today, however: this would be the finest, luckiest, most effective Devastator attack of the entire war.

The Wildcats and American bombers were distracting the few Japanese fighters aloft, and Brett's torpedo planes were able to line up their attacks unmolested. *Shōhō*, staggering under the blows received already, had steadied on a southeasterly course, her crew desperately fighting the fires. With Captain Izawa blinded to further attacks by the smoke and flames enveloping his ship, VT-2 executed a perfect anvil attack, with six Devastators converging on each bow quarter.

One torpedo, with a mind of its own, foiled its electrical circuit and released too soon, plunging to the bottom of the ocean. Another torpedo wouldn't release at all and stubbornly clung to its carriage, but ten fish went into the water and, to the amazement of their pilots, five struck home.

Shōhō was rocked by explosions on both sides. The engine room was obliterated by one torpedo and the ship began to slow, completely devoid of power, gaping holes torn in her hull. Hundreds of sailors perished below decks from the torpedoes, joining the hundreds more killed topside and on the hangar deck by the bombs.

The *Lexington* attack had finished *Shōhō* before the *Yorktown* air group could even get on station.

By 1135, *Shōhō* was nothing more than a target ship, dead in the water, on fire, and surrounded in smoke. It was hard for the *Yorktown* pilots to see the ship, but it didn't stop them from trying to attack anyway. Eleven more thousand-pound bombs pummeled *Shōhō*. VT-5 bored in and successfully launched ten more torpedoes. It was a completely unnecessary coda. At least two of the torpedoes cleaved the hull; several more went off, but they probably exploded short of the ship against some of the large pieces of debris surrounding the shattered vessel.

Observing from above, Lt. Cmdr. Jim Flatley, CO of VF-42 and a pilot who would go on to win considerable glory, began to wonder why all the aircraft snarling below him were piling on a victim that was already doomed. Japanese cruisers were still nearby, fat and vulnerable targets, and only one or two planes were paying any attention to them. Flatley also observed that even though there were two group commanders present, along with six squadron COs, no one was coordinating the attack. He realized that if there had been a designated strike director on scene, observing the battle on a macro level, there would have been better management of all the assets. Flatley filed these thoughts away for the debrief.

The six fighters that *Shōhō* had managed to get into the air did all that they could to defend their ship, but the odds were overwhelming. The two overmatched Claudes were quickly dispatched, with the loss of both their pilots, after putting up a brave but futile fight.

Warrant Officer Imamura, in his Zero, slashed at VS-2's Ensign Tony Quigley, shooting out most of his controls. Quigley was forced to pull away from the fight. Knowing he could not make it back to

Lexington, he landed on Rossel Island, where he was later rescued by the Australians.

Imamura had even more success in a subsequent attack on Lt. Edward Allen, XO of VS-2. Imamura caught Allen just as he was most vulnerable, pulling out of a dive after dropping his bomb on *Shōhō*. Using his 7.7-millimeter guns to track into Allen's SBD, Imamura blasted Allen's craft with 20-millimeter cannon fire and dropped him directly into *Shōhō*'s wake. Allen had won the Navy Cross for his part in defending *Lexington* from the Japanese bombing attack of February 20, but on this day his skill could not save him.

Imamura would not live much longer than Lieutenant Allen. VF-42's Lt. j.g. Walter Haas spied Imamura fleeing from another attack, chased by his squadron mate, Ensign Ed Bassett. Imamura's speed advantage was leaving Bassett in the clouds, but Haas had the altitude and attack angle and bore down on Imamura from above. He riddled Imamura's fuselage, which quickly burst into flames and surprised Haas. The Zero headed for the water only a thousand feet or so below. Haas watched as Imamura popped open his canopy and stood on his seat, preparing to bail out. At that instant, the Zero slammed into the water and blew itself into oblivion. Lieutenant Allen had been avenged.

Of *Shōhō*'s eight Zeros, one was shot down and four were destroyed aboard ship in the bombing attacks, which included a fatal injury to one of the Zero pilots. The three remaining Zeros had no carrier. After the battle, all three flew to Deboyne Atoll, where they were forced to ditch in the lagoon.

Lieutenant Commander Flatley, and all the other pilots, had now seen the Zero in combat for the first time. Its speed and maneuverability made a powerful impression on them—but so did its vulnerability. Even a few rounds hitting a Zero seemed to "smoke it" readily. Flatley made another observation about the day's combat, one that would prove extremely valuable: some of the smoke the pilots observed coming from underneath the Zero after an attack was often the extra gray exhaust gasses caused by aggressive application of throttle. This confused the American pilots at first and caused Lieutenant Commander Flatley to caution, "Set them on fire before you take your guns off them."[56]

1131
BRIDGE, IJN CARRIER *SHŌHŌ*
There was hardly a square foot of *Shōhō*'s six-hundred-foot-long flight deck

---

56. Flatley.

not on fire. Flames and smoke billowed from every aperture below the flight deck, too, all along the hangar deck. All of her aircraft still aboard had been destroyed or blown over the side of the ship. No fewer than seven gaping holes in her hull, all below the waterline, were taking in huge cascades of water. She was dead, powerless, and without any functional firefighting equipment. The surviving crew members were stubbornly trying to save their ship any way they could, but it was obvious to Captain Izawa that it was too late. He looked around his shattered bridge. The flames were already higher than the coaming. Every window was blown out, all electronics silenced, the helm drifting. Two mangled sailors lay dead at his feet. All the rest of the surviving bridge crew were wounded and waiting for his next command. There could only be one order to give at that moment, and he gave it: "Abandon ship. Inform the crew."

Four minutes later, at 1135, *Shōhō* slipped beneath the surface. Only 203 of her 834-man crew survived. It was a staggering and deeply mortifying loss for Admiral Gotō, who ordered his MO Invasion Force to turn around and head north at high speed.

As the *Yorktown* and *Lexington* air groups reformed and headed back to their ships, Lt. Cmdr. Bob Dixon sent off a short message that echoed across the Pacific and around the world: "Scratch one flattop!"

THE AGONY OF *SIMS*

1201

USS *SIMS* AND USS *NEOSHO*

As one group of Americans headed back in triumph, another was about to suffer a cruel defeat. At 1201, Lieutenant Commander Takahashi's 5th Carrier Group bombers, thirty-six in all, descended on *Sims* and *Neosho* with a terrible resolve.

Takahashi personally led one section of four Vals against *Sims*. The Vals dropped to less than 2,000 feet and lined up, one behind the other, to fly up *Sims*'s stern, intending a longitudinal attack on the lone destroyer.

On the bridge, Lieutenant Commander Hyman ordered a frantic zig-zagging in order to upset the aim of the Japanese pilots. The Vals stayed with the ship, and as soon as they were a few hundred yards astern they dropped their five-hundred-pound bombs in succession. The first bomb fell into the sea harmlessly as *Sims* dodged away. The second bomb landed atop the No. 2 forward torpedo mount and continued through the deck to the forward engine room, where it finally exploded. Every sailor in that space was ripped apart instantly. *Sims* slowed to a stop and all the lights went out. A second bomb landed atop the afterdeck house, angled downwards, and blew apart the after engine room. Six of the eight life rafts were also destroyed. Survivors guessed that the final five-hundred-pound bomb hit the No. 4 five-inch gun aft, killing everyone stationed within it, plus every sailor at the nearby machine guns. The bomb also tore a gaping hole in the deck, from one side of the ship to the other. *Sims* was wrecked from stem to stern and lost dozens of her crew.

Up on the bridge, Captain Hyman desperately tried to save his ship from further savaging.

"Off! Everyone but the quartermaster off the bridge!" he shouted. "The rest of you get down to the main deck, help the repair parties! Start throwing anything you can over the side!"

Hyman knew his ship was crippled, maybe fatally, but perhaps lightening the load would help. The engineering officer and several crewmen frantically tried to free the mangled forward torpedo tube array to get its dead weight dumped over the side.

Sims had two large whale boats. One was smashed; the other had been holed. Chief Signalman R. J. Dicken managed to get the damaged boat into the water and, by stuffing life jackets into the hole in its side, he kept it afloat. Dicken started circling the ship, picking up men who had been tossed into the water.

On the bridge, Lieutenant Commander Hyman tried to signal *Neosho*, but without any power, he had no success. Moments later, a loud and sickening crack was followed by a lurching that could be felt throughout the ship. *Sims*'s back had been broken. The keel was split and the ship started buckling, pulling itself apart right aft of the stack.

Sims started settling at the stern, pulling the bow down after it. Men jumped over the sides. As the bow was being dragged under, several survivors heard someone, maybe several men, still firing away with the No. 2 gun forward in a last, pyrrhic stab at their enemies.

Sims plunged under water, trapping Hyman on the bridge. Water poured into the stack as it went under, and a tremendous explosion occurred just beneath the surface. *Sims*'s forward section, already submerged, was blown fifteen feet out of the water, crashing down seconds later and crushing many of the survivors. Dozens of men in the water were killed by the concussion of the explosion. To this day it is not known if the boilers blew, or perhaps several depth charges, left on the deck, exploded as the hull sank.

The valiant little *Sims* was gone. Chief Dicken managed to rescue fourteen survivors. He hauled them aboard the whaleboat and set out for *Neosho*. Two of the men he picked up were so badly wounded that they died before the day was out.

THE SAVAGING OF NEOSHO

The other thirty-two bombers in Takahashi's strike force descended on *Neosho*. Despite the obvious mismatch, *Neosho*'s men gave a good account of themselves—at first.

As a relatively new ship (commissioned August 7, 1939), *Neosho* had two geared steam turbines to drive her dual shafts at a decent eighteen-plus knots. She was equipped with eight modern anti-aircraft guns: four five-inch guns (two forward, two aft) and four 20-millimeter Oerlikon anti-aircraft cannons.

As the Vals dove on the oiler, all of *Neosho*'s guns were firing, hitting four of Takahashi's planes. Two of the Japanese planes were blown apart, another caught fire and slammed into the water nearby, and one, severely damaged, was forced to retreat.

Of the remaining twenty-eight aircraft, thirteen pulled themselves out of the fight as *Neosho*'s flak intensified. Fifteen Vals dropped a single five hundred-pound bomb each. Eight were near misses; seven hit their quarry. One bomb penetrated through the main deck to the fire room and exploded, causing numerous casualties and rendering *Neosho* immobile. The oiler slowed to a dead stop and listed to port, eventually heeling over as far as thirty degrees. Fires erupted everywhere and thick, black smoke billowed into the sky. The only thing that kept *Neosho* from sinking immediately was the fact that all her main fuel tanks were empty, having been drained by *Yorktown* and *Lexington* the day before. The buoyancy of those empty tanks proved providential.

This single, savage attack was all that was necessary to begin the long, slow demise of *Neosho*, but one Val that had been badly damaged managed to circle back. In a last, dying gesture, the pilot of the flaming aircraft plunged squarely onto *Neosho*'s stern, plowing into the No. 4 gun, killing all its sailors plus several more on deck, and severely burning the ship's XO, Lt. Cmdr. Francis Firth.

As the Japanese finally broke off, Commander Phillips was faced with a mortally wounded ship, scores of dead, dozens wounded, and many badly burned. The suicidal Japanese pilot, the blasts, and the bombs unnerved many in the crew, especially in the after part of the ship where the damage had been the greatest.

Commander John Phillips, commanding officer:

> Shortly after the last bomb dropped, the Commanding Officer ordered all hands to "Prepare to Abandon Ship but not to abandon until so ordered." A messenger sent by the Executive Officer from aft came to the Commanding Officer stating that he had been sent to find out what

the orders were regarding abandoning ship. The Commanding Officer told him to tell the Executive Officer, "Make preparations for abandoning ship and stand-by." The Commanding Officer had no knowledge of the condition of the Executive Officer. At about 1230, the Commanding Officer ordered the two motor whale boats to be lowered to pick up personnel who had abandoned ship without orders, and to tow all life rafts back to the ship. All undamaged life rafts, seven in number, had been set adrift without orders from the bridge . . . In the after part of the ship, two direct hits, a suicidal dive of a plane, and the blowing up of at least two boilers, along with several near misses, occurred. It is believed that the destruction of the escort vessel with no other ships in sight, combined with the violent shocks from the several bomb hits and near misses, in many cases rendered personnel incapable of logical thought. It is known that many of the personnel aft, due to the flame resulting from the suicidal dive, smoke, and escaping steam, believing they were trapped with the ship sinking, jumped over the side. The number of men who were critically burned or injured in the after end of the ship, and who jumped over the side, is not known. The two motor whale boats placed men on the rafts and took as many in the boat as the boat officer in each case considered safe. They did not tow the life rafts back to the ship. When the boats returned to the ship, without life rafts, and loaded in excess of capacity with survivors, many of whom were badly injured and severely burned, it was too near sunset to send them back to attempt to locate, and return with, the drifting life rafts.[57]

Below decks, fires raged. Super-heated steam flooded the engine room from the ship's ruptured boilers. If the pressure could not be corralled, there would be no way to reoccupy the engine room. No engine room meant no power, and therefore none of the ship's surviving systems, including winches, motors, machinery, or radios.

The bomb that hit the engine room not only crippled a vital section of the ship, it decimated the ship's mobile repair party, led by Chief Water Tender Oscar Peterson, a proud, dedicated, and professional sailor.

Peterson had joined the Navy at age twenty-one in 1920 and had spent nearly all the twenty years since at sea, though he did have a wife and two sons living in California. As a member of *Neosho*'s commissioning crew, he had helped bring the new oiler into the fleet and had been with the ship when she narrowly escaped the rain of Japanese bombs on Pearl Harbor.

57. Phillips.

Peterson's repair party had been on duty in the crew's mess, right next to the upper level of the fire room. When the Japanese bomb exploded, the steel hatch between the fire room and the mess deck was blown in, sending a red-hot curtain of fire and shrapnel into the galley. Every sailor in Peterson's party was wounded, including Peterson, whose face and hands received second- and third-degree burns. As a water tender,[58] Peterson knew the seriousness of the situation in the engine spaces—and what it would mean to the ship and its surviving crew if nothing could be done to stop the high-pressure steam from blowing off.

Despite his excruciating pain, Peterson managed to crawl past the shrieking boilers on his hands and knees. He knew the location of the four steam shut-off valves on the bulkhead within the shattered space. One by one he managed to reach up and secure each line, but as he did so his face, shoulders, and arms were exposed to more scalding, high-pressure steam. As the last valve was finally closed, Peterson slumped to the deck. Most of the skin on his upper body, face, and head was gone.

Peterson was among the rescued but succumbed to his burns while en route to Australia. He was buried at sea on May 13. He would be awarded the Medal of Honor posthumously, the first of four earned during the Battle of the Coral Sea.[59]

Pharmacist Mate Third Class Henry Tucker, twenty-three, one of the ship's medical staff, saw shipmates leap away from the crippled vessel and then flounder in the flaming oil that clung to the surface of the sea. He saw other, badly burned men trying to crawl aboard the drifting rafts. Without hesitation, Tucker grabbed as many containers of tannic acid as he could carry and leapt into the sea himself. He swam from raft to raft, applying handfuls of the soothing jelly to as many men as he could reach. He refused a place for himself on any of the life rafts and kept working as long as he could. In the terror and confusion, Tucker disappeared. His selflessness was not forgotten, and those few who survived told Tucker's story. His family would receive a posthumous Navy Cross in his honor.

58. A watertender was a crewman aboard a steam-powered ship who was responsible for tending to the fires and boilers in the ship's engine room. This rate existed from 1884 to 1948, when it was officially changed to "boilermaker"—then, in 1968, to "machinist's mate."

59. Peterson's official Medal of Honor citation reads: "For extraordinary courage and conspicuous heroism above and beyond the call of duty while in charge of a repair party during an attack on the USS *Neosho* by enemy Japanese aerial forces on 7 May 1942. Lacking assistance because of injuries to the other members of his repair party and severely wounded himself, Peterson, with no concern for his own life, closed the bulkhead stop valves and in so doing received additional burns which resulted in his death. His spirit of self-sacrifice and loyalty, characteristic of a fine seaman, was in keeping with the highest traditions of the U.S. Naval Service. He gallantly gave his life in the service of his country."

1230, MAY 7
USS *NEOSHO*
Commander Phillips:

> I ordered that the two remaining undamaged life boats be lowered, with the
> idea that we would pick up the men who had abandoned ship. I also wanted to
> round up the life rafts, fearing that we'd ultimately need them if the ship foun-
> dered. The boats were soon full of survivors and returned to unload them. By
> the time the men were off-loaded, the life rafts had drifted out of sight and
> the sea was starting to kick up with force five waves. It was no longer safe nor
> practicable to go chasing after the rafts. We began the day with 21 officers and
> 267 crew and passengers [civilian technical representatives]. After the attack,
> one officer was dead, another four were missing. Nineteen crew members had
> been killed and another 154 were missing. We continued broadcasting our
> distress calls using our last position, as plotted by the ship's navigator.

What Captain Phillips did not know was that his navigator, in the heat of battle, had misplotted the ship's last position. An attempted rescue of *Neosho*'s
stranded and drifting sailors would begin from a spot almost thirty miles
away from where the crew continued to suffer and die.

Neosho, by 1230 on May 7, was a drifting, nearly powerless wreck. Water
was rising inside her hull and the decks were beginning to crack and buckle. It
seemed she would break apart at any moment. Captain Phillips still believed,
though, that the hull remained the safest place for her surviving crew. He was
hopeful that the distress call and their position report had been picked up (it
was) and that rescue ships would be on the way soon (they were, but to the
wrong coordinates).

Somehow, *Neosho* stayed afloat during the night of May 7. One auxiliary
transmitter was working, but the task force was too busy on the morning of
May 8 to attend to the distress calls; besides, sea search and rescue was the
responsibility of Task Group 17.9, based at Nouméa. This group had a dozen
PBYs assigned, and two were already out, looking for survivors. Fletcher had
also sent the destroyer *Monaghan*, but she was more than thirty miles away.

May 9 was spent trying to keep the ship from turning turtle: she had
a twenty-six degree starboard list. Any equipment not bolted down on the
starboard side was tossed overboard. The men began making sails, masts,
rafts, and floats—anything they could use for a boat.

On May 10, an Australian Hudson bomber finally found the floating
wreck. *Neosho* was able to signal the plane, which circled several times but
flew off to the south without indicating its intentions. It was never heard from
again, and no such aircraft filed any report.

THE BATTLE OF THE CORAL SEA: MAY 7, 1942   129

By dawn on May 11, the officers were desperate to take action; the ship was clearly settling further. They held an "abandon ship" conference late morning, and charts were checked to determine the best direction to strike out for the Australian coast. They were to start leaving the ship at noon.

Miraculously, an American PBY patrol plane discovered them at 1130. It, too, circled and flew off to the south, but this time the PBY was able to locate the destroyer USS *Henley* a short distance away. *Henley* cranked on flank speed and was alongside *Neosho* ninety minutes later.

Henley removed all the survivors by 1412. Captain Phillips requested that *Henley's* CO finish off the wreck so it would not remain a hazard to navigation or be a derelict for the Japanese to explore. *Henley* sank *Neosho* with two torpedoes and some five-inch rounds. The rescuing vessel circled the area looking for other missing men, but found no one. She then headed to Brisbane to off-load the wounded and the rest of the crew.

After safely landing at Brisbane, Captain Phillips was able to reconstruct his track (he still hoped to find his missing men) and it was then he finally discovered the egregious error made by his shell-shocked navigator. *Henley*, in company with another destroyer, USS *Helm*, charged back to the correct coordinates on May 14.

Adjusting for weather and drift, *Helm* found an empty *Neosho* whaleboat on the 16th. On the 17th, *Helm* came upon one lonely life raft with four survivors. One man died shortly after being picked up, and the remaining three told a horrifying tale of men losing their minds, leaping off the raft, and swimming away to find land. The men ate what little food there was right away and drank all the water quickly. All the rafts floated away from one another, and this small group never saw the other rafts again. There was no leadership or discipline. Of the sixty-eight men in the original group of rafts who left the ship, only these three lived to tell the tale.

Commander Phillips completed an after-action report for the commander in chief, US Pacific Fleet, on May 25, 1942, while temporarily aboard USS *Wright* in Sydney, Australia. A careful reading uncovers the pride Commander Phillips had in the men who persevered and the disdain he felt for those who failed in the performance of their duties.[60]

1427, MAY 7

TASK FORCE 17.3, ADMIRAL CRACE'S GROUP

To the west of the main body of Task Force 17, Admiral Crace's ships forged ahead at twenty-five knots toward the Jomard Passage. Due to radio silence,

60. Phillips.

Crace's task force had no idea that *Shōhō* was being blown to bits, *Sims* was beneath the waves with nearly all her crew lost, and *Neosho* was a floating wreck.

Task Force 17.3 was steaming in a modified diamond formation with the destroyer USS *Perkins*, DD-377, on point. The flagship, the heavy cruiser HMAS *Australia*, was in the center flanked by two more destroyers, USS *Farragut* (DD-348) to port and USS *Walke* (DD-416) to starboard. The light cruisers HMAS *Hobart* and USS *Chicago*, CA-29, brought up the rear.

Unbeknownst to Admiral Crace, his flotilla had been spotted twice on May 7. Unluckily for the Japanese, these sightings were wildly inaccurate and navigationally incorrect. A land-based seaplane from Deboyne reported a "battleship" in company with two cruisers and three destroyers seventy-eight miles due south of Deboyne, heading northwest, at 1240. This was HMAS *Australia*. Shortly thereafter, at 1315, a land-based bomber out of Rabaul found an "American carrier" 115 miles southeast of Deboyne heading west. This was also HMAS *Australia*, and the position reported by the Japanese pilot was forty miles to the southwest of the true position.

Desperately wanting to believe he finally knew where the American task forces were operating, Admiral Inoue accepted these reports at face value. Inoue was convinced he was dealing with a battleship force that was slightly east of an American carrier force. He ordered admirals Takagi and Hara to eliminate these threats in all haste.

In the meantime, the Task Force 17 main body, with *Lexington* and *Yorktown*, was 150 miles farther east of the positions Inoue had; more ironically, TF17 was actually between Crace's ships and Admiral Hara's carriers. Even if Admiral Hara had known the correct coordinates, he was still not in a position to do anything about his enemies. The morning strike was still being recovered, and, frustratingly, *Zuikaku*'s bombers had somehow gotten lost in the weather and were missing. Hara could not afford to leave them behind. He was forced to delay the relaunching of the strike that Admiral Inoue demanded.

This did not mean that Task Force 17.3 was unassailable—quite the opposite, in fact. Land-based torpedo planes and bombers stumbled across Admiral Crace's forces at about 1427. The torpedo planes, all Bettys, were from the same unit that had attacked *Lexington* with such ferocity back in February. The bombers were all Type 96 Nell aircraft from a new bomber unit that had been assigned to Rabaul.

The two groups of IJN aircraft commenced what several observers later described as a ferocious but somewhat uncoordinated attack. The largest ship in the formation, Crace's flagship, *Australia*, seemed to draw the most attention, but superb ship handling and crazy, high-speed turns thwarted all attempts to torpedo or bomb the ship. No ship in the formation, in fact, was hit directly by any of the bombs or torpedoes dropped. After their initial attack runs, several aircraft strafed the ships with machine guns. The worst damage in this assault occurred on board USS *Chicago*, where seven sailors, topside, were hit by bullets or fragments. Two of these men later succumbed to their wounds.

The Japanese got the worst of the fight, by far. All the TF-17.3 ships claimed credit for shooting down enemy planes, but most reports were "enthusiastic" and several others were outright fantasy. A wild melee of flak, cannons, bullets, and buzzing aircraft ensued, and what is known with certainty is that four Japanese planes went into the drink. But it proved impossible to determine which ship's gunners had done the deeds. After taking their lumps, the Japanese retired to the north, heading back to base. They dutifully reported to their commanders that they had sunk a *California*-type battleship and damaged one other battleship and a light cruiser. Since no Allied ship was more than slightly damaged, it seemed that that the Japanese, too, could be guilty of combat inflation.

Shortly after the Japanese retired, another group of three bombers appeared over the horizon, at a very high altitude. As they passed over Crace's ships, they unleashed a salvo that fell harmlessly among the flotilla, although a couple of the bombs were uncomfortably close to USS *Walke*. The offending aircraft were photographed from USS *Chicago*, and when the film was developed it showed clearly that the attackers had been US Army B-26 bombers. No reports have surfaced to identify the planes specifically or to understand why they attacked. It was likely a case of mistaken identity and poor combat discipline. Admiral Crace made his feelings known at a later combat debriefing ashore, and witness accounts say he was livid.

1830

ADMIRAL HARA'S CARRIER GROUP

The Japanese were stunned. Yes, they had sunk two minor American vessels, but they had lost an aircraft carrier, albeit a small one. Their MO invasion force had been forced to turn back, at least temporarily. Numerous irreplaceable aircraft crews had been lost, and not once did a single Japanese carrier pilot lay eyes on the American flattops.

Shame and consternation pushed Admirals Takagi and Hara to make one more try before daylight faded. Improbably but accurately, at 1500, one lone Japanese floatplane had sighted the US Navy carriers and was shadowing them from a distance. Hunching over their charts and fuel data, the Japanese admirals were able to determine that they might be able to launch a strike against the Americans and still recover their aircraft before the end of the day.

Twelve dive bombers and fifteen torpedo planes, including several already exhausted crews that had been flying all day, were flung into the sky from the decks of *Zuikaku* and *Shōkaku* at 1830. They were sent off on a southwesterly heading with instructions to fly a search leg out to 230 miles. If they found nothing, they were to return.

1747

RADAR ROOM, USS *LEXINGTON*

"Contact! Bearing 144 degrees, distance forty-eight miles! Looks like . . . a formation, maybe. They're moving fast, and about 15,000 feet altitude."

Red Gill had eight Wildcats in the air already, but four, from *Yorktown*, were low on fuel. The other four, from VF-2, had enough for Gill to send them zooming out to confront the radar threat. He recalled the four fighters from VF-42 and simultaneously directed six fighters aboard *Lexington* to get into the air, led by Lt. Noel Gayler. He also launched eleven more from *Yorktown* under Lieutenant Commander Flatley.

Lieutenant Commander Paul Ramsey, who flew on "Wildcat One," recounts the sortie:

> The weather was murky as hell. We were in and out of rain squalls and it was starting to get dark. Nasty weather for this type of business. Gill gave us a couple of course corrections, based on radar, and, damn it, if he didn't put us right on top of them. About 30 miles out, there they were, right below me, scooting in and out of the clouds. Looked like Zeros. I took my wingman, George Hopper, and dove on 'em. I counted nine altogether, flying in a "V" formation, five-two-two. I opened up at about 700 yards on the last Jap in the right hand "V." I hit him right away. Amazing, he didn't flinch or dive or maneuver. He just blew up. That gave me a clear shot at the plane next to him. I just pressed on and kept firing. The second plane went down, too. Damn near hit him, though, as I blew by. We were pretty close.

In the darkness, Ramsey had mistaken the nine Kates, all from *Zuikaku*, as Zeros. The remaining seven torpedo bombers scattered into the clouds.

Lieutenant Junior Grade Paul Baker, a former NAP promoted recently from chief petty officer to commissioned status, dashed into the clouds behind one of the Kates. Baker was an accomplished and well-liked pilot who had gotten his wings in 1935. Baker's wingman, Ensign Bill Wileman, lost track of his partner momentarily. Wileman was hesitant to duck into the clouds with so many other aircraft wildly flying about. Sure enough, seconds later, Wileman witnessed a brilliant flash and an explosion in the clouds to his left. Baker and his plane were never seen again, but one less Kate was in the sky as well.

Lieutenant Commander Flatley soon arrived, and for the next ten minutes the opposing aircraft flailed away at one another in the bad weather and gathering gloom. It was, essentially, a battle of fighters against heavily laden torpedo planes and twin-engine bombers. The Vals and Kates had the advantage in firepower with extra gunners, but they fell, one by one, to the swifter, more maneuverable Wildcats. Seven Japanese planes were downed; two more were badly damaged and later had to ditch. In addition to the loss of Lieutenant Junior Grade Baker, Ensign Les Knox was last seen chasing an enemy plane into the darkness. He was never heard from again. One more Wildcat was heavily damaged but managed to land aboard *Yorktown*.

1930, MAY 7

One last, bizarre incident would cap the day's frenetic activities. Lieutenant Commander Roy Hartwig, CO, USS *Russell*:

> As darkness started to fall, I was on the bridge, with *Russell* steaming on a parallel course with *Yorktown* and *Lexington*. We were in between the two big carriers. I saw lights from eight aircraft on our port beam. It looked like they were forming up to land on the Lex. My first thought was, "Our boys! Thank God they're back!" But as I stared a little harder, something didn't look right. These planes were twin engine jobs with fixed landing gear. I didn't recall that we had any planes like that.

Commander Harry "Beany" Jarrett, CO, USS *Morris*, DD-417: "The silhouettes didn't look right. I had our signalman blinker over to *Lexington* asking if we had any twin engine planes airborne."

Lieutenant "Red" Gill, FDO, USS *Lexington*: "They appeared to want to land, and were flashing their running lights. I thought, 'What the hell?' because I knew that we only had one aircraft left in the air at that time. Who could these guys be? The lead plane was very close to coming aboard when it became apparent to the LSO that they didn't have the correct countersign."

Stanley Johnston, war correspondent: "Right at that moment, our last plane, a missing scout, returned. He knew right away that these were not our guys and he started blasting away. We could see his red tracers as he fired. Sparks flew from the last plane in formation."

The nearby destroyers jumped into the fight and the cruiser USS *Minneapolis*, CA-36, unlimbered its guns, too. The Japanese pilots, who had somehow mistaken *Lexington* for one of their own carriers, finally caught on. One by one they shut off their running lights, pulled up and away, and sped off. Lady Lex's radar tracked them outbound. Thirty miles away from Lex, the planes seemed to orbit again; then, one by one, the blips fell off the radar screen.

It took a few moments, but the significance of this last radar contact with the enemy finally sank in: the aircraft that had just tried to land were obviously carrier-based planes, and they had been expecting to find a carrier in the vicinity of *Lexington* and *Yorktown*. They had the wrong ship, at first, but they soon found the right one thirty miles away. The two powerful task forces, desperately trying to find one another all day, were practically on top of each other.

2200

USS *NEW ORLEANS*

The "No-Boat," as her crew dubbed her, cruised silently alongside *Lexington*, guarding her flank. Should there be any action the next day—which seemed more than likely—the cruisers would act as floating anti-aircraft batteries. Lieutenant Howell Forgy, USS *New Orleans*'s senior chaplain, was no stranger to hostile action. His baptism of fire had come, as it had for many, on December 7, at Pearl Harbor. Forgy had become more than a little famous for his performance during the first day of war. Not permitted, as a man of the cloth, to handle weapons, he nonetheless assisted the men of *New Orleans* as they tried to battle the Japanese. The officer in charge of the ammunition locker aboard the cruiser was still ashore that Sunday morning, so Forgy, with others, battered the locks with axes to get to the ammo. Once the guns were firing, Forgy went up and down the line, slapping the men on the back and shouting out loudly, "Praise the Lord and pass the ammunition!" Forgy later admitted the line "just came to [him]" spontaneously, but the story of his inspiration was repeated over and over and quickly turned into a popular song that was performed by some of the biggest bands and recording stars of the day. Forgy wrote in his diary on the eve of this battle, "A sober yet confident tension hung over the ship."

~

Darkness finally enveloped the Coral Sea. It had been a bloody and confusing day, with mistakes and losses on both sides. By sundown on May 7, the true positions of all the opponents had been sorted out and the correct composition of all the battle groups was finally known. It looked like May 8 would be a decisive day.

USS *Lexington* (CC-1) as a battle cruiser, her original design, in 1919. *Library of Congress, LC-DIG-npcc-29701*

Opposite page: Rear Admiral David Taylor, Rear Adm. William Moffett, Congressman Frederick Hicks, Congressman Clark Burdick, Congressman Philip Swing, and Rear Adm. John Robison with models of the *Lexington*-class carrier conversion. Navy Department, Washington, DC, March 8, 1922. *US National Archives, 80-CF-395b*

USS *Lexington* (CV-2) on her building ways at Quincy, Massachusetts, on October 2, 1925, the day before her launching. *US National Archives, 80-CF-21126-7*

Lexington passes through the Panama Canal during her shakedown cruise, March 25, 1928. *US Navy National Museum of Naval Aviation, 2013.005.022.003.040*

Lexington's first air wing, 1929. *US Navy National Museum of Naval Aviation, 1996.488.011.005*

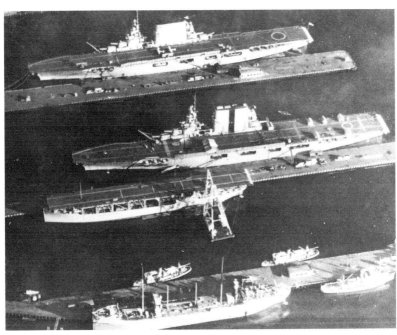

The entire 1929 US Navy carrier fleet: USS *Lexington* (top), USS *Saratoga* (center), and USS *Langley* at Bremerton, Washington. Note the vertical stripe on *Saratoga*'s stack; *Lexington*'s stripe is horizontal around the top of the stack. These were added so pilots could tell which ship was which (but it was not always successful!). *US Navy National Museum of Naval Aviation, 1996.488.001.004*

Lexington fires her 55-caliber, 8-inch guns in 1928. They never fired a shot in anger and were removed just after Pearl Harbor. *US Navy National Museum of Naval Aviation, 1996.488.011.002*

Lexington in Lahaina Roads, Maui, US Territory of Hawaii, mid-February 1933. *US Navy*

A US Navy landing signal officer on board *Lexington* uses flags to guide an OL-8 amphibian to a recovery on board the ship. The aircraft is returning from a relief mission to Managua, Nicaragua, in the wake of a devastating earthquake. *US Navy National Museum of Naval Aviation, 1996.488.020.001*

Lexington underway, early 1930s; note the aircraft taking off from the bow. *US Navy*

A flight deck crew pushes an SBD-2 Dauntless aircraft into position aboard *Lexington*, 1941. *US Navy National Museum of Naval Aviation, 1996.253.570*

Lexington leaves San Diego, California, on October 14, 1941, with F2A-1 fighters parked forward, SBD scout-bombers amidships, and TBD-1 torpedo bombers aft. Note the fake wave painted on her bow to give a false impression of speed to an enemy ship or aircraft. *US National Archives, 80-G-416362*

Aerial photograph of Ford Island, Pearl Harbor, US Territory of Hawaii, taken November 10, 1941—a month before the attack on Pearl Harbor. Battleship Row is on the left of the photo and *Lexington*, at her mooring, can be seen on the right. *US National Archives, 80-G-279385*

Lieutenant Edward O'Hare and his F4F Wildcat pictured in April 1942, right after O'Hare became the first navy "ace" of World War II. *US Navy*

Lieutenant Commander "Jimmie" Thach (foreground) and Lt. "Butch" O'Hare (background) in flight near Naval Air Station Kaneohe, Oahu, Hawaii, April 10, 1942. *US National Archives, 80-G-10613*

USS *Neosho* (AO-23) under attack on May 7, 1942, in a photo taken by a Japanese aircrew photographer aboard one of the planes that bombed the ship. *Imperial Japanese Navy Photo Archives, captured by the US Navy after the conclusion of World War II*

Lexington during the Battle of Coral Sea as seen from USS Yorktown early on the morning of May 8, 1942. *US National Archives, 80-G-16569*

Lexington under attack during the Battle of Coral Sea, 1130 hours, May 8, 1942. *US Navy*

Lexington at 1700 hours on May 8, 1942. The crew musters on the flight deck in preparation to abandon ship—note the ship's port list and the fact that she is already down by the bow. *US National Archives, 80-G-16811*

Damage to *Lexington* after a bomb hit near the port forward 5-inch gun gallery. This is where so many marines were killed and wounded. *US National Archives, 80-G-16807*

Explosion amidships aboard *Lexington*, 1727 hours on 8 May 1942: the first of the death blows. *US National Archives, 80-G-7406*

Torpedo damage to *Lexington* as seen from starboard forward catwalk, May 8, 1942. The torpedo blister and part of the hull have been blown outward. *US National Archives, 80-G-16804*

Cruiser USS *Minneapolis* picks up Lexington survivors, May 8, 1942. *US National Archives, 80-G-7392*

A G4M "Betty" bomber, hit by anti-aircraft fire, goes down near *Lexington*'s bow after unsuccessfully trying to smash into the ship. *US National Archives, 80-G-16638*

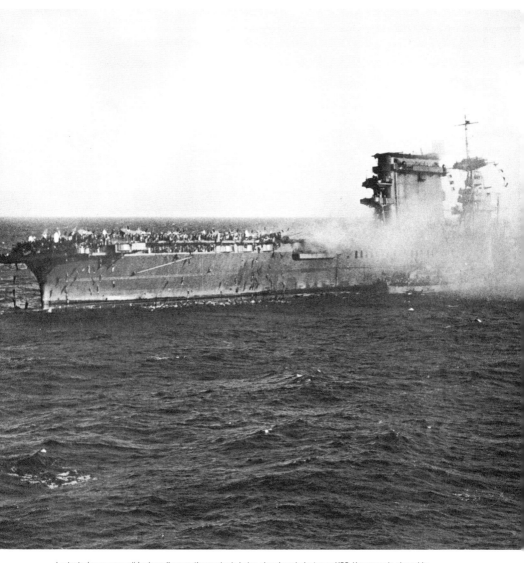

Lexington's crewmen slide down lines as the carrier is being abandoned; destroyer USS *Hammann* is alongside, rescuing crewmen. *US National Archives, 80-G-7398*

Shōhō, torpedoed and exploding, photographed by a pilot from *Lexington* on May 7, 1942. *US National Archives, 80-G-17026*

Light carrier *Shōhō,* in Yokosuka, Japan, on December 20, 1941, shortly after her conversion from a seaplane tender. *Maritime History and Science Museum, Kure, Japan*

USS *Lexington* (AVT-16), underway for training exercises in 1968. *US Navy*

CHAPTER 9

THE BATTLE OF THE CORAL SEA
MAY 8, 1942

RIGHT AFTER DAWN ON MAY 8, the temperature soared to a humid ninety-seven degrees. The skies over *Lexington* were clear and blue—not a cloud in sight. It was the worst possible atmospheric condition for Task Force 17: any Japanese snooper aircraft could spot them dozens of miles away. Admiral Fletcher would have preferred to be in and out of rain squalls—at least until the battle. Luckily for the Japanese task force, however, they were experiencing exactly that type of rainy weather at their position more than 150 miles away.

The opposing navies had shifted during the night. The MO Striking Force of Admiral Takagi had moved north and Task Force 17 had headed west. Both admirals wanted space between their armadas, believing this would be best for aircraft operations. The pilots, after all, would be doing most of the fighting.

Admiral Hara launched seven search planes beginning at 0615, sending them in the vicinity of Task Force 17's last known position, adjusted for assumed course and estimated speed. At the same time, Takagi turned his whole fleet southwest on what he hoped was the right intersect course. Land-based reconnaissance planes were launched from both Rabaul and Deboyne.

Admiral Fletcher gave *Lexington* search duty for the morning, and Captain Sherman launched eighteen scout planes. Twelve scouts flew off to the north and east, believing (correctly) that this was the likely sector for finding the Japanese; but, just to be cautious, six scouts were sent to the south. Sherman didn't want to be surprised by any Japanese force that might be lurking there, undetected.

As the day began, between *Zuikaku* and *Shōkaku*, Admiral Hara had ninety-five operational aircraft available: thirty-seven Zero fighters, thirty-three Val carrier bombers, and twenty-five Kate attack planes. His surface forces, none of whom would ever see any opposing ship during the course of the day, consisted of the two carriers plus two heavy cruisers, six destroyers, and a fleet oiler.

Admiral Fletcher had 117 flyable aircraft: thirty-one fighters, sixty-five bombers, and twenty-one torpedo planes. The TF-17 surface ships consisted of carriers *Lexington* and *Yorktown*; five cruisers (*Minneapolis, New Orleans, Astoria, Chester,* and *Portland*); and nine destroyers (*Phelps, Dewey, Farragut, Aylwin, Monaghan, Morris, Anderson, Hammann,* and *Russell*). By daybreak, USS *Monaghan* was absent, as she had been sent off at 0116 to search for survivors from *Neosho* and *Sims.*

The surface ships of both forces would have one primary role: to perform as floating anti-aircraft batteries. The carriers' goal was to annihilate each other. For the Japanese, destroying or disabling the US Navy flattops was the key to getting their MO Invasion Force moving again and on to Port Moresby. For the Americans, stopping the Japanese was paramount. The survival of Australia was at stake.

The Japanese carriers were relatively new, both having been commissioned in 1939. *Yorktown* had been commissioned in 1937 and Lady Lex in 1928. The Japanese carriers were faster and more maneuverable than *Lexington*, but *Yorktown* compared favorably. What *Lexington* might have lacked in speed and agility the old girl made up for with two key technological advantages: radar and IFF. The radar was crude and sometimes unreliable, but when it worked properly it often allowed the Americans to stay one step ahead. The IFF (Identification: Friend or Foe) gear was also new and had not been deployed to all aircraft—the *Yorktown* planes did not yet have it—but its simple radar-coded "reflectors" worked quite well. Contained in small black boxes carried aboard each plane, IFF allowed the FDO to identify friendly aircraft on the radar.

Admirals Fletcher and Fitch had a decided advantage in aircraft, at least in terms of raw numbers. The Japanese had lost a shocking number to the Allies during the previous day's fighting. All eighteen planes from the sunken *Shōhō* were gone, plus the Wildcats and Dauntlesses had knocked down another nine. Admiral Crace's forces had accounted for four more as had the doomed *Neosho.* American losses totaled six aircraft and three fatalities.

However, the Devastators, although they had been successful in attacking a stationary, mostly undefended target (*Shōhō*), were problematic.

Against determined opposition, they became easy targets with their painfully slow attack speeds and limited ability to maneuver during the torpedo delivery phase. The Japanese torpedo/attack Kates were much more of a threat.

The Japanese pilots were more experienced, but the US Navy fliers were catching up.

All in all, neither force held any overpowering advantage. The day would belong to who could hit the hardest, fight with the greatest skill, shoot the straightest—and amass the most luck.

0552

BRIDGE, USS *LEXINGTON*

"Sound General Quarters." Bugles and alarms began to go off all over the ship. The dark skies were turning opaque and the temperature was starting to rise. The sea, however, was calm: long, gentle rollers rocked the ship as she sliced through the waves at fifteen knots.

The stampeding feet of over two thousand men thumped the decks, the soles of their shoes clanging on hundreds of ladders as they scurried to their battle stations. Sailors left heaping plates of steak and eggs behind on the mess decks as they gulped down a last slug of coffee and grabbed pieces of toast to go. The butchers set down their carving knives, leaving slabs of beef, pork, and lamb swaying on their hooks. The bakers left trays of bread and rolls in the ovens, on timers, as they beat feet to their assigned GQ stations. The ship's band members turned into stretcher bearers, yeomen dropped their pencils and took up clipboards on which to keep score, aircraft mechanics set aside their wrenches and volunteered to become ammo handlers, pharmacist mates put aside their pill dispensers and grabbed emergency medical kits, mess boys joined repair parties, and chaplains donned helmets and tucked Bibles into their pockets. The marines stripped off their dress blouses, donned bulky flash garb, and ran for their anti-aircraft guns. The morning muster would be on station.

"Set Condition Zed," Sherman intoned. At those words, the call to the highest level of shipboard lockdown, metal hatches in more than six hundred compartments all over the ship started slamming shut. Wheels spun, driving latches home; handles were dogged down; and electrical switches were thrown, setting locking mechanisms to closed. Lady Lex was made as watertight and buoyant as the marine engineering of her designers had allowed.

"The smoking lamp is out," Sherman finally added. This would be more annoying to the chain-smoking skipper than just about any other man on the ship.

In both engine and boiler rooms, the temperatures were already well over one hundred. The blowers were roaring, but they were only exchanging the hot, dry air from the overheated spaces within for humid, slightly less warm air from without. Stripped to the waist, pale-skinned, and glistening in sweat, the boiler technicians, machinist's mates, and enginemen continued to toil under debilitating conditions.

Within the deserted passageways, the linoleum floors gleamed under layers of highly polished, flammable wax. All interior and exterior metal surfaces were covered with combustible enamel paint. Extra ammunition was stuffed into every available space. Aviation gas tanks that had been shoehorned into a hull never intended to accommodate them were held in place, mostly along the port side, by metal brackets welded to the bulkheads. Electric motors that had never been made safe against errant sparks continued to whirr and whine in nearly every compartment.

Up on deck, more than three dozen pilots were already sitting in their cockpits, nervously twisting switches and checking gauges, propellers turning, while the engines warmed. All across the flattop, men moved between the aircraft, navigating what they called the "Dance of Death" between the slashing blades. Last-minute wipe-downs were being performed by the plane captains. Aircraft handlers were completing the complex jockeying of aircraft prior to the anticipated launches. Ordnancemen rechecked fuses and couplings among the bombs and torpedoes; others fiddled with the ammunition storage doors, ensuring the belts of bullets would not jam. The sailors in charge of refueling were carefully storing their hoses and mopping up spills. The launch officers paced back and forth near the ship's big island, waiting for the signal to "Go!"

In the catwalks and gun mounts all down both sides of the ship, men were fidgeting with fire control levers, gun sights, and ammo lifts. Gleaming canisters of brass tipped with high explosives waited to be thrown into the breeches. Guns were racked back to make sure they were clear and ready to fire. Gunners melted in the warm sun under pounds of heavy flash gear and steel helmets.

The tropical sun continued to climb, beating down on those above deck and cooking the sides of the ship, roasting the men stationed in the interior spaces. The minutes dragged by, stretching into uncomfortable hours.

0600

FLIGHT DECK, USS *LEXINGTON*

Aviation Ordnanceman 2nd Class Walter Hassell:

> We knew this was our day of battle in the Coral Sea—the day for which all
> our training and preparation had pointed. We hoped we had learned our
> lessons well. . . . Up until that day, unlike the flight crews who had per-
> formed so well and valiantly, we of the ground crew and ship's company
> aboard *Lexington* had been but spectators in the war. All this was to change,
> and we knew it would not be too many hours away.[61]

0625

ADMIRAL'S COUNTRY, USS *LEXINGTON*

Correspondent Stanley Johnston had had a rough night. He hadn't
turned in until 0400. He and the XO, Cmdr. Mort Seligman, had been
fiddling with some personal recording equipment that Seligman had
brought aboard the ship. The two men, rapidly becoming fast friends,
thought that it might be interesting if they began putting on disc some of
their reports about the war. It would sure beat filling out the usual endless reams of paper. From midnight until 0200, they had experimented
with taking the accounts of a couple of the squadron leaders, Ramsey
and Dixon, and had liked what they heard. Still, Johnston had dispatches
he needed to get out; so, from 0200 to 0400, he had been banging away
on his typewriter, the old-fashioned way. Johnston's quarters aboard
Lexington were within the spaces assigned to Admiral Fitch, his staff,
and any guests, in what was termed "Admiral's Country." They were
convenient and relatively luxurious, for shipboard digs, but Johnston's
bed was right under one of the topside, flight deck metal flanges that
aircraft rolled over when taking off. The resultant loud *Clang!* signaling
that air ops had commenced became Johnston's daily alarm clock. Three
loud clangs from scouts taking off at 0625 were finally enough to awaken
the exhausted Johnston.

0820

SCOUTING TWO

One of the clangs that had gotten Johnston out of his rack was supplied by
the Dauntless scout plane flown by Lt. j.g. Joseph G. Smith. The young pilot
had taken off on a northeast vector and had been told to fly out two hundred miles. A little over halfway out, Smith had started to run into a warm

61. Hassell.

front that forced him in and out of dense clouds and pelting rain. At 0820, he spotted his quarry. He hit the radio switch.

"Contact!" he shouted. "Two enemy CVs, four CAs, many DDs, bearing 006 degrees, distance 120 miles from Point Zed, course 120, speed 15."

This was what the Americans had been waiting for and needed so desperately—confirmation of the enemy and his position. There was just one problem: the atmospherics through which Smith was then flying garbled his transmission. *Lexington* never even heard that it was Smith on the radio. All they got was "two CV . . . four CA . . . three DD. . . ." There was no call sign, position, course, or speed. Worse was that *Lexington* couldn't call back without risking her own position.

0822

ZUIKAKU KATE

It was too late anyway. A Kate from IJN carrier *Zuikaku*, flying a nearly reciprocal heading from Lieutenant Junior Grade Smith, and lurking in the high clouds, radioed back to his ship at 0822, "Have sighted the enemy carriers. Location 205 degrees and 225 miles from your position, course 170 degrees, speed 16 knots." This message got through cleanly and was in Admiral Hara's hand at 0830. Petty Officer First Class Kenzō Kanno, observer, was broadcasting in the clear, but no one aboard *Lexington* was picking up his transmissions and the CXAM radar never spotted him.

0845

ENGINE SPACES, USS *LEXINGTON*

Far below the confusion on the bridge and the frantic activity on the flight deck, six men strained and sweated to keep the boilers and the engines functioning. They were only six among a couple of hundred "snipes" then on duty, but the remarkable thing about them was that they were all machinist's mates and they all shared the same last name: Patten. They were all brothers from one family in Iowa. Gilbert, Marvin, "Bick" (Clarence), Allen, "Bub" (Ray), and Bruce had all been serving on USS *Nevada* when she was bombed and nearly sunk at Pearl Harbor. All were transferred to *Lexington*. These were the days before the tragedy of the Sullivan brothers,[62] and the US Navy still allowed close family members to serve together, thinking it produced harmony and positive public relations. Remarkably, there were two more Patten brothers with military inclinations: Ted had served with his siblings on *Nevada*

---

62. Five brothers from the Sullivan family of Waterloo, Iowa—Joseph, Francis, Albert, Madison, and George—served together aboard USS *Juneau*, CL-52. All were killed when *Juneau* was torpedoed and sunk at the Battle of Guadalcanal in November 1942.

but had finished his service in October 1941 and been discharged. (He would reenlist immediately after Pearl Harbor but did not reunite in service with his brothers.) The eighth brother, Wayne, was too young to sign up; he was known as "Patten Pending." Additionally, Floyd, their father, was granted a waiver for age and at fifty-two was also allowed to join the navy. Thus, eight Patten men at once wore US Navy blue. The next few hours of May 8, 1942, would have a tremendous impact on this family.

0837

ADMIRAL'S BRIDGE, USS *LEXINGTON*

Admiral Fletcher wisely bowed to his classmate's considerable experience in aviation and carrier command and turned over tactical control of the aircraft aboard both *Yorktown* and *Lexington* to Admiral Fitch at 0837. Fitch, however, was still in a quandary over the contact report he had received from Lieutenant Junior Grade Smith. It had been confirmed, at 0833, by Smith's gunner, who managed to key a more readable typed report. Moments later, that message was reconfirmed by Lt. Cmdr. "Scratch One Flattop" Dixon, Smith's CO, who was also flying in the area. There was still one challenge, however: Smith had referred the Japanese contact data to "Point Zed" and not to *Lexington*'s actual position. He had been so briefed. Point Zed was a geographic coordinate away from the actual position of TF-17, so if the Japanese were listening they would not get the task force's true position. Fitch was not convinced the pilot knew the difference. Nonetheless, Fitch had to act. At 0838, he ordered both *Lexington* and *Yorktown* to start launching their strike groups. Smith did report exactly as he had been told, but in one of those fateful quirks of history, his estimate was forty miles off. The error, however, worked in favor of the Americans due to the maneuvering of the Japanese and US Navy task forces, one toward the other. In fact, it put the US Navy right on target, just as if it had been planned that way.

0900

FLIGHT DECKS, IJN CARRIERS *SHŌKAKU* AND *ZUIKAKU*

Admiral Hara wasted no time. At 0900 he ordered his pilots to man their planes. By 0910 both carriers began launching their strike forces, and by 0915 the first elements of the strike were in formation and heading off toward the reported position of the American ships. The entire strike was under the operational command of Lt. Cmdr. Kakuichi Takahashi, the same officer who had led the strike that sank *Neosho* and *Sims*. Takahashi had sixty-nine planes, and it is significant to note that he was in complete control of all the planes from both *Shōkaku* and *Zuikaku*, all of whom were drilled to fight as one cohesive unit. This was a different approach than that taken by the Americans.

0920

CENTRAL STATION, USS *LEXINGTON*

Buried under layers of steel, three levels below the flight deck, was a cavernous space called Central Station. This compartment, located amidships, stretched across an expanse of *Lexington* about twenty feet wide. Six inches of armor plate protected the occupants overhead. Fuel tanks were sandwiched between the port bulkhead and the outer hull, and water tanks were likewise wedged on the starboard side. Under GQ conditions, the space was bathed in an eerie, bluish light meant to be easier on the eyes. A huge steel conference table, bolted to the deck and surrounded by twenty chairs, was the dominant feature of the space. A dozen telephone handsets were screwed down to the tabletop. The room was ringed with corkboards to which were pinned various charts and diagrams outlining features of the massive ship. The forward bulkhead held a number of repeaters, instruments that would repeat the actions of the main gauges they were enslaved to: an inclinometer; a compass; RPM dials for the engines; temperature, pressure, and wind speed indicators; and more. There was a huge bank of cut-out switches and backup controls for various valves, pumps, motors, fuel, water, and firefighting equipment. These would be used if other crewmen who would normally control these systems were incapacitated. In short, Central Station was the ship's nerve center, monitoring station, emergency room, and backup for nearly every non-aviation function of the ship.

The officer in charge of Central Station had even more power than the captain to physically control *Lexington*. He could, in fact, run the ship if the senior officers were killed or incapacitated. That officer, on that day, was Lt. Cmdr. Howard R. Healy, whom just about everyone called "Pop." Annapolis class of 1922, Pop Healy had served in a number of surface ships before coming aboard *Lexington* as the damage control officer. He had also taught at the Naval Academy, commanded the destroyer USS *Dorsey*, DD-117, and served a tour at the US Navy Torpedo Station at Newport.

Healy was a pug of a man, on the hefty side, soft-spoken, and revered by his men. He was whip smart and knew every dial, gauge, lever, cut-off, and system in Central. It would be his job to keep Lady Lex out of trouble in a fight. In addition to his phones and equipment, Healy had charge of five separate flying squads of one hundred men each: mobile repair parties that could be sent wherever they were needed. Each repair team was commanded by one of Healy's trusted officers and was populated by machinists, metal-workers, electricians, ship fitters, hull technicians, welders, firemen, boiler men, carpenters, and ordinary seamen of size and strength. They were superbly trained and knew where the emergency equipment was located, including mobile breathing apparatus, fire hoses, pumps, and CO_2 extinguishers. There wasn't much they couldn't do to make things right, and everyone from the captain on down believed their central, protected station was invulnerable.

0925

FLIGHT DECK, USS *LEXINGTON*

Yorktown's strike force was aloft and on its way. Commander Bill Ault, *Lexington*'s CLAG, was anxious to get his planes off the deck and catch up with the *Yorktown* aircraft. By 0925, all thirty-six planes in Ault's section were airborne. In addition to Ault and his three SBDs, VF-2 sent nine Wildcats under Lt. Noel Gayler's direction, as well as twelve Devastators commanded by Lieutenant Commander Brett and eleven more SBDs under the wing of VB-2's Lieutenant Commander Hamilton. The *Yorktown* group, somewhere out ahead, had been broken into two sections. Lieutenant Commander Bill Burch, CO of VS-5, was leading all the bombers of both VS-5 and VB-5, with fighter escorts from VF-42. The second element was Lt. Cmdr. Joe Taylor's VT-5, consisting of nine wave-hopping Devastators. Commander, *Yorktown* Air Group (CYAG), Lt. Cmdr. Oscar Pederson wasn't part of the strike force—although he wanted to be. *Yorktown*'s skipper, Captain Buckmaster, had grounded him; he wanted someone he could trust as his FDO, and under heated protest Pederson had stayed aboard to fill that role as well as CYAG. The net result of all this jockeying was that seventy-five American aircraft were headed into battle without a unified strike commander. Each section—indeed, each individual squadron—would operate independently, although each skipper had received specific orders to coordinate his attacks. The results would reflect a serious flaw in US Navy carrier attack doctrine.

0945

SIGNAL BRIDGE, USS *LEXINGTON*

Stanley Johnston:

> After our planes took off I wandered up to the Signal Bridge. I was looking for Captain Sherman. I found him in his Emergency Cabin, just behind the bridge. He was practically living in this little space these days. He seemed calm and collected, ready for whatever might lie ahead. He told me we had all the steam built up we would need, ready to jump to thirty knots

if we had to. He also speculated on the hours ahead: He was quite convinced that as our planes, and the *Yorktown*'s, forged ahead a similar—maybe even larger—Jap air armada was seeking us out simultaneously. He said, and I wrote it down, "I feel that at the present time an air attack group cannot be stopped. It's likely that the position will be similar to that of two boxers, both swinging a knockout punch at the same time, and both connecting."

The signal bridge is twenty-five feet above the flight deck; and, though narrow, it commands a sweeping view of all activity topside. Today, the plate glass windows were all un-latched and snugged inside their casements giving the Captain and his bridge crew an unimpeded view of all air operations and any enemy activity that might sweep in upon us, which seemed certain. Captain Sherman was fairly convinced that nothing would happen for some time yet, so I settled in to wait.[63]

1000

MESS DECKS, USS *LEXINGTON*

They stood by patiently, a group of about one hundred men, gathered on the mess deck. They had no specific GQ station, so all sat quietly or chatted in small groups. They were the "Battle Reserve," a conglomeration of all ranks and rates who would—singly, in pairs, or in groups—leap up, once called upon by Central, to take up the positions of those killed or wounded. They might be sent to a gun position, an ammo hoist, a blasted engine room, the radio shack, a damage-control party, or wherever else they were needed. At 1000, thirty-two of them, all cooks and bakers, were tasked with hauling water, coffee, fruit, and sandwiches to the men topside, toiling in the heat, sitting at their guns, waiting for something to happen.

1030

SIGNAL BRIDGE, USS *LEXINGTON*

Stanley Johnston:

> Capt. Sherman had a little solid black cocker spaniel, named Admiral Wags, aboard ship with him. Normally Wags was always at the captain's heels. But as the little pup was terrified by the sound of the ship's guns whenever these were fired, he was out on an extended leash anchored in the skipper's emergency bedroom. The line was just long enough to allow him to poke his nose into the chartroom or see into the bridge.

63. Johnston, 178.
64. Johnston, 181.

This arrangement was his battle station. He was put there at about 10 o'clock, and for sometime afterward he showed a mournful nose and ear at the door.[64]

1055

USS *LEXINGTON*

By 1050, the entire crew had been at battle stations for nearly five hours. The tension was so thick it could have been sliced up and served on toast. Topside, the men on station at their guns were wilting in bulky, heavy flash clothing. Steel helmets baked the heads of those who couldn't find any shade. Air crewmen, without planes to fuss over, wandered the flight deck aimlessly. Gun barrels were hot to the touch, and not a shot had yet been fired. Below decks, perspiring enginemen gulped down salt tablets by the handful and tried to find some relief near a blower. Captain Sherman paced his bridge. Admiral Fitch, twelve feet higher on his own small bridge, did the same. Snatches of the faraway air battle filtered back to the crew. Some men on deck could even see a bit of the fight on the horizon as *Lexington*'s shield of SBDs and Wildcats picked off a stray Japanese flying boat trying to snoop on the task force. The ship's senior chaplain, Commander Markle, had once again been anointed emcee for the crew by Captain Sherman: whenever a bit of news came in from the pilots, Markle would get on the 1MC and relay it. Several men, scattered about the ship, were also on *Lexington*'s radio net, listening to the airmen's broadcasts and passing on their reports to the men nearby.

At 1055, the tension snapped: "[T]he *Lexington* and *Yorktown* simultaneously registered what appeared to be a large group of bogeys bearing 020 degrees, distance sixty-eight miles and closing. Such a strong contact had to portend the long-expected enemy carrier strike on Task Force 17."[65]

1058

FIGHTER DIRECTION, USS *LEXINGTON*

Lieutenant Gill had eight fighters on CAP, but they had been aloft a long time and would soon need fuel. He brought those eight Wildcats back to the ship, circling overhead, so they could land quickly if need be. These fighters would be his close-in CAP. Gill then launched his last nine Wildcats. Five were from *Lexington*, under Lieutenant Commander Ramsey, and four were from *Yorktown*, led by Lieutenant Commander Flatley.

There were also eighteen SBDs aloft, on patrol to defend against enemy torpedo planes. Sherman had long believed that a carrier needed more than

65. Lundstrom, 310.

the standard eighteen fighters, but he had been unsuccessful in getting the higher-ups to agree (and there was still a critical shortage of capable fighter aircraft in the fleet). To compensate, Sherman had been using some of his scouts as fighters. They were not deployed in air-to-air dogfights, as true fighters would be, but Sherman believed they could be used for close-in support, such as anti-torpedo plane patrol. That day, the SBDs would get a severe test of Sherman's plan. Unfortunately, however, even though the Dauntlesses were acting as fighters they were not placed under the operational control of the FDO, who would have had the best overall picture on how to use them. They remained under Captain Sherman's thumb, which would be another fateful error.

1100

SIGNAL BRIDGE, USS *LEXINGTON*

Stanley Johnston:

> About this time, a great deal began to happen. Thinking back later I realize a thousand and one impressions were registering that I wasn't even conscious of at the time. Chiefly I was busy for the next few minutes getting my microphone and telephone circuits straightened out. With lightning suddenness the fleet was in direst danger. One minute we had been shouldering our way through the Coral Sea billows in what might have been a pleasure cruise, the next we were prepared to fight for our lives.[66]

From this moment forward, correspondent Johnston, on the Signal Bridge, had a bird's-eye view of the battle. He collected all his impressions on the jury-rigged recording system he and Commander Seligman had cobbled together—but it was all lost when *Lexington* went under.

1100

35 MILES SOUTHEAST OF *LEXINGTON*, 14,000 FEET

Lexington and *Yorktown* were five miles apart, surrounded by their escorts, when Lieutenant Commander Takahashi's strike group spotted them at 1100. Takahashi made his attack plan quickly and skillfully. At 1109, he sent all eighteen of his torpedo attack planes to 4,000 feet, accompanied by all eighteen of his Zeros. He figured that the torpedo planes would need the most protection as they commenced their attacks. Takahashi left the actual disposition of the torpedo planes to that section's leader, Lt. Cmdr. Shigekazu Shimazaki. Lieutenant Takumi Hoashi

66. Johnston, 183.

was also freed to deploy his Zeros as he saw fit. Takahashi kept all thirty-three bombers under his control and deployed them in several vees as they dropped down to 10,000 feet and closed the target. The torpedo planes, with fighter escorts, would attack first and Takahashi would then go in with his bombers, splitting them at the last possible moment into two groups, one for each American carrier. It was a well-coordinated " one-two" punch.

1110

FIGHTER DIRECTION, USS *LEXINGTON*

Believing that the Japanese torpedo planes presented the greatest threat to his ship, Lieutenant Gill instructed six of the nine Wildcats to go low in the direction of the estimated threat vector. He had them at 020°, outbound, at 1,000 feet. He sent the other three Wildcats in the same direction but told them to climb to 10,000 feet and then wait "until we see what develops." Gill, though a well-respected officer and pilot, had, nonetheless, made four critical errors. First, he assumed that the Japanese torpedo attack planes would react and maneuver like the Devastators—that is, that they would have to come in low and slow. He should have known better. The IJN Kates were much more capable bombers. They certainly had to attack at a low angle, but they could do it faster than the Devastators and still maneuver while aiming their torpedoes. Second, he failed to take the weather into account. *Lexington* was moving toward the front that the Japanese had been hiding in all morning. There were layers of clouds in the area. All of the Wildcats he sent low flew under and past the oncoming Japanese, who were above one of those cloud layers. By the time this mistake was discovered, it was too late for these fighters to attack their intended targets. Third, Gill did not send the other Wildcats high enough. The Japanese bombers were 4,000 feet above the Wildcats as the fight began. Gill certainly knew his fighters were slow climbers. Once the Wildcats found the Vals, they were forced, initially, to engage them from below, which was a disadvantageous attack angle. Fourth, Gill should have gotten the Wildcats that were circling over *Lexington* back on board and refueled when he had the chance. They were running out of gas just as the Japanese were pressing their attacks.

1112

JAPANESE TORPEDO STRIKE, INITIAL ATTACK

Lexington grew larger in Lieutenant Shimazaki's windscreen. He did not know, for certain, that it was *Lexington*. His recognition training only led him to conclude it was a *Saratoga*-class aircraft carrier—and a big one. It loomed so large, in fact, that Shimazaki decided to hurl fourteen of his eighteen torpedo bombers at her—he sent only four of his Kates after the smaller *Yorktown*. The attack was to use a classic anvil tactic: the fourteen Kates would come at Lady Lex in two waves of seven planes each. Four Kates on the right side of the first vee would launch their torpedoes aimed at the port bow. The other three Kates, on the left side of the vee, would drop on the starboard bow. All seven fish would thence be coming at *Lexington*'s bows from a relative forty-five degree angle. If Captain Sherman did nothing, all seven torpedoes might strike the ship. If he turned away, he might be able to avoid one group of torpedoes while the second group smashed into the side of the ship then facing them. Adroit ship handling might be able to twist the ship enough to avoid them all. The problem was that massive old Lady Lex had a slow helm and a lousy turn ratio. By 1112, Shimazaki was set up and ready, with all his planes boring in on the big ship ahead. His aircraft dropped to less than 200 feet. He could see flashes from the anti-aircraft guns start twinkling, and outside his cockpit red tracers began to zip by.

1109

"AGNES RED," 12,000 FEET

As a young aviation cadet from Iowa, Edward R. "Doc" Sellstrom had wanted to be a doctor, but the war had disrupted his plans. He signed up for pilot training, and by March 1941 he had been commissioned an ensign and had his wings. In the February clash when Butch O'Hare earned his Medal of Honor, Sellstrom was awarded a Navy Cross for downing a Japanese flying boat as well as one of the Betty bombers that was trying to sink *Lexington*. His skill at gunnery and his terrific flying had earned him a spot as his skipper's wingman. That's exactly where he was shortly after 1100 on May 8, on Lieutenant Commander Ramsey's wing as he, Ramsey, and Ensign George Markham—designated cohort "Agnes Three"—struggled to get high enough to intercept the Japanese bombers bearing down en masse for the Lady Lex.

Finally, at 1109, Sellstrom spotted them: "Skipper! Eleven o'clock right up from you. Can't you see them straight up from you?" he shouted into his radio.

Ramsey saw them, but he didn't know what he was looking at. Were they bombers or fighters or both? He became fixated on getting higher, getting in among them, whatever they were, and shooting down as many as he could.

Sellstrom glanced over his shoulder and caught sight of something even more chilling than the mass of enemy aircraft above: Shimazaki's torpedo bombers were zooming in from below. He could see no other defenders anywhere nearby.

"Skipper!" he shouted again, "Look down! Torpedo bombers, headed for the task force!"

Ramsey did not reply, still focused on the planes above. Sellstrom had a split second to make a decision. He could continue to struggle for altitude, to get behind the threat above, then try and chase it down; or, he could dive immediately on the targets below, guns blazing.

Without permission, he peeled away and plunged downward. Sellstrom knew he was risking the wrath of his commanding officer, but he believed the torpedo planes were the greater threat.

Sellstrom was on the torpedo bombers before they knew he was there. With the advantage of the tremendous speed he had picked up in his dive, he sliced through the right-hand side of the rearward vee and cleanly picked off one of the Kates, which flamed up and spun into the water. This got the immediate attention of three of the Zeros. Rolling, spinning, and diving, the four planes careened after one another through the clouds.

1116

IJN CARRIER ATTACK GROUP

Shimazaki's torpedo attack juggernaut rolled on. A minute later, four miles out from *Lexington*'s, the thirteen remaining Kates blew by and through the screen put up by eight Dauntlesses from *Yorktown*'s VS-5. The scouts were caught between Shimazaki's vees with no time or altitude advantage. Several of the hapless pilots never even witnessed the torpedo planes speeding by, but a moment later they felt the sting of the Zeros. In rapid order, Lt. j.g. Earl Johnson, Ensign Samuel Underhill, and Ensign Edward B. Kinzer were blasted from the skies, their Dauntlesses flaming and spinning into the sea. Ensign Kendall Campbell's SBD had its tail blown off by a buzz saw of cannon fire before looping crazily into the waves. Kinzer had dropped a thousand-pound bomb on *Shōhō* the day before; Johnson had earned a Navy Cross for heroism in the attacks on Tulagi; Underhill, a graduate of Yale and Harvard Law School, had also bombed *Shōhō*; and Campbell had earned a Navy Cross for the New Guinea raids. Four brave pilots, all holders of the Navy Cross, were dead in under a minute. Each would have a destroyer built and named after him in the coming months.

It was beginning to look as if Captain Sherman's pet theory concerning the Dauntless as a faux fighter was being blasted full of holes, but *Lexington*'s screen of SBDs would have better luck. Scouting Two had taken a higher altitude than VS-5, and by the time Shimazaki's planes were nearby they had started to descend even lower, easing back their speed to drop their weapons. Nine SBDs swung around and chased the Kates, who were, by then, only five thousand yards from their drop points. VS-2 did not have to face the Zeros, either, at least at first: the Japanese fighters were tangling with the remnants of VS-5, and three of them were still trying to shoot down Sellstrom. Before their escorts returned to cover them, Shimazaki lost two Kates to the pilots of VS-2.

～

One of those two doomed Kates was shot down by Lt. j.g. William E. Hall, a scout pilot from VS-2. Hall had already tasted victory on May 7 when he had been one of the pilots to drop a thousand-pound bomb on the unfortunate *Shōhō*. Later on May 8, after the torpedo and bomb attacks against *Lexington* and *Yorktown* had been completed and the Japanese began to run for home, a grand melee developed between the fleeing planes and the American pilots defending their ships. The Japanese Zeros became particularly aggressive. Two Zeros jumped Lieutenant Junior Grade Hall and riddled his plane with bullets. Hall was seriously wounded in both ankles from fragments coming up through the bottom of his ship, but he somehow pushed through the pain and executed a series of deft maneuvers to escape the Zeros. Hall and another VS-2 pilot, Ensign John Leppla, went after the four antagonizing Zeros with a vengeance, and between the two of them shot three down. Fighting blood loss, pain, and immobility in his lower legs, Hall somehow managed to get his plane back to *Lexington*, where he executed a near-perfect landing despite his injuries and the severe damage to his Dauntless. Medics hauled the nearly comatose Hall out of his aircraft. The plane captains took one look at Hall's riddled ship and simply decided to push it over the side. Hall's heroics over two days of intense combat earned him one of the four Medals of Honor to be earned at the Battle of the Coral Sea.

～

As Shimazaki's Kates drew inside *Lexington*'s three thousand-yard defensive circle, the ship's anti-aircraft guns took over her defense. The five-inch guns, accompanied by the Oerlikons, put up what should have been a wall of steel, but every one of Shimazaki's eleven remaining attackers made it through nearly untouched.

1116,

SIGNAL BRIDGE, USS *LEXINGTON*

Stanley Johnston:

> About this time the *Lexington*'s own batteries of more than 100 guns
> break into flame. There is the sharp, "wham, wham, wham, wham" of the
> 5 inchers, the staccato bark of the 1.1 inchers (37 mm) and the rushing
> yammer of the 20 mm batteries. A hellish chorus, uneven, jerky, but so
> forceful that it leaves you, here on the bridge, gasping in the partial vacuums
> created by the blasts. Out on the open bridge we are above the gun muzzles
> and with the first firing our nostrils are stuck by the reeking cordite of the
> driving charges.[67]

1117

BRIDGE, USS *LEXINGTON*

Captain Sherman needed all of his ship-handling skill that day, and then
some. The torpedo bombers bearing down on him first appeared as tiny
specks, low on the water, three to starboard, two to port.

Sherman later wrote: "It was beautifully coordinated. From my bridge I
saw bombers roaring down in steep dives from many points in the sky, and
torpedo planes coming in on both bows almost simultaneously. There was
nothing I could do about the bombers, but I could do something to avoid
the torpedoes."[68]

He rapidly did the mental math and combined it with his experience
and tactical savvy. He watched five distant splashes leap up from the ocean.
The three to starboard had landed first, so they were the bigger threat.

"Right full rudder, hard to starboard!" he bellowed. Agonizing moments
later, the old girl shuddered and began an achingly slow turn to the right.
Sherman could see the frothy wakes in the water ahead, and even before
they reached the bow he yelled again:

"Left full rudder, hard a-port!"

As the mighty bow of the ship bit back into the waves, the onrushing
torpedoes streaked down the sides of *Lexington*, one to starboard, two to
port. Sherman had beaten Shimazaki's first salvo. His next frantic turn had
foiled the second as the other two deadly fish flashed by harmlessly.

That left six more Kates, but Sherman's deft dancing was about to endure
a stumble.

67. Johnston, 185–186.
68. Hoehling, 68.

1118

Shimazaki's first attack had missed, but *Lexington*'s violent maneuvering had put Sherman in a box. Flight leader Lt. Tatsuo Ichihara's element was right behind Shimazaki and they were ready. Ichihara had another anvil attack lined up, three to starboard, four to port. He was the lead bomber in the starboard element, and he bore down hard, less than two thousand yards from *Lexington*, reaching for the torpedo release lever. As his fingers curled around the handle, a brilliant, violent sun exploded in his face and he was no more.

Sherman saw the Japanese torpedo plane explode in midair as one of his SBDs riddled it with slugs. The Dauntless pilot must have hit the torpedo warhead. The two Kates on the same trajectory abruptly pulled up, aborting their attacks, confused by the massive fireball of their leader. It was already too late for *Lexington*. Anticipating the torpedo tracks, Sherman had already shoved his ship starboard, leaving his port side exposed with no time to veer away. The four surviving Kates were on top of him.

1119

Lexington's enormous bulk was dead ahead for Ichihara's remaining strike planes. They could hardly miss at this range, even though the huge ship was already starting its swing to the left. All four pilots launched their torpedoes at less than 250 feet altitude and only seven hundred yards away. They were almost too close. Two of the torpedoes plunged deep and flew harmlessly under *Lexington*'s keel. Three of the Kates managed to streak by *Lexington*'s bow beneath the level of the flight deck. Sailors on the ship could actually look down at the planes and pilots as they flashed by below them. The fourth Kate was less fortunate: *Lexington*'s anti-aircraft crews were all over the hapless bomber. Bands of tracers slammed into the plane, which started streaming fuel immediately. It rolled over on its back and plowed into the sea, coming apart underneath the bow of the carrier.

Stanley Johnston, watching the action from his high vantage point, described the scene:

> Right here I see the results of our battery training. The forward 1.1 battery has the range on that first Jap. I see their shells, bright crimson tracers, tearing through the wings and fuselage. This plane wavers, begins a slow roll to its left and veers off just enough to pass in an inverted position just under our bow. As it glides by I see flames coming from the tail, and the machine smashes itself into the water fifty feet off our starboard bow. The

port forward 5-inch battery manned by the marines concentrates its fire on the second Jap. As this plane zooms to cross almost directly over these guns, they hit it squarely with a shell. The explosion blows it to bits, its engine plunging into the water almost at the foot of the battery. Shreds of its wings and tail surfaces slither along the carrier's deck like sheets of paper swept in front of a gale. I can't see what happens to the crew—and I'm not interested.[69]

1120

The Japanese Type 91 aerial torpedo was dubbed the "thunder fish," and for good reason. It was the standard (in fact, the only) IJN aerial torpedo—the same one that had been used at Pearl Harbor. The Type 91 was a whopping eighteen feet long and weighed almost 1,900 pounds, just shy of a ton. It was reliable, had a range out to two thousand yards, flew through the water at forty-two knots, and packed 450 pounds of high explosive into its warhead. It was a contact weapon, which means that when it struck home, the mass of the torpedo behind the warhead would drive the strikers into the detonator, resulting in a tremendous bang.

The Lady Lex felt the first Type 91 bite at 1120. The thunder fish slammed into the hull on the port side, somewhere between frames 60 and 65, which put it slightly ahead of the leading edge of the bridge and island. The ship was immediately rocked by a shuddering explosion that rattled dishes, shook loose items, and bounced a few people around below decks. The hydraulic system for both the ship's elevators was rocked and jammed, causing the huge slabs to drop down a few inches until they hit their safety stops. They would be useless for the remainder of the day.

There were other effects, even more insidious, even if they were not immediately noticed. The blast ruptured at least two or three of the gasoline storage tanks on the port side. These tanks were among those that were shoehorned in after the original battle cruiser hull had been designed and built. As a precaution, these jury-rigged gas tanks were surrounded by freshwater storage tanks, several of which were also holed. The explosion most likely caused *Lexington* to start dumping aviation gasoline into the surrounding ocean and emptied water tanks that could have been used to fight fires. The blast also jarred loose fittings and cracked additional gasoline tanks. Unbeknownst to the crew, gasoline began to seep into the interior of the ship and the vapors began to creep through all the surrounding spaces.

---

69. Johnston, 186–187.

1121

A minute after the first thunder fish slammed home, a second one did the same. This torpedo struck at frame 85, almost dead amidships, also on the port side.

The portside torpedo blister did its job and absorbed much of the impact, but boiler rooms 2, 4, and 6 were breached and partially flooded. Extensive fractures occurred in many of the pipes in the three boiler rooms, and all these spaces had to be taken off line by the ship's engineer. It made only a slight difference in the ship's propulsion capability, however, and *Lexington* was still able to course ahead at a steady twenty-five knots.

Stanley Johnston:

> The *Lexington* shudders under our feet, and a heavy blast spouts mingled flame and water on our port side forward. A torpedo explosion, and I can see the wakes of others streaking toward us. . . . I notice that some of them are porpoising. . . . Their wicked noses look to me like death incarnate. I have the illusion they are alive, and breaking water to peek at us, only to dive again after making sure of their courses. . . . "Wham"—again the whole ship is shaken. Another torpedo. And at the same place, on our port bow. Another spout of flame enclosed in seawater. While we are still staggering under the lurch as the great old ship heaves and shakes itself, a lookout in sky forward [just above the bridge] calls out "dive bombers."[70]

Aviation Ordnanceman 2nd Class Walter Hassell:

> I could not imagine anything that would take a ship almost fifty thousand tons and shake it like a dog would shake a bone, but that one torpedo did it. I recall my first reaction was that we would probably have to go back to the States and the navy yard for repairs, and that didn't seem bad. Later, another torpedo struck, and then in a few moments it seemed another. [Actually, two torpedoes, followed by bomb hits.] We could feel the deck tilt as we started to list to port, and we knew we were in big trouble, and still it continued. By now, I wasn't thinking about the navy yard. I was thinking about my life insurance policy and how long it would take care of my wife and two sons.
>
> Perhaps the worst damage, although it would not be noticed for several hours, was that the port fire mains had been ruptured: they had to be secured and taken off line. Should there be a fire on the port side of the ship, the crew would not be able to fight it effectively.

---

70. Johnston, 187–188.

The two holes in the hull and the venting of so much gas and oil into the surrounding water let a considerable amount of ocean into the affected spaces. Shortly after the torpedo attacks, the *Lexington* began a list to port that went as far as seven degrees before Lieutenant Commander Healy could begin to correct it. Healy, ensconced in his chamber far below, began throwing switches, counter-flooding with his starboard tanks.

1122

As the remainder of the torpedo planes skittered away, dancing with the deadly anti-aircraft fire and hornet-angry American fighters, it was the bombers' turn to try and do their worst. As in the torpedo attack, Lieutenant Commander Takahashi divided his group between the two carrier targets. He would lead nineteen Vals against *Lexington*, and Lieutenant Tamotsu Ema would attack *Yorktown* with fourteen.

Takahashi's cohort pushed over from 14,000 feet, aligned in a long string, and plunged downward to their target. The Val came in at a shallower dive angle than the American Dauntless: sixty degrees versus the Dauntless's seventy to eighty-plus. This gave *Lexington*'s deck gunners more time and a better angle to try and shoot them down. The Japanese pilots did not waver. A wall of tracers flew upward, but the Vals kept coming. *Lexington*'s gunners scored hits, mostly from the 1.1-inch guns, but only one Val burst into flames and fell away from the attack before releasing its bombs. The rest, even those that had taken hits, pressed on. At 1,500 feet, they finally pickled their ordnance.

Many of the bombs used that day against *Lexington* and *Yorktown* were of the five hundred-pound type. Each Val could carry one such bomb or, alternatively, two 60-kilogram (132-pound) bombs. The bombs were generally contact fused, but most would penetrate at least a first layer of thin steel (such as a bulkhead) before exploding. Some bombs had delayed fuses, but it is not known whether any were used on this mission.

In this attack, only two out of possibly twenty-six bombs that the Japanese dropped scored direct hits. Another five were characterized as "near misses." All the near misses exploded on impact with the water and were close enough to do some damage. Titanic geysers of water plumed on both sides of the ship, and for a moment the walls of water almost completely obscured the ship's profile.

71. Hoehling, 68.

1123
BRIDGE, USS *LEXINGTON*
Captain Sherman:

> As I saw a bomb leave one of the planes, it seemed to be coming straight
> for where I stood on the bridge. Had I better duck behind the thin armored
> shield? If it had my name on it, I thought, there was no use dodging, and if
> not, there was no need to worry.[71]

The first direct hit (likely a 132-pound bomb) caused extensive damage
to Admiral Fitch's quarters, along the port side, forward, near frames 55
through 58. Part of these spaces served as a temporary storage area for
some of the shells being used by the nearby five-inch guns. A number of
the five-inch shells were split open and the powder inside combusted, but
miraculously none of the warheads exploded. The lip of the flight deck in
the immediate area was pushed upward, but not enough to impact flight
operations. The admiral and his chief of staff lost their living spaces, and
their overstuffed chairs were the items the fire crews found most difficult
to extinguish.

It was the loss of life at the nearby gun positions that was the worst
news, however. Gun mounts 2, 4, and 6 were the most severely affected.
These were positions manned by the marines. Over a dozen leather-
necks were killed instantly, with another half dozen mortally wounded.
Three wounded marines would succumb later, aboard other ships. It
was a disaster of immense proportions for *Lexington*'s relatively small
Marine Detachment.

Captain Ralph Houser, USMC, was the CO of the Marine Detachment.
He had been nearby when the bomb hit, but was not wounded. The shocking
tableau of the first bomb's aftermath had him crazed with grief and anger.
Several of his proud marines were dead at their gun positions, charred
beyond recognition, frozen in place—just like the bodies at Pompeii after
the volcano, some said. Others had been cast into misshapen forms, missing
limbs, eviscerated, or decapitated. Several men lay moaning on the blasted
deck, bleeding, many with gaping wounds. Houser and the medical team
dashed from one man to the next, trying to stop the fountains of blood,
applying battle dressings or layers of tannic jelly to cover the frightful
burns. It was a scene of absolute carnage. Aviation Ordnanceman 2nd Class
Walter Hassell:

> I walked to the forward edge of the flight deck, where the Marine detach-
> ment was charged with manning two of the 5-inch anti-aircraft guns.

That was where my friend Sergeant Larry Peyton was gun captain and in charge of the battery. The sight that met my eyes, and stunned my soul, was a gapping [sic], jagged hole in the deck just aft of gun No. 2. . . . The effect of the concussion on the Marine gun crew was beyond description. There were at least six or eight bodies lying around the shattered gun. There were still a few Marines from the sheltered side of the No. 1 gun sitting dazed and quiet beside their silent gun. My friend Larry Peyton was not among them. I knew then that he had been one of those who did not make it.[72][73]

There had been tragic secondary damage in the interior spaces near the Admiral's Quarters as well. Although it was never entirely clear why they were in the vicinity as neither man's GQ station was in that area, both Cmdr. Walter W. Gilmore, the senior supply officer, and Cmdr. Wadsworth Trojakowski, the chief dental surgeon, were discovered inert in a nearby passageway. Both were dead, with no visible wounds.

The senior chaplain, Commander Markle, an ex-marine rifleman from World War I, rushed to the area as soon as he heard there were casualties among the marines. As he ran through Admiral's Country, he found Gilmore face down on the deck. His first thought was that his overweight friend had had a heart attack, so Markle started artificial respiration. Moments later, he was joined by the senior medical officer, Commander White, who was also rushing to aid the marines. He examined Gilmore and told Markle that nothing could be done. He guessed that the concussion from the bomb blast had flattened all of Gilmore's internal organs, killing him instantly. White had seen these types of injuries before. The same seemed to be true for Trojakowski, whose body lay nearby.

The nearby coding room, where all radio intercepts were deciphered, was obliterated. The thin bulkheads were knocked flat and several spaces sandwiched together. Half a dozen men died in this space, including Ensign Robert H. Zwierschke of the Supply Corps, who was the duty officer for the coding room during the battle.

Shortly after the attacks, Chaplain Markle described the area near Admiral's Country:

[I] found a hospital corpsman administering tannic acid jelly to the patients and generally caring for the wounded. They were horribly burned. Their

---

72. In fact, Sergeant Peyton did survive, and he was one of the very last off the ship. He led a cheer for Captain Sherman before departing to a lifeboat.
73. Hassell.

clothing and shoes had almost been blasted from them and some were almost naked. . . . Some had burned eyes and had to be led through the passageway. I took charge and got them stretched out on cots. . . . We greased them with tannic acid, and gave injections of morphine to those in great pain, making a red cross on their foreheads with Mercurochrome so no one would give them another injection. . . . There was chaos and turmoil, smoke and fumes and bedlam.[74]

Stanley Johnston, too, faced loss:

Immediately after the [bomb] attack I came down [from the signal bridge] to get my typewriter and found all of this section devastated, still burning, and soaked with the chemical fire extinguishing fluid. Before the battle hundreds of 5-inch shells had been stacked all around to be near that gun position; these were now scattered throughout the whole section.

Relatively few of them were exploded but the continuing fire and heat caused their charges to swell. This pushed the projectile [warhead] out of the brass powder cases of scores of them. Shortly after the projectile would fall away the fire would get to the powder charges and burn with a great rushing "sssssssssss" throwing out a searing tail of flame. They reminded me of the giant firecrackers we used to break in half and then light to see the powder hiss and burn.[75]

Johnston's typewriter, all his notes, the copies of his dispatches, and the recordings that he and Commander Seligman had so excitedly prepared were all gone.

The second bomb, most likely another sixty-kilogram bomb, struck the port side of *Lexington*'s enormous stack housing. The strike was high on the funnel but only a few feet above the portside .50-caliber machine gun platform. It detonated on contact, but the metal surrounding the stack was relatively thin and, as a result, fragments of the bomb and shrapnel from the stack blew in all directions, even punching all the way through to the starboard side.

The machine gun platforms, added in the 1935 retrofit, were the highest guns on the ship and the most exposed. It was a hot, noisy, and dirty perch. When the ship was speeding along, like it was that day, the stacks roared and pumped out spouts of fumes and lots of heat. On top of that, the sun beat down on the gunners from above and waves of heat reflected back on them from the steel surrounding the stack.

74. Hoehling, 91.
75. Johnston, 203.

The bomb slammed in right above the heads of the men manning the machine guns on the port side. Half a dozen sailors were killed instantly, including Seaman 2nd Class Tom Hart. Down below, on the flight deck, Hart's older brother, Machinist's Mate 3rd Class Joe Hart, looked up a fraction of a second after the noise of the bomb reached his ears. He saw a large puff of "dirty, yellow smoke" followed by "great clouds of thick, black smoke or soot from the stack."

The Hart brothers had been aboard *Lexington* since Pearl Harbor. That very morning they had been together at breakfast when the GQ alarm went off. Joe started sprinting for his plane captain station on the flight deck, and Tom ran for the machine gun platform on the stack. As they split up, Tom shouted back over his shoulder to Joe that they'd surely be "seeing some more excitement!" Joe remembered his brother's earlier bright-eyed enthusiasm as he gazed up at the damaged stack and was gripped by "a funny feeling."[76]

Shrapnel from the bomb that struck the stack housing blew backward toward the station known as "sky aft." This was a fire-control platform located on the back side of the stack, high up and almost level with the machine guns. Lieutenant Junior Grade E. M. "Max" Price was standing on the open platform, shielded only by flimsy canvas, directing his batteries of .50-calibers. As the echoes from the bomb blast skittered away, he turned to speak to his boss, the gunnery officer. He opened his mouth, but nothing came out. As his eyes glazed over, he fell to the deck, face down, at the gunnery officer's feet. A large piece of ugly shrapnel protruded from the back of his head. The gunnery officer kneeled down and bent over Price, gently removing his silver collar bars. He placed them in his shirt pocket, making a mental note to include them in Price's effects, all the items he would later send home to Price's parents.

The near bomb misses were spectacular in terms of noise and creating large water spouts, but they did very little damage, except to the port side near the boat pocket amidships (frames 84 to 97). The three 20-millimeter gun platforms in this area featured hinged, semi-circular front deck-plates that could be raised for normal steaming and lowered for action. One near miss sent such a powerful shot of seawater upward that it blew all three platforms up and jammed them shut, taking these weapons out of action and nearly drowning several of the gunners.

Another near miss was a whisker away from catastrophe. A bomb flew through the narrow space between the funnel and the bridge, exactly at bridge level. The random dynamics of the arc of the bomb, the flight path of the plane that dropped it, and the relative motion of the ship could have allowed it to strike steel instead of air. Miraculously, it passed through the opening. Had it struck home, it would have killed everyone on the bridge, including Captain Sherman and probably Admiral Fitch, who was only a few feet higher on the Admiral's Bridge, just above. It did bisect the cord controlling the ship's siren, which sent the whistle into a continuous, high-pitched shriek that pierced eardrums and exacerbated the frayed nerves of everyone near the ship's bridges.

Fireman Vernon Highfill was at his station several decks below, in charge of maintaining several critical generators. He got a frantic call from the bridge to kill the whistle. He jumped up and ran to the ladder leading to the next deck, where he knew the steam-control valve for the siren was housed. He managed to shut it down and dash back to his post, much to the relief of the entire topside crew.

1128

SHIP'S DISPENSARY, USS *NEW ORLEANS*

Lieutenant Forgy's battle station was two decks below the main deck of the cruiser *New Orleans*, in the ship's dispensary, or hospital ward. Of his limited vantage point, Forgy wrote:

> You can't see what's going on, you don't know where the enemy is and there is nothing you can do to release the dammed-up emotions multiplying inside your mind. I looked out at the sweating men at the ammunition hoist and envied them. They were keeping busy and their minds were on their jobs—not filled with flashes of fear and uncertainty. . . . You couldn't hear any words over the ear splitting banging of the guns. . . . We all lay flat hugging the deck. Some corpsmen crawled under the cots. Others snuggled against the bulkheads for added protection. I lay there with my face against the cool deck and looked through the doorway at the ammunition crew. The men were working like parts of a well-lubricated machine as they grabbed each shell and pushed it through a hole in the bulkhead to the men at the next hoist. I wondered how they could maintain the back breaking pace without missing or dropping a shell. The guns above us were firing so rapidly now that the deck beneath me shook continuously. It slapped back and forth against my cheek. Dozens of thoughts and half-thoughts raced through my mind. I looked up at the overhead and wondered what I would do if we were hit. If an armor piercing shell found us, I thought, it would probably come through the quarterdeck, the main deck, and let go right here. Maybe one of those Jap planes had already sent a torpedo at us. Well, down here we'd never know it until it hit. I wondered how I could get out of here if we did take a hit and the water began

to pour in. Odd, I had never thought of that before. A fellow should always think of how he can get out of a place in an emergency. . . . There was no letup in the barking of the guns topside. It was almost a continuous roar now, like a huge machine gun with the trigger held down. . . . I looked across the room to one of the boys in the cots. He reached under his pillow and pulled out a little blue ring box. In it was a diamond he had bought at Honolulu to give to his girl back in the states. I knew he was wondering now whether he would ever live through this to see the girl he wanted for his wife.[77]

1129
SIGNAL BRIDGE, USS *LEXINGTON*
A marine reported to the bridge with an "urgent" message for the XO. The young marine saluted smartly, handed a folded paper to Commander Seligman, turned on a heel, and left. Expecting dire news from deep within the ship, Seligman anxiously unfolded the sheet. He scanned the paper, frowned, crumpled the note, and tossed it in a nearby shit can.

Stanley Johnston, standing close by, asked, "What's the bother now?"

Seligman turned back to the air battle and fuming with incredulity replied, "Someone wants me to worry because we have a case of measles aboard."

$\sim$

As the dive bombers peeled away, heading back to their ships, it was their turn to face the gauntlet of continuing anti-aircraft fire and the planes guarding *Lexington*. Several of the Val pilots, as they sped away, gave their gunners a shot at raking *Lexington* with their 7.7-millimeter machine guns. It was a last insult to add to the injuries already inflicted.

As men fell around him, nineteen-year-old Pvt. Raymond Miller refused to leave his post. Bleeding profusely from his wounds, he shunned relief and medical attention, continuing to heave the five-inch shells needed by his gun. He held on until the end of the action, when he finally fell to the deck, a round cradled in his arms. He was dead. Miller was written up for a Navy Cross, which was, after several weeks, finally approved. There was a problem, though: Private Raymond Miller did not exist. The home address and next of kin he had given were fake.

77. Hoehling, 76-77.

The truth was finally unearthed. "Raymond Miller," who had lied about his age, ran away from home, and enlisted in Seattle, Washington, was actually Jesse Rutherford Jr. from Chanute, Kansas. Rutherford, born January 12, 1923, and underage, had fled after his mother had refused to sign his enlistment papers. In the days before computers and instant identity checks, it was relatively easy to skip to another town, lie about your name and age, and sign up. Many recruiters were looking the other way anyway, as the needs of the service and casualties mounted.

To his Marine Corps buddies, Rutherford was "Miller" until after he was killed. Even his official Navy Cross citation was written in his assumed name. His bravery, however, was genuine. It was a sad surprise for Rutherford's shocked mother, who was not leavened by his award. A year later, Mrs. Rutherford christened a brand-new Navy destroyer escort launched in her son's real name, USS *Jesse Rutherford*, DE-347.

1129

VS-2 DAUNTLESS

In the wild melee after the main fight, as Lt. j.g. William Hall and Ensign John Leppla were tangling with four Zeros, one of the Japanese pilots shot up the Dauntless flown by VS-2's Lt. j.g. Roy Hale Jr. Hale was wounded and his plane badly damaged. He angled his Dauntless to *Lexington*'s stern, desperately hoping to effect an immediate landing. The twenty-four-year-old Naval Academy graduate, class of 1938, whose birthday was two days away, struggled to keep his ship airborne as he curved back to the flight deck. The nervous gunners aboard *Lexington* and the nearby cruiser *New Orleans* mistook Hale for one of the Japanese attack planes and opened fire.

As John Lundstrom writes, "[T]he SBD was hit by a torrent of antiaircraft fire from the *Lexington* and surrounding vessels and splashed off the cruiser *New Orleans*'s starboard bow. The crew did not survive."[78]

Lieutenant Junior Grade Hale's death and that of his gunner were officially recorded as killed in action, and Hale was posthumously awarded a Distinguished Flying Cross for "extraordinary achievement in aerial combat." Another destroyer escort, this one christened USS *Roy O. Hale*, DE-336, was launched in his honor a year later.

1139

BRIDGE, USS *LEXINGTON*

The guns started to fall silent, but the deafening roar of the battle was still ringing in the ears of all, above and below decks. It was hard to believe, but

78. Lundstrom, 330.

only twenty-three minutes had passed since the initial Japanese torpedo drops. In that short span, twenty-six years of design and development and thousands of hours devoted to the Fleet Problems had been tested and validated. The first carrier-versus-carrier battle had been waged and *Lexington* had survived. All that remained to be determined was the fate of her air wing and the outcome of the battle against the opponent's flattops.

On the bridge, Captain Sherman began to call for damage reports from all departments. His major concern, of course, was the six degrees list to port, which Lieutenant Commander Healy had already assured him was under control. The flight deck was pockmarked with bullet holes, but the sturdy teak planking had held up well and the damage was insufficient to hinder flight operations. The loss of the elevators was a problem, but one that could be repaired quickly. The big ship was leaking oil and aviation gas from the hull punctures, but the damage-control teams were already using prefabricated repair kits to plug the holes. Sherman felt that Lady Lex wasn't done yet.

The viewpoint of the rest of the crew was a little more cautionary. Although they had survived, beating back the best the Japanese navy could throw at them in the process, the crew knew the damage was not slight. Many of the men began to speculate on a return to the yards, either Pearl or maybe even Bremerton, which would mean shore leave and time with families. The air officer, Commander Duckworth, was even predicting aloud that *Lexington* would need at least three months in dry dock.

A couple of stubborn fires still burned forward, near the chief petty officers' mess and the Admiral's Quarters, but the firefighters reported that they would soon be "under control." Sherman turned his attention to getting his airmen safely aboard. The quartermaster on the bridge logged, at noon, "Steaming as before."

While the men shook off the fear, horror, exhilaration, and adrenaline, deep below, in the bowels of the ship, unbeknownst to most, the seeds of *Lexington*'s destruction, sown at her birth, were about to germinate.

1120

LEXINGTON AIR STRIKE GROUP

At the very moment the Japanese began to assault their mother ship, *Lexington*'s air group was about to stumble on the Japanese MO Strike Force. Things had not gone well since their 0945 takeoff. The weather had worsened and wreaked havoc on any sense of coordination for CLAG Cmdr. Bill Ault's plan of attack.

There was no way of predicting exactly what the weather would have been over the enemy's carriers, but the "weather guessers" back at the ship had not been optimistic. They were right, and when the first American air units arrived at their target area, they found lowering skies and rain. It might have been more prudent to hold off on the air strikes until the weather over the target area improved.

The *Lexington* air group went at the target without the benefit of coordination with the *Yorktown* strike group. This was, in retrospect, a serious tactical error. It allowed the Japanese to defend themselves more easily and strike back at their attackers in segments. At the very least, the *Yorktown* strike group could have coordinated by radio once the engagement had commenced, but they did not even do that; thus, Commander Ault was left in the air both literally and figuratively. He had run out to the very end of his assigned search leg, some two hundred miles, and found nothing while the *Yorktown* group was already making their attacks. The *Yorktown* pilots were already heading back before the *Lexington* air group could get in the game.

The *Yorktown* strike group had started their assault on the MO Force at 1057. They attacked in two sections, one primarily of bombers and the other of torpedo planes escorted by most of the fighters. Without radar, the Japanese were caught completely by surprise. They had left thirteen Zeros behind as an air defense, and they were busy. But in the ensuing melee, they knocked down only two SBDs, both from VB-5. The navy airmen claimed they had downed eleven Zeros, but the true total was more modest: three altogether. The *Yorktown* pilots also claimed they had sent three torpedoes into *Shōkaku* and pummeled her with six thousand-pound bombs. Once again, the actual scores were less impressive. Not a single torpedo found its mark, and only two bombs struck home. Those two bombs were devastating, however, at least to *Shōkaku*'s air operations. There was extensive damage to the flight deck and hundreds of casualties on the open flattop and on the hangar deck below. *Zuikaku* escaped untouched, lucky enough to be able to duck in and out of squalls. The *Yorktown*'s air group had completed its attacks and was already leaving the area by 1115.

One of the VB-5 bombers that was lost, and one of the thousand-pound bombs to strike *Shōkaku*, belonged to Lt. John J. "Jo Jo" Powers. The young aviator and graduate of Annapolis, class of 1935, had spent his first five years of commissioned service aboard ships. He petitioned for aviation service and received his wings in 1941. He was sent to VB-5, where, by early 1942, he had become the squadron's gunnery officer and an advocate for pushing the envelope of bombing doctrine. Powers preferred to extend his dives farther, and get in closer, than anyone else. In the Tulagi raids, his first actual combat, he had placed ordnance on one destroyer, which ultimately sank, and scored near misses on two Japanese transports. On May 7, he was one of the pilots who successfully put a thousand-pound bomb into *Shōhō*, but he did so by diving well below the recommended safe diving recovery altitude.

In what would become great irony in hindsight, Powers gave a lecture to his squadron mates on the evening of May 7 after the *Shōhō* incident and shared his ideas on lower release points. He stressed the danger of greater vulnerability to enemy anti-aircraft fire as well as the higher possibility of getting caught up in one's own bomb blast. If he swayed any of his fellow bomber pilots, it was not recorded.

The next morning, as the VB-5 pilots left their *Yorktown* Ready Room for the day's mission, Powers said, "Remember, the folks back home are counting on us. I'm going to get a hit if I have to lay it right on their flight deck."

He pushed over from 18,000 feet, screaming down on *Shōkaku*. Toward the end of his dive, one of the Zeros tagged Powers with a 20-millimeter round, near his fuel tank. Gas and flames started streaming from his plane. Both he and his gunner were seriously wounded, but Powers pressed his attack. He passed well below the recommended 1,000 feet before dropping his bomb, striking *Shōkaku* directly behind the island and squarely on the flight deck he had sworn to hit. Powers initiated a pull-out at about 200 feet, but he was too low and his plane disintegrated in the blowback from his own bomb. Fragments of the Dauntless, Powers, and his gunner splashed into the Coral Sea next to the wounded *Shōkaku*.

The daring exploit, though reckless, became a favorite story of President Roosevelt, who presented Powers's family with a posthumous Medal of Honor later in the year.

Ault, like his opposite number from *Yorktown*, divided his group into two sections. He led his own small pod of four bombers, along with six Wildcats and eleven torpedo planes. The second section was under the command of VB-2 CO Lieutenant Commander Hamilton and accompanied by three more fighters. At 1120, Ault was staring at an empty sky and an open ocean. The enemy was nowhere in sight. He started a box search to the west.

Ten minutes later, Ault saw wisps of smoke on the water and knew that he must be looking at the remnants of the *Yorktown* attack. A carrier shot across an open patch of ocean between some clouds. It was burning, and looked to be in serious trouble, but it was still steaming at a high rate of speed (*Shōkaku* had not been damaged below the waterline and was still capable of making thirty-plus knots). Ault finally decided to get on the radio. He ordered his group to circle up and get ready to go in. Unfortunately, Hamilton was lost in the clouds nearby and had no idea where Ault and his planes were. Ault decided he couldn't wait—another tactical error that can be chalked up to overzealousness and inexperience. He dove in with the aircraft he had at hand.

Ault did not see *Zuikaku*. Her lookouts spotted Ault's group as they circled up. *Zuikaku*'s captain radioed a warning to *Shōkaku* and her CAP, which was still in the air, unable to land. He alerted his own Zeros aloft as well. Now the Americans were caught by surprise. Several Zeros jumped on the Wildcats and the torpedo planes, and the others went after the fighters that were escorting the bombers.

Commander Ault decided to forego the usual screaming dive from 18,000 feet. He elected instead to use a flat glide-bombing approach. It worked. The patrolling Zeros never saw his planes. Ault and his pilots settled on the wounded *Shōkaku* as their prey and one by one they eased in over their target. Three thousand-pound bombs went away, one striking the imperiled *Shōkaku* near the island structure and causing even more damage to the flight deck and the hangar deck below. One SBD, flown by Ensign John Wingfield, could not release its bomb. When told he still had his ordnance slung beneath his carriage, Wingfield peeled away to conduct another attack. He was never seen again.

Lieutenant Commander Brett's Devastators had a clear field. The Zeros decided to chase the Wildcats instead of the torpedo planes. Two of Brett's intrepid pilots bore down on *Shōkaku* from the port side and launched their fish. *Shōkaku*'s captain deftly spun the helm away and both torpedoes missed, but in so doing he set up his starboard side for a classic anvil attack by Brett's nine remaining aircraft. All of the pilots dropped on the fully exposed target and, incredibly, all nine torpedoes missed as *Shōkaku* again pirouetted away from the erratic American fish. The bravery of the "Torpecker" airmen was overmatched by their antiquated aircraft and ineffective munitions.

Up in the clouds, Lieutenant Commander Hamilton's group remained hopelessly lost. They heard, on the radios, the fight going on below them, but they could not get into it. They narrowly missed colliding with a group of enemy Zeros, but that was as close as they came to any action. Fearing the rapid diminishment of his fuel supply, Hamilton finally ordered his pilots to jettison their bombs and return to the ship, shortly after noon.

Ault's piecemeal attack disintegrated into dozens of separate skirmishes, hither and yon, skipping throughout the clouds. Several pilots became disoriented, including Commander Ault himself. One Zero, piloted by Petty Officer 1st Class Kenji Okabe, a veteran fighter pilot from *Shōkaku*, chased Ault into the overcast, but not before peppering his aircraft with dozens of 7.7-millimeter slugs. Ault was hit in both his right arm and leg. His gunner, Petty Officer 1st Class Bill Butler, was mortally wounded. Ault's plane began streaming fuel and losing power. He ducked down close to the surface and tried to raise *Lexington* on the radios, desperate to get a compass heading back to the ship. Lieutenant Red Gill heard his radio call, but at that moment *Lexington* was under the most furious part of the Japanese attacks and no one could render Ault any assistance.

Low on fuel, wounded, nursing a failing aircraft, and heading in the wrong direction, *Yorktown* picked up Ault's last transmission shortly after 1454: "From CLAG. OK, so long people. Remember, we got a thousand-pound hit on the flattop." He probably knew he was going to die, yet his last, plaintive message was from the warrior within, wanting credit for striking a significant blow on the enemy. He was never heard from again.

The price for Ault's strike had been steep. Three Wildcats and their pilots had been lost, and another fighter was later forced down at sea, though the pilot was rescued. Three Dauntlesses were lost with their crews, including Ault, and one ditched near Rossel Island, where the pilot and gunner were rescued. The loss of *Lexington*'s air group leader was a blow, but his counterpart in the Japanese strike group, Lieutenant Commander Takahashi, was also lost, shot down as he raced back to *Shōkaku* with the disappointing news that his pilots had failed to sink either of the American carriers.

1150

BRIDGE, IJN CARRIER *SHŌKAKU*

Captain Takaji Jōshima knew that his ship had had enough. Three large bombs had devastated his flight deck, making further aircraft operations impossible. More than a hundred of his crew were dead and another hundred or more wounded. His ship's ability to continue in the fight was nil; in fact, he was probably more of a liability, a floating, burning magnet for more enemy attacks.

Jōshima radioed Admiral Hara seeking permission to withdraw. He still had full propulsion capability, and his aim was to get to a repair facility as quickly as possible, maybe Kure back in Japan. The fate of his aircrews worried Jōshima, but there was nothing he could do for them: those who had survived the day's battles would have to seek refuge aboard *Zuikaku* or whatever nearby land bases they could reach with their remaining fuel.

1230

IJN HEAVY CRUISER *MYŌKŌ*

At 1230 hours, after conferring with Hara, Admiral Takagi gave permission for Captain Jōshima to withdraw with all due haste and head north, to Japan, in company with the heavy cruisers *Kinugasa* and *Furutaka* plus two destroyers. Ten minutes later, at 1240, Hara and Takagi both agreed that they needed a timeout. There were planes from two flattops to recover, and they would soon be inbound. The pilots were already chattering about having downed "dozens" of enemy planes and "sunk" two carriers. If this were true, both Japanese admirals agreed that it would be glorious news of a great victory. In the meantime, they needed an assessment of their remaining strength and their staffs needed a breather to consider their next moves. Takagi turned his remaining ships north and prepared to recover his aircraft.

1315
FLAG PLOT, USS *YORKTOWN*
Meanwhile, to the south, at Task Force 17 flag plot aboard *Yorktown*, Admiral Fletcher was assessing his own situation. *Yorktown* had not escaped the battle untouched. The ship's speed and agility and Captain Buckmaster's outstanding seamanship had kept *Yorktown* out of the path of the four torpedoes thrown at her, and avoided thirteen out of the fourteen attempts to bomb her. The one bomb that did strike home was a near disaster, however. John Lundstrom describes the devastation:

> At 1127, one 250-kilogram "ordinary" bomb (semi-armor-piercing) struck the center of her flight deck forward of the middle elevator. Leaving a clean twelve-inch hole in the flight deck, the bomb penetrated four more decks (totaling almost two inches of steel) and detonated in an aviation storeroom, fifty feet below the flight deck. The force of the blast destroyed the compartment and the surrounding area, stove in hatches up to the hangar deck, and damaged bulkheads. Small fires ignited in several locations, venting dense, black smoke to the flight deck.[79]

Before finally exploding four decks down, the bomb blew through the space where Repair Party No. 5 was waiting to respond to any emergencies. Twenty-eight-year-old Lt. Milton E. Ricketts was the O-in-C (officer in charge) of the repair team. Most of Ricketts's team was killed or seriously wounded when the bomb tore through the compartment, hitting them where they stood. Ricketts, mortally wounded, managed to get to a nearby fireplug, open the valve, roll out a length of hose, and place water on the fire below before literally dropping dead with his hands on the hose. His selfless act of valor prevented the fire from spreading to the ammunition stored nearby and earned the Annapolis Class of 1935 graduate the Medal of Honor.

Sixty-six sailors were killed or seriously wounded in this one bomb blast. Three fire rooms were temporarily put out of commission, reducing

79. Lundstrom, 328.

the ship's speed to twenty-five knots. The flight deck was not crippled, however, and the damage from the other near misses was minor.

The Japanese pilots were either completely fooled or given to great exaggeration, or both. The Japanese aviators excitedly radioed that they had hit *Yorktown* with two torpedoes and eight to ten bombs. The gigantic spouts of water that engulfed *Yorktown* from the near misses and the plume of thick, black smoke from the one bomb that did strike home led them to conclude—or at least report—that they had sunk the carrier.

As the morning strikes came back, Fletcher discovered that *Yorktown* had only seven Wildcats fit for further duty. More than twenty planes were still missing, and the weapons officer inventoried only seven torpedoes remaining. The status of *Lexington*'s air group was unknown. Fletcher had also received overinflated reports concerning the large number of Zeros his pilots said were still available to the enemy.

Captain Buckmaster reported accurately to Admiral Fletcher that the fire from the bomb strike was out (thanks to Lieutenant Ricketts) and that the damage was not critical. Fletcher was receiving mixed reports on the amount of damage to his other carrier, however, and the messages worried him. Admiral Fitch was being cautious about *Lexington*'s ability to continue the fight. Fletcher was also starting to hear something about "an explosion" aboard *Lexington*, an event that had occurred well after the battle.

At 1315, Fletcher radioed Fitch, "In view of [reported] enemy fighter plane superiority and undamaged carrier [*Zuikaku*], I propose retiring. What do you think?"

At 1324, a preoccupied Fitch replied only, "Affirmative."

Fletcher sent back, "Tomorrow may rearm this ship with your planes and renew attack."

Fletcher was worried about *Lexington*, and it seemed to him that both sides had probably been reduced to one carrier each.

1500

IJN CARRIER *ZUIKAKU*

As the Japanese crews came back aboard *Zuikaku*, from her own air wing as well as from *Shōkaku*, two things became apparent to admirals Hara and Takagi. First, the day's losses, combined with the crews and planes lost the day before, were staggering. Twenty-two more aircraft, and their crews, were gone. Many of the remaining planes were damaged, some extensively. Twelve aircraft were so badly damaged that the Japanese sailors simply pushed them over the side. The aircraft losses from both days left barely enough planes to supply one carrier's air wing, never mind two.

Second, the returning airmen were adamant that they had sunk the "*Saratoga*-type" carrier (*Lexington*) and had at least badly damaged and probably had sunk the other (*Yorktown*). The one Japanese pilot who knew the truth could not tell it: Lieutenant Commander Takahashi, the strike leader, had lingered behind his returning aircraft, darting in and out of the clouds to avoid detection. When the smoke of battle finally cleared, he was shocked to discover that *Yorktown* was no longer on fire and that "*Saratoga*" was landing aircraft and steaming away at twenty-five knots. He raced back to the MO Strike Force anxious to deliver this sobering news. Minutes later he met up with a stray Wildcat, flying in the opposite direction and above him, piloted by VF-42's Lt. j.g. Bill Leonard. Leonard was escorting home a badly shot-up SBD, but the target racing below him was too tempting. It was all too easy to turn, drop down, and fire into an enemy that was totally unaware of his presence. The Val pilot—Takahashi—didn't even try and evade. Takahashi's plane rolled over and plunged straight into the ocean.

Buoyed by the reported sinkings of the enemy, but sobered by the loss of so many planes and aviators and low on fuel, Takagi, at 1500, ordered the MO Striking Force to turn around and head north. The battle was over. There would not be, at least for the moment, any invasion of Port Moresby.

Thus with the withdrawal of the contending forces, the Battle of the Coral Sea was over. Task Force 17 had accomplished exactly what was expected of it, the defense of Port Moresby. Fletcher's force had blunted the first of several expected Japanese thrusts into the South Pacific. The trouble was that Task Force 17 had got itself grievously bloodied in the process.[80]

$\sim$

As the guns fell silent, the grim statistics were totaled by both sides. For the IJN, over the course of the battle from May 4 through 1600, May 8, the losses were as follows:

1 light carrier lost (*Shōhō*) with 18 planes and 631 KIA

1 fleet carrier damaged (*Shōkaku*) and out of action, 108 KIA

1 fleet carrier's air wing (*Zuikaku*) smashed (and unable to participate in any actions for weeks, making it unavailable for the Battle of Midway)

87 carrier aircraft destroyed with the loss of 90 aircrew KIA

---

80. Lundstrom, 354.

5 land-based Betty bombers destroyed, 35 KIA
2 Mavis seaplanes destroyed, 20 KIA
3 Alf type floatplanes, 9 KIA
1 destroyer sunk (*Kikuzuki*), 12 KIA
3 minesweepers sunk, 51 KIA

For the Allies and Task Force 17, for the same period:

1 fleet carrier (*Yorktown*) slightly damaged, 40 KIA
1 fleet carrier (*Lexington*) severely damaged, 100 (+) KIA (to 1600 hours)
1 fleet oiler (*Neosho*) sunk, 175 KIA
1 destroyer (*Sims*) sunk, 178 KIA
1 heavy cruiser (*Chicago*) slightly damaged, 2 KIA
35 carrier aircraft destroyed with the loss of 35 aircrew KIA

Sadly, this would not be the end of the Allied tally.

CHAPTER 10

"WE CAN'T SAVE HER, CAPTAIN"

1233, MAY 8, 1942
CENTRAL STATION, USS *LEXINGTON*

Lieutenant Commander Healy had repair crews running all over the ship. The reports coming back were encouraging, for the most part. All the fires were out except for that nagging bit of business in the Admiral's Quarters. The upholstered furniture and the fancier trappings associated with flag rank were proving not to be worth the trouble, at least not that day. Thick, black smoke was still making the job difficult, although the actual area of the fire seemed to be rather small. Healy told his men to stay at it.

The inclinometer was finally level again—maybe just a smidgeon too much to starboard—but he could correct that pretty easily. Commander Duckworth had been anxiously awaiting a "clear deck" signal so he could launch a new CAP—just in case the Japanese were inclined to continue the fight.

Healy rang up the air boss: "Ducky, it's Healy. I'm showing a level deck, almost. I think you're OK to launch."

"Great, Pop, thanks. What about the fires? I need to get these birds gassed up."

"If you use the starboard tanks and pumps you'll be OK. No reports of damage or any fires on that side."

"Roger, thanks."

"Portside boiler rooms are pumped dry, too. 'Heine' will be lighting them off again momentarily."

"Pop. . . . You think we're going to be OK?"

"I think we're going to make it. Now get those boys in the air."

"Thanks, Pop. You got it. Ducky out."

Healy replaced the receiver. *Do I really believe what I just told Duckworth?* he wondered to himself.

He looked up at his status boards: a lot of red lights were still on, too many switches were still open, repair parties were still struggling. *Well, hell, doesn't do any good to be negative,* he thought silently. He picked up the phone to call the chief engineer.

Topside, Commander Duckworth signaled his crew to get the next launch moving. Five Wildcats were gassed and ready, and off they went, sent aloft to guard the skies overhead. Seven Dauntlesses were next. They would fly out toward the last known positions of the enemy to scout the Japanese task force.

With the exception of a few wisps of smoke from the forward fires, the jagged hole in the stack, and the thin trail of fuel oil streaming in her wake, Lady Lex, for all intents and purposes, looked to be ready for whatever the Japanese might send their way.

1242
IC MOTOR GENERATOR ROOM, USS *LEXINGTON*

Aviation gasoline is a mixture of various hydrocarbons that make its fumes denser—thus heavier—than ambient air. The portside aviation gas tanks were shielded by the hull, empty space, and water tanks, but there was no question that they had been shaken violently by the torpedoes that slammed into the vessel. Had they been penetrated, they might have exploded. But what if they were cracked, or if the brackets that secured them to the bulkheads came loose? There was no way to inspect the tanks directly—not without getting behind the bulkheads. Members of the repair parties, medical teams, and the firefighters all reported "smelling fumes," however, which was not a comforting indicator.

What no one realized was that the vapors, weighing more, sank to the level of the decks and began to wend along the passageways in the area, seeping into cracks and bulges made in the bulkheads as a result of blast damage. Even some of the fuel itself slithered down the decks, unnoticed in all the smoke and water from the fire hoses. Like a phantom reptile, the deadly fluid snaked along, looking for an ignition source to sink its ghostly fangs into.

Finally, some of the combustible fumes and flammable liquids found their way into the IC Motor Generator Room, near the chief petty officers' mess, on deck three. A powerful odor of gas immediately welled up in the vicinity of the General Workshop and the CPO spaces, and all personnel were told to clear the area. "IC" stood for "internal combustion," just like a conventional automotive engine, and *Lexington* had a number of these motors installed in a special compartment used to produce electricity. The engines were critical to maintaining vital systems on the ship and therefore were not "secured" (shut down) during or immediately after the attacks. In all probability, one or more of these motors, still running, had been jarred loose or misaligned enough to cause it to generate sparks. All it would take was one spark coming into contact with the leaking gas or vapors.

At 1242, that's precisely what happened. An enormous explosion rocked the ship.

1243

BRIDGE, USS *LEXINGTON*

"What in God's name was that?!" Captain Sherman shouted as he was nearly thrown off his feet. The powerful shaking of his ship was even worse than what he had felt when the torpedoes had punched into the hull.

All over the ship, men were knocked flat, equipment jammed, hatches flew open, dishes crashed, and Lady Lex, as enormous as she was, was pushed a few feet sideways. Smoke poured, once again, from her wounded port bow area.

Valves cracked, additional pipes burst, and more gas ignited. A huge conflagration swept the lower decks in the area near the IC Motor Generator Room, the CPO Mess, the General Workroom, Admiral's Quarters, and, most significantly, Central Station.

The massive fireball consumed every molecule of oxygen, literally sucking the air out of the lungs of the men nearby and replacing it with searing flame. Twenty-five men in Central Station, including steadfast Lieutenant Commander Healy, were killed instantly, burned from the inside out and then incinerated into carbon, beings barely recognizable as human forms. Central Station ceased to function.

Annunciators on the bridge went out as did steering control. Sherman's only way to control the track of the ship was by an alternate voice circuit to a helmsman at the trick wheel, aft.[81] New fires broke out and thick, brown smoke plumed upward from the forward elevator shaft. Damage-control teams, already exhausted, raced to the scene.

Some men remembered the blasted area as a charnel house. They had to pull and push aside charred bodies to fight the growing fires; other survivors were severely burned, several mortally. Band members and pantry boys hefted stretchers or pulled men from the shattered spaces.

---

81. The trick wheel is an alternative ship's wheel, usually located in an after compartment and used for emergency steering if control of the rudder from the bridge is lost.

Sailors with their clothes burned off their bodies stumbled, naked, down smoking passageways.

The concussion of the blast blew forward and aft, its hot breath seeking any empty space in its path. The ship's senior doctor, Commander White, who was working in the medical bay near the bow, was blown off his feet and slammed into a bulkhead, fracturing both ankles.

Back on the bridge, Captain Sherman steadied himself and barked out commands. He desperately needed to know the status of his ship. Commander Duckworth had gotten all the flyable aircraft off the deck, but the surviving fighters, bombers, and torpedo planes from the morning strike had yet to return. Would they be able to land?

1300

FORWARD DISTRIBUTION ROOM, USS *LEXINGTON*

The space immediately in front of Central Station was the Forward Distribution Room. Maintained mostly by the ship's electricians, it was the nerve center for all electrical power distribution. The same blast that wiped out Central Station killed or wounded nearly all the men in Forward Distribution, too. The space was filled with thick, acrid smoke, the kind produced when insulation and wiring catches fire. Circuit boards were crippled, switches shattered, and paint melted off the bulkheads. Breathing was impossible, yet Electrician's Mate 2nd Class Robert Meeks would not leave his post. Wounded and in pain, Meeks found a gas mask. He donned it and began trying to reestablish some systems. He tackled the communications circuits first, knowing how vital it would be to the bridge, in particular, to talk with other areas throughout the ship. He kept at his task while the fires and smoke grew around him. He was successful in regaining some limited comms, which provided Captain Sherman a link with his engineer and the repair teams—crucial given the loss of Central Station. Meeks stayed at it until his oxygen ran out, then he fell unconscious and collapsed to the deck.

Chief Electrician's Mate Jack Brown was also in Forward Distribution at the time of the explosion. He was knocked unconscious by a piece of flying shrapnel that gouged a nasty, bloody gash in his skull. He came to within moments, crawled from the smoke-filled space, and staggered to a nearby location, where gas masks were stored. He managed to don a mask, crawled back, and begin searching the Distribution Room for survivors. He discovered several men who were already beyond help, but in untangling the mangled bodies he found one man alive at the bottom of a pile of the dead. He hauled the man out and dragged him to safety. He plunged into the hell of that compartment again and found Electrician's Mate 2nd Class Meeks suffocating on the deck. Strength ebbing, Brown pulled Meeks up to a sitting position, grabbed his shirt collar, dragged him backwards, and stumbled out of the deathtrap one more time before collapsing himself.

A medical team arrived and began treating Brown, Meeks, and the other wounded. Both Meeks and Brown, who performed above and beyond the call of duty, survived and received the Navy Cross.

1330
FORWARD REPAIR PARTY NO. 4

The choking smoke, twisted metal, oily water, and stubborn fires surrounded them. Lt. Fred Hawes, in charge of Repair Party No. 4, was without direction. His boss, Lieutenant Commander Healy, was dead along with most of his staff. He did not know where his team's efforts were needed most, so Hawes decided to tackle what was right in front of them, and that looked to be a great deal. This part of the ship was a twisted wreck. Men were trapped and would certainly die if they could not be extracted. He could hear their screams, their moans, their pleas for help. Hawes and his men forged ahead. Jagged pieces of steel and glass ripped into their clothes and their flesh. Sizzling metal, still incandescent, singed their hair and burned their skin. The fumes choked them, forcing them to vomit—there were not enough masks or breathing equipment to go around. Using mauls, pry bars, saws, and their bare, bleeding hands, Hawes and his men coaxed open hatches that were jammed shut and pushed warped bulkheads out of the way, shoving aside twisted steel. The fires reached for them and the smoke overcame them, but they pressed on. Hawes himself collapsed twice from smoke inhalation. One by one the men separated the living from the dead; they left the dead behind and tried to save the living. Before the fires forced them back a final time, Hawes's team managed to pull twenty survivors out of shattered areas that would have become crypts if Hawes had not been there. Hawes was nearly dead from heat exhaustion, burns, and smoke when it was all over. His heroics earned him, too, a Navy Cross.

1342
FORWARD ACCESS TRUNK, USS *LEXINGTON*

Four men were trapped in the forward access trunk where the water was rising. The access trunk is essentially a crawlspace that allows entry to the under sections of the interior hull. The four sailors trapped inside the space had been sent into the dark and cramped confines to assess what damage the torpedoes had done to the forward portside section of the hull. The subsequent explosions had shifted machinery and entangled the men in piping. Gas was seeping into the space, to boot. Lieutenant John Gorman, an assistant engineering officer, was desperately trying to save the four men. The effort required manning a portable hand pump to keep the water at bay, wrestling with the damaged equipment entrapping the sailors, and trying not to breathe the noxious fumes that were making them dizzy. Gorman frantically pumped the water down a few inches, jumped back into the trunk to work on freeing the men, then jumped out again to pump out more water. It was a race against time, water, and fumes. The space would be a death trap if the gas erupted. Gorman eventually freed all four grateful sailors. His fortitude and tenacious bravery were also rewarded with the Navy Cross.

1352
FLAG PLOT, USS *YORKTOWN*

As concerned as he was about faithful old *Lexington*, Admiral Fletcher had an entire task force to consider. If *Lexington* was out of action, the loss of his other carrier would be catastrophic. *Yorktown* was damaged, though not fatally. His pilots had also told him that the Japanese had either lost a carrier or at least it was too badly damaged to continue. That left them with one undamaged carrier to Fletcher's two cripples. The odds were poor.

"Chief of Staff, radio Fitch. Tell him to send all his undamaged aircraft to *Yorktown*. Tell him to get ready to detach. I'm sending *Lexington* back to Pearl."

1355
FLAG PLOT, USS *LEXINGTON*

The stubborn fires aboard *Lexington* would not go out, and the rumblings below deck continued. Admiral Fitch signaled his concerns to Fletcher, but Fitch was also working another problem. From the reports of the returning pilots, it seemed there had been an inordinate number of Japanese aircraft swarming Task Force 17 and defending their carriers. There were too many planes for just two carriers. Was there a third IJN carrier? Fitch and Fletcher knew that *Kaga* was at sea, but they did not know exactly where. There had been reports that she was in the vicinity of Truk, and if that were so it was entirely possible that she was within striking distance. The Americans could be in serious jeopardy.

1406
FIGHTER DIRECTION, USS *LEXINGTON*

It was useless. The radar was jammed. Lieutenant Gill did not know whether it had sustained a combat malfunction or if the fires had damaged the power grid below decks and burned the motors out. Reluctantly, he informed *Yorktown* of his situation and turned over fighter direction to Lieutenant Commander Pederson.

1414

FLIGHT DECK, USS *LEXINGTON*

The last of the strike aircraft were recovered by 1414. The deck crew had undertaken Herculean efforts to get all the aircraft back aboard and re-spotted. Making room for the returning aircraft was problematic: a jammed elevator and suspicious fires forward made half the deck unusable.

Five Wildcats, twelve bombers, and eleven torpedo planes made it back to *Lexington* safely. As the air crewmen landed and alit from their planes, they were surprised to see concern on the faces of the ship's crew. From the air, there had been little sign of the ship's agony. Most were shocked to learn of the damage, the fires, and the destruction below decks.

1422

FLAG PLOT, USS *LEXINGTON*

Fitch was convinced that another Japanese carrier was lurking in the area. He radioed Fletcher: "Strong indication additional enemy carrier has joined up." Fitch believed it had to be *Kaga*. What Fitch and Fletcher did not know was that the *Kaga* sighting had been erroneous. The Allied planes from Australia had confused her with *Shōhō*. *Kaga* was still sailing south from Japan, where she had been undergoing repairs after striking a reef in February. She had set sail from Sasebo on May 4.

1430

USS *YORKTOWN*

That settled it for Fletcher, albeit reluctantly. Insufficient fighter aircraft, too few torpedoes, a low fuel state, no oiler, two damaged carriers, and the possibility of two undamaged Japanese carriers made the decision easy: Task Force 17 would withdraw and head for calmer waters near Australia. *Lexington* would head back to Pearl, if she could.

1445

FORWARD ELEVATOR WELL, USS *LEXINGTON*

Firefighting crews were trying to tackle the blazes in the forward third of the ship with less and less success. Hoses snaked down the forward elevator well in an attempt to get water closer to the primary point of attack. The men noticed that the floor of the elevator was awash with brown hydraulic fluid—not a good sign. At 1445, another enormous blast rocked Lady Lex from somewhere deep in the elevator well. The force pushed the heavy elevator up through the flight deck about a foot above the surface of the flattop. Gigantic clouds of smoke and steam poured from the well and all the openings in the forward part of the ship. The hangar deck was engulfed in smoke and flames, and the only aircraft still down on the hangar deck, a damaged Dauntless, caught fire and added itself to the conflagration. The entire bow of the ship was on fire, and anyone still in its confines was either dead or doomed.

Sherman had his duty signalman flash to *Yorktown*: "*Lexington* has serious explosion."

1452

SIGNAL BRIDGE, USS *LEXINGTON*

Message to USS *Yorktown*: "This ship needs help."

1505

FLAG PLOT, USS *YORKTOWN*

Admiral Fletcher: "Tell Fitch I'm taking tactical control. Tell Admiral Kinkaid to send *Phelps*, *Morris*, and *Anderson* to assist *Lexington*."[82]

1525

FORWARD FIRE ROOMS, USS *LEXINGTON*

Another massive explosion tore through the bulkhead plating in the vicinity of the forward fire rooms and smashed the uptakes. This eliminated more than half of the ship's propulsion system and further damaged the fire mains, shutting off the water needed to fight the fires forward and on the hangar deck. Anything else the crew might do was a holding action. The fires were out of control and would relentlessly walk from fore to aft, consuming the ship compartment by compartment.

On the bridge, Captain Sherman lost mechanical steering completely. The only way he could maneuver the ship was by shifting the engines. *Lexington*'s speed was cut to about fifteen knots, and she was careening wildly through the formation. Admiral Kinkaid told all of his escorting vessels to open up the range around the giant ship. She was a dying hulk, madly thrashing the seas.

Yet Sherman still believed. The Great Barrier Reef was only four hundred miles away. Maybe he could get there and beach his ship on the reef, put out the fires, and save her.

1540

OUTSIDE THE BRIDGE, USS *LEXINGTON*

Lieutenant Charles Williams, an assistant supply officer, stood outside the entrance to the bridge, sweaty, panting, covered in oily grime and smoke

---

82. "Kinkaid" was Rear Adm. Thomas C. Kinkaid, commanding officer of Task Group 17.2, consisting of the cruisers *Minneapolis*, *New Orleans*, *Astoria*, *Chester*, and *Portland*; plus, the destroyers *Phelps*, *Dewey*, *Farragut*, *Aylwin*, and *Monaghan*.

smudges. He was nearly doubled over from smoke inhalation and the exertion of the climb to the bridge.

"Permission to speak to the captain," he gasped to the officer of the deck.

"He's a little busy now, Lieutenant," an irked OOD growled back at the frazzled supply officer. "What can I do for you?"

"Well, I just want the captain to know I tried, that's all."

"Tried what, exactly?"

"To get the money."

"Money? What money? What the hell are you talking about?"

"There's three hundred thousand dollars in cash in the ship's safe. Or there was. Probably burned up by now. But I tried. I couldn't get to it. The money. The safe is on fire—or surrounded by fire. Couldn't do it. . . ."

The OOD softened. "Well, Mr. Williams, I'm sure you did your best, but I can assure you that money is about the last thing on the captain's mind at the moment. But I'll tell him—that you tried. As soon as he has a moment."

"Good. Great . . . thanks," Williams sighed, then turned to go back below and help fight the fires.

1600
FIRE ROOMS AFT, USS *LEXINGTON*

With the death of Lieutenant Commander Healy, chief engineer Cmdr. "Heine" Junkers had assumed command of the damage-control efforts below as well as directing the functioning of the powerplant. The damage-control parties were doing heroic work and dying in the process, but they were losing. The ship's powerplant was failing rapidly.

The turboelectric drives that had once powered an entire city, that were revolutionary at the time they were designed and built, were unreliable in the shock of combat. The older geared engines were hardier, less vulnerable to the pounding that ships took as the result of torpedo attacks and bomb strikes. Water in the engine rooms proved to be more problematic for electric motors than for the old oil-fired ones. Flooding made a mess of electrical switches and commutators; wipe-downs and repairs took more time than the engineers had available.

With his last remaining electrical circuit, Junkers called the captain on the bridge.

"We can't save her, Captain. The fires down here are out of control. I'm losing propulsion throughout the system. The boilers are falling offline—all of them. My men are dying down here, Captain." Junkers fell silent, sweating in the 125-degree heat, gasping for air, waiting for Sherman's reply.

Sherman held the phone to his ear for a long second. He stared ahead, at the vast and languid Coral Sea. He watched the smoke pouring skyward. Men still rushed about him, trying desperately to do anything to help. He felt the deck swaying beneath his feet as the big ship thrashed. He knew it was over, too.

"All right, Heine," he finally breathed into the phone, "get the men up. Get 'em up on the flight deck. Secure the powerplant. Let off the steam."

"Aye, Captain. I'm sorry . . . we did the best . . ."

"It's all right, Heine. I know you did. Get the men up—now please."

Moments later *Lexington* started to slow, drifting in an uncontrolled circular spiral. Great gouts of steam poured from the wounded boilers as the engineers opened the valves. The great old warship gave up her last breaths.

It won't matter much now, Ted Sherman thought to himself. He reached into his pocket, pulled out a cigarette, and lit up.

1601

FLAG PLOT, USS *YORKTOWN*

Admiral Fletcher radioed Kinkaid and told him to stand by *Lexington* with the cruisers *New Orleans* and *Minneapolis* and the destroyers *Morris*, *Anderson*, *Hammann*, and *Phelps*. Kinkaid was to escort *Lexington* home, if possible, but if not, to rescue her crew and then send her to the bottom if she wouldn't go herself. Fletcher did not want the Japanese to have a trophy.

1630

USS *LEXINGTON*

The XO had been all over the ship. As the first major explosion rocked *Lexington*, Commander Seligman had been on his way forward to the sick bay, to check on casualties. The blast picked him up and blew him through an open hatch, slamming him painfully against a bulkhead. Nothing was broken. Seligman became a human dynamo, racing from one crisis point to the next, directing rescues, repairs, or evacuations. In between, he raced up to the bridge to make reports. He became the eyes and ears on the crisis that Captain Sherman desperately needed. The XO was the second to last man to leave the ship. He could not have done more short of laying down his own life. He would receive a Navy Cross for that day's work, his second award.

1645

USS *LEXINGTON*

Another officer who rose to the challenge was *Lexington*'s senior medical officer, Arthur J. "Doc" White. Beginning with the first casualties until the end of the evacuation, Commander White was in constant motion. As the fires spread throughout the ship, he had to keep his wounded charges moving from one safe location to another until ultimately they had to be removed from the ship. He conducted dozens of triages for severely wounded men; he administered applications of gallons of tannic acid to the numerous burns; he directed the efforts of the entire medical staff with efficiency and courage throughout the fight. He did all this on two fractured ankles, injuries he received during the first major explosion at 1247. The fifty-three-year-old professional naval surgeon would receive his Navy Cross shortly after the battle.

1652
BRIDGE, USS *MORRIS* (DD-417)

The plucky little *Morris*, skippered by Cmdr. Harry B. "Beany" Jarrett, pulled in close to *Lexington*'s hull—so close that the massive steel sides of the carrier, riding on the swells of the Coral Sea, pounded down on the bridge wing of the smaller destroyer. That did not matter at that moment. The job was to get hoses from the destroyer working to fight the fires aboard *Lexington*. Jarrett also needed to get close enough to start evacuating some of *Lexington*'s crew, which *Morris* had begun to do. The puny hoses were not equal to the flames, but *Morris* executed an orderly evacuation of nearly five hundred sailors.

1707
FLAG BRIDGE, USS *LEXINGTON*

Admiral Fitch casually leaned over the side of his Flag Bridge, immediately above the Ship's Bridge. Ted Sherman was right below him. In a calm but firm voice, Fitch called down to Sherman, "Well, Ted, let's get the boys off the ship."

"Heartbroken" is how Sherman later described his feelings at that moment. But he immediately issued the directive to abandon ship. A flag hoist announcing the captain's intentions was hauled up.

Aviation Ordnanceman 2nd Class Walter Hassell:

> The flight deck—at least the after port side where I was waiting—was fairly quiet. Men spoke softly to each other, each trying to buck up the courage of the other. Some were quietly sobbing, others praying and some others just sitting there deep in their own private thoughts. . . . The evacuation was as orderly as was possible under those conditions. . . . The remainder of us [left] after carefully removing our shoes . . . and I was amused to notice that the waterway at the edge of the deck was neatly lined with shoes, most with

a blackout flashlight tucked in them, exactly the way we normally stowed them under our bunks so that we would know just where they were in the dark. Habits are hard to break. And now, the sight of those shoes provided a comic relief to the tragic event taking place.

Some men casually dove the fifty feet from the flight deck into the warm waters of the Coral Sea, but most went down the knotted lines strung over the side of the ship, hand under hand. A few enterprising air and flight deck crew yanked the small rubber life rafts from the planes that still sat on the flight deck and took to the waters in the small inflatables. The surrounding rescue ships launched whaleboats and began pulling the men from the water. A few dozen of the stronger swimmers stroked over to the cruisers and destroyers hovering nearby and crawled up the cargo nets strung over the sides.

The many wounded and severely burned were carefully lifted by metal stretchers from *Lexington* directly to the decks of *Anderson* and *Hammann*, two other destroyers that had pulled alongside.

The abandonment took about an hour, during which there were two more terrific explosions, one amidships and one further aft. The fires were working their way to the stern and had started reaching the stored warheads. The biggest concern was a stockpile of torpedoes that had not been jettisoned due to the failure of the electric torpedo winch. If they were to explode simultaneously, it could tear the ship in half.

1730

BRIDGE, USS *HAMMANN*

After working alongside *Lexington* for a number of perilous minutes, the destroyer *Hammann* started to carefully back away. Lieutenant Commander Arnold True, CO:

> [It] was a difficult maneuver due to the fact that the Lex was drifting down on *Hammann* [but] the maneuver was successful and we got clear. We were not more than fifty yards away when a magazine on the *Lexington* exploded, blowing out the side of the ship where the *Hammann* had been moored about three minutes before. Had we been a few minutes later getting away, the tons of metal thrown out by the explosion would have badly damaged *Hammann* and killed a lot of men.[83]

Hammann did not get away without tragedy completely: Pharmacist's Mate 2nd Class Vernon Weeks, the corpsman for VF-2, had just been taken off a life raft. A piece of shrapnel from the blast punctured his skull and he died instantly. Weeks was the only casualty of the entire rescue operation.

1830

FLIGHT DECK, USS *LEXINGTON*

As Admiral Fitch left the ship to be picked up, feet dry, by a whale boat from *Minneapolis*, he turned to Sherman and cautioned him that there would be no "funny business," by which Fitch meant he would not condone any old-fashioned nonsense about Sherman going down with his ship. Sherman assured the admiral that his intentions were otherwise.

After the admiral safely departed, Sherman and Commander Seligman walked the flight deck one last time. By 1830, Sherman was convinced that they had not left a single living soul aboard the dying ship.

Seligman, growing more nervous by the minute, waiting for the torpedoes to cook off, nervously asked his captain, "Sir, don't you think it's time we went over the side?"

"Just one more thing, XO," and with that, Sherman turned and jogged back to the island structure and ducked inside.

Seligman was aghast. *What in hell is he doing?* he worried. *Is he going to disobey Fitch after all and go down with this wreck?*

A few seconds later, Sherman reemerged. He had ducked into his emergency cabin to retrieve something. He jogged back to Seligman's side, clutching his best-dress, gold-braided captain's hat. He tossed aside his fore-and-aft cap and clapped the big, fancy cover on his head at a jaunty angle.

"OK, now I'm ready," he grinned. "I've heard that there's a shortage of good, gold thread until after the war. I didn't want to lose my best cap and have to get one with the cheap stuff. Let's go."

With that, he motioned for the XO to grab the rope in front of them and start down. Sherman wanted to be last off the ship. Seligman obeyed, and was followed by his captain. The two men were about halfway down the rope when another titanic explosion rocked the ship. Both men fell into the water but were safely hauled out by men from *Hammann*, then transferred to a launch headed for *Minneapolis*. Captain Sherman's fancy, gold-braided hat was still firmly planted on his head.

～

From the time that Captain Sherman gave the abandon ship order at 1707 until *Lexington* would finally be put out of her misery at 1841, a remarkable 2,735 of her complement of 2,951 evacuated the ship. To pull that off, hundreds of desperate acts of courage and simple human kindness took place in ninety-four

83. Hoehling, 177.

minutes. A look back at the record of valor represented by the awards given to the rescuers underscores this point.

The destroyers *Anderson*, *Hammann*, and *Morris* bore the brunt of the rescue efforts in assisting *Lexington*'s survivors. The ships circled the stricken carrier looking diligently for men in the water or pulled in close to the sides of Lady Lex to haul off the ship's company and wounded men. *Morris* and *Anderson* were battered by the thrashing *Lexington* several times when they moved in close to the hull. *Hammann* was showered with burning debris as she came alongside during one of *Lexington*'s massive explosions. Each of the three destroyer skippers had to exercise the utmost care not to run over men in the water, suck them into their props, or crush them between their hulls and *Lexington*. Every time they came close aboard, these daring commanders risked their ships. *Lexington* would have been ripped apart if the torpedo warheads on board had cooked off. If that had happened, any ship nearby would have been doomed as well. With the exception of Vernon Weeks, not a single instance of drowning or injury was recorded during the entire rescue operation. Each of the skippers—Lt. Cmdr. John K. B. Ginder (USS *Anderson*), Cmdr. Harry B. Jarrett (USS *Morris*), and Lt. Cmdr. Arnold E. True (USS *Hammann*)—received the Navy Cross for their magnificent performances during this crowded hour and a half.

Two young ensigns from USS *Hammann* likewise received Navy Crosses for their heroics during the rescue operation. Ensigns Ralph Holton and Theodore Krepski were each in charge of a large motor whaleboat. Darting in and around *Lexington*'s hull, each officer rescued dozens of men from the oily waters surrounding the ship. Both whaleboats were hit by flaming debris and constantly in danger of being crushed or rammed, yet each ensign expertly handled his tiny command with skill and courage.

Boatswain's Mate 2nd Class Albert Jason was working one of the few boats that made it off *Lexington* to assist her own crew. Acting as coxswain, Boatswain's Mate 2nd Class Jason steered his boat in and out of debris fields, picking up dozens of men and taking them to safety aboard the rescue ships. At one point, the boat's propeller became fouled by debris. Without hesitation, Jason dove over the side and under the boat to free the prop. Once the engine was working again, Jason continued to rescue more men. Several times, he was forced to dodge burning objects hurled down from above as *Lexington* tore apart. Jason saved many lives via his courage and expeditious boat handling.

This was not his first brush with this type of rescue operation, however. Only four days prior, he had picked up two downed *Lexington* aviators who had crashed on Guadalcanal after the Tulagi raids. In a remarkably similar scenario, he earned the Navy and Marine Corps medal for that mission.

His citation reads, in part: "On a strange uncharted coast, in complete darkness and squally weather, within action range of enemy forces and in shark infested waters, he dived overboard to clear a fouled propeller and later swam through a heavy surf to carry a line to the beach and bring off an exhausted man."

For his skill and courage on May 8, Jason was honored with the Navy Cross. Unfortunately, he did not live to receive it. After *Lexington*, Jason was reassigned to USS *Hammann*. One month later, the ship was torpedoed and sunk at the Battle of Midway while assisting the stricken *Yorktown*. Jason was MIA and presumed killed.

Aviation Ordnanceman 2nd Class Walter Hassell, who was himself rescued by the cruiser New Orleans:

> The ships circling around, well away from the men in the water, were careful not to get too close because of the danger of their propellers to the swimming men and rafts. I saw that a cruiser, with cargo nets hanging from her side to provide a means for the men swimming to get aboard, was very slowly approaching our area. I slipped out of my life jacket and, using my fastest overhand swimming stroke, headed for it. Luckily, I timed it just right and got alongside just about amidships. I grabbed the cargo net and started to climb up. Aboard and alive, I wrapped myself in a blanket one of the crewmen handed me and sank down on the deck to rest. Another kind soul brought me a cup of coffee and gave me a cigarette, both of which I sorely needed. It was 7:30 p.m. I had been in the water one hour and 40 minutes. My watch had stopped. It was not waterproof and must have stopped running shortly after I landed in the water.

There were a thousand other unrecorded acts of courage as one shipmate helped another down a rope, onto a vessel, or out of the water. Men aboard the rescuing ships stripped their quarters of blankets and sheets to wrap around the chilled and wounded. The men emptied their lockers of extra clothes and shoes to give to the men from *Lexington* who had lost everything except the clothes they were wearing. The rescue effort was a remarkable testament of the bonds between men at war.

1841

USS *PHELPS*, DD-360

In what was certainly the saddest action he ever initiated, Lt. Cmdr. J. E. Edwards, CO of the destroyer *Phelps*, was ordered by Admiral Kinkaid to sink *Lexington*. The burning hulk, her entire hull glowing cherry red in the gathering twilight, was not only a hazard to navigation but a gleaming beacon to any enemy ships or aircraft in the vicinity. One by one, *Phelps* pumped five torpedoes into the stubborn survivor.

It took another hour for her to succumb, but the Queen of the Flattops finally slid beneath the surface at 1952 hours. She took twenty-six officers and 190 brave sailors down with her. Moments after she finally disappeared, a massive underwater explosion rocked the area. The captain of *Phelps* thought his ship had been torpedoed; twenty miles way, *Yorktown* and her accompanying escorts heard and felt the blast. In reality, the fires aboard *Lexington* had finally reached the torpedo warheads.

One quarter of all the US Navy carrier forces in the Pacific had just plunged to the bottom of the Coral Sea, some two thousand feet below. A remarkable 92 percent of her crew had been rescued, however, and she had given an excellent account of herself in the face of the enemy. If Admiral Taylor had still been alive, he would have been proud of his handiwork.

CHAPTER 11

"WE BEG THE PRIVILEGE TO PRODUCE ANOTHER *LEXINGTON*"

ALMOST IMMEDIATELY, Captain Sherman and Commander Seligman began canvassing the rescue ships for a tally of Lex's remaining crew to get an accurate count of the living and a correct record of the missing and the dead. There was another purpose to the count, however: Sherman wanted to keep the surviving members of the crew together and, as soon as possible, get them all aboard a replacement carrier and back into the fight. He wanted a complete record and to know the status of every sailor. They were still under his command.

Sherman's official after-action report, which he completed and submitted to the commander, Pacific Fleet, on May 15, 1942, asked specifically "[t]hat a new carrier, the first available, be re-named *Lexington* to carry on the traditions of that great ship. That the officers and men survivors of *Lexington* and her air group be retained together as a unit, to man the new *Lexington*. This will be of the utmost value for morale, not only to these men but for the country as a whole, and will best utilize this group of well-trained, seasoned, and tested officers and men."[84]

It was a pipe dream, and Sherman probably knew it, but he wanted to express his preferences nonetheless. For one thing, shortly after the Coral Sea, Admiral King placed him on the promotion list to rear admiral. As soon as the paperwork was completed, he would be given survivor's leave

84. Sherman

and reassigned, with his new flag, and it wouldn't be as the CO of an aircraft carrier. He had become too senior for such a command. He would also be sporting a new decoration: the Legion of Merit, with combat "V," awarded for his exemplary performance in handling *Lexington* during the Coral Sea engagements.

Admiral Fitch made a similar recommendation for keeping the crew together and giving them another carrier, as did Admiral Fletcher; but the needs of the service, whatever they might be, would ultimately determine the disposition of the crew.

After three months in Washington, DC, serving on the staff of the chief of naval operations, Sherman was sent back to the Pacific as commander of Carrier Task Force 16, Admiral "Bull" Halsey's old command.

All six of the indomitable Patten brothers survived the sinking. Allen, Marvin, and Bub went overboard and were rescued by the destroyer *Morris*. The cruiser *New Orleans* saved Bick, Bruce, and Gilbert. Neither set of brothers knew the whereabouts of the other until both ships reached Tonga Island. All were sent home to Iowa, where they went on a War Bond drive that successfully raised millions of dollars. In July 1942, they were joined in service by the seventh brother, Wayne, who was no longer "Patten Pending." Wayne went off to Navy boot camp; Gilbert, Allen, and Bub were sent to the escort carrier USS *Altamaha* (CVE-18) and would be joined by Wayne as soon as he finished basic training. Marvin, Bick, and Bruce were sent to the troopship USS *Monticello* (AP-61), the former Italian luxury ocean liner SS *Conte Grande*; Ted went to the troop carrier USS *J. Franklin Bell* (APA-16).

After the sinking of USS *Juneau* in November 1942 with the loss of all five Sullivan brothers, the Navy clamped down on brothers serving aboard the same ships, and all eight Pattens were reassigned and scattered, with Marvin going to the new *Lexington*, CV-16. Amazingly, all eight brothers survived the war without a scratch.

The Navy did not release the news of the loss of *Lexington* until June 12, 1942, five days after the US victory at the Battle of Midway. Outside of those who were on board Lady Lex and their families, the loss of the ship was most profoundly felt among those who had built it and by the residents of the town of Lexington, Massachusetts. Hundreds of the original shipyard workers at the Fore River Shipyard, men and women who had swarmed over her decks as she rose in the ways, were still hard at work. The entire shipyard felt a powerful bond with "the old lady," and the workers were mad as hell that the Japanese had sunk her. For the denizens of Lexington town, it was as if a piece of their Revolutionary War sacrifice and glory had been ripped away.

As recounted in a profile by the navy's *All Hands* magazine, "The following day [June 13] the townspeople formed a committee and launched a campaign to have another vessel carry the name *Lexington* to war. The quest was enthusiastically taken up by the workers at Quincy Shipyard."[85]

On June 16, 1942, Secretary of the Navy Frank Knox received a telegram in his office in Washington, DC:

> Twenty-three thousand workers at Bethlehem's Fore River Yard where the *Lexington* was built, respectfully urge you to give the name *Lexington* to your carrier CV-16. We glory in the achievement of that fine ship, the sacrifice of which, to many of us, is a personal loss. We pledge our utmost efforts to build ships with all the speed and all the skill that is in our power. We beg the privilege to produce another *Lexington*.

It was a powerful missive, and Knox, being a crafty old former newspaperman, knew a perfect public-relations ploy when he saw one. He hustled over to the White House, telegram in hand, and showed it to President Roosevelt. Both men agreed that the request should be granted. Knox telegraphed his enthusiastic approval to the shipyard.

The Navy already had an *Essex*-class carrier hull on the ways at Fore River. It had barely been laid down but had already been designated CV-16 and was scheduled to become USS *Cabot*, after the first English explorer to trek North America. That was quickly changed to *Lexington*. Good to their word, the shipyard workers produced the new *Lexington* in record time: fourteen months from start to finish and a year ahead of schedule. The ship, with Capt. Felix Stump in command, was commissioned on February 17, 1943.

The *Essex*-class carrier was the backbone of the US Navy's capital ship program from its inception, in 1943, through the 1970s. A remarkable twenty-four *Essex*-class flattops were constructed, including CV-16. At 36,000 tons (full load), the new *Lexington* was almost as long as her predecessor (824 feet, versus 888 feet for CV-2). She had geared steam turbines instead of turbo electric drives and could do better than CV-2's thirty-five knots. She hosted 2,600 officers and enlisted men, sported 62 guns of various calibers when built (all removed by 1967), and could host 96 aircraft (later 110).

In the new *Lexington*, the Navy applied many lessons learned from the years of experience it had gained with the old *Lexington* and its fate in the Coral Sea. With newer, heavier aircraft and less deck space, catapults became necessary. The elevators on CV-2 had sometimes jammed during fleet exercises and combat conditions, making all or part of the flight deck

85. Ford, 4.

unusable; CV-16 would have two flight-deck elevators but would also sport a third elevator on the deck edge along the port side.

Air conditioning was incorporated into the powerplant design to provide the crew comfort as well as cooling for the ever-growing machinery needs. Aviation fuel tanks were integrated into the hull design—they could still be damaged by torpedoes or mines, but they were equipped with counter-flooding. Gas could be pumped overboard, if need be, and the tanks were isolated from the interior crew spaces. Electrical equipment was shielded to prevent sparks and installed away from areas where flammable materials existed in quantity.

As much as possible, flammable materials were eliminated altogether throughout the ship. Deck surfaces were no longer slathered in linoleum; lead-based paints replaced enamels; stuffed furniture was replaced with stark plastic and metal; and as many empty spaces as possible were packed with asbestos (the dangers of lead and asbestos not yet being known). The teak deck gave way to steel covered in a material similar to asphalt.

Firefighting equipment was increased in quantity and quality. Oxygen masks, self-contained breathing equipment, hazard suits, and fireproof gloves were updated and also multiplied. Specialized training programs for damage control and firefighting were designed, deployed, and made mandatory for certain shipboard personnel.

Tactics also changed, and fortunately, these changes took place almost immediately. Air Wing commanders had learned that squadron attacks had to be better coordinated. Sending in torpedo squadrons without adequate fighter cover was suicidal—proven again with the luckless VT-8 at Midway. Bombers, as Ted Sherman had believed, could be used protectively as well as for scouting and bombing missions. The number of fighters aboard a carrier needed to be increased so that they could handle the critical roles of protecting the strike aircraft as well as the mother ship. If air wings from different ships were tasked with the same mission, they would have to be coordinated as one strike group—something the Japanese had been doing from the outset.

Fighter direction aboard the carrier that was in tactical control of the air mission also needed to be better coordinated and equipped. Newer, more powerful radars were coming along, as well as larger command centers. The miniscule space allocation for the FDO was beginning to morph into more of a combat information center, or CIC.

One of the Americans' biggest disappointments at Coral Sea was the dismal performance of the anti-aircraft guns and gunners. Cruisers, destroyers, and the mounted batteries on the carriers all scored poorly. Given the amount of lead they pumped into the sky, in some cases putting up virtual walls of bullets in front of their Japanese targets, the kill ratio was still pitiful.[86]

The gunners simply couldn't keep up. Their aim points were invariably behind their targets. Even leading the aircraft and using their tracer rounds as spotters, the bullets didn't arrive before the speedy Zeros and attack planes had sped ahead of the ordnance. The "Mark 1, Mod Zero Eyeball" was no longer a match for the technology, and certainly not with the ranges involved. It became apparent that modern fire-control computers and automatic guns were the only solutions to the gunnery challenge.

The bomber pilots, time and again, complained about the fogging of their bombsights. Pilots typically took off in tropical temperatures at sea level and then climbed to altitudes of 10,000 to 17,000 feet, where they encountered below-zero temperatures. On attacking, they plunged from 17,000 feet back down to 1,000 feet. Due to the radical altitude changes and rapidly fluctuating temperatures and atmospheric pressures, their sights would invariably cloud over. Admiral Nimitz called this situation, at the Battle of the Coral Sea, the "outstanding material defect of the 3-day action."[87] This unhappy situation brought on an all-out development effort that finally resolved the issue in late 1943, when the Navy began deploying reflector-type bombsights that proved far superior to the telescopic sights used at Coral Sea and Midway.

Medical and Supply Departments learned valuable lessons from Coral Sea as well. Emergency medical kits were stocked all over carriers after Coral Sea. Dr. White and others discovered that the application of emergency bandages and tapes, along with morphine sticks and burn medications, as soon as possible after injury made a difference in saving lives and speeding recovery. The serviceable but hard to handle tannic acid jelly was soon replaced by more manageable paraffin canisters.

Supply departments began to concentrate on battle necessities rather than providing as many different solutions to the needs of as many sailors as possible. The new *Lexington* might not carry a pack of rosin for a violin bow, but it would stock far more beans, bandages, and bullets.

Ammunition storage would be much less haphazard. With CV-2's basic battle cruiser design, no consideration had been given to the proper stowing of the huge quantities of aviation ordnance that was required. As a result, belts of bullets, torpedo warheads, and five-inch gun rounds had been stuffed into any available extra space. One of the main reasons that the admiral's quarters aboard Lady Lex had become such a charnel house after the first Japanese bomb was that a number of five-inch rounds had

86. Admiral Smith, in his post-battle report, wrote: "The performance of the 5-inch batteries was uniformly poor with much wild shooting. The 1.1 and 20-mm guns were more effective, but extremely wild."
87. *Combat Narrative: The Battle of the Coral Sea*, 51.

been stored within it, as an afterthought. It is most likely that the concussion from one of these rounds killed both the ship's senior supply officer and senior dental surgeon.

The Japanese were learning, too. No fewer than forty-one admirals had a hand in some aspect of the planned Port Moresby invasion and the Coral Sea actions. Admirals Yamamoto and Inoue both took steps to slim down the chain of command.

Their anti-aircraft gunners did not perform any better than their American counterparts. The Japanese were also far behind in the development of firing control solutions and radar. Their experiences in the Coral Sea made both these deficiencies top priorities.

The American pilots surprised their Japanese adversaries. Up until that point, the Japanese had ruled the skies as well as the seas. The Chinese Air Force proved to be no real competition for the Japanese airmen; other opponents, the British in particular, had been flying ancient airframes from scattered and poorly coordinated land-based facilities. The US Navy's carrier pilots were a different story. They were aggressive, fearless, and tenacious. Even though they were flying slower and less maneuverable aircraft, they stayed in the fight. Their airplanes could also take tremendous amounts of punishment and had heavier weapons. The Japanese quickly realized that their advantages of speed and dexterity could be overcome by American armor and self-sealing gas tanks.

In assessing the outcome of the Battle of the Coral Sea, many historians have summed it up as a tactical victory for the Japanese but a strategic victory for the Allies. The Japanese had enjoyed an unbroken string of victories in the Pacific Theater since the outbreak of hostilities in 1939, but the halt of the Port Moresby invasion broke their streak. While the IJN bound up its wounds, the Americans gathered strength. Thanks, also, to a lucky break in deciphering the next objective, the Americans were able to gain a decisive advantage for the next round. The loss of one Japanese light carrier at Coral Sea plus denying the IJN's two heavy carriers for the fight at Midway was profound.[88] When four fleet carriers were lost at Midway, the momentum was taken away from the IJN permanently.

Bucking convention, this author would also give the tactical victory at Coral Sea to the Allies, based on the following definition: "A tactical victory may refer to a victory that results in the completion of a tactical objective as part of an operation or a victory where the losses of the defeated outweigh those of the victor."[89]

---

88. *Shōkaku*, of course, was damaged extensively and needed repairs. *Zuikaku*, though undamaged, had lost so many planes and aircrew that she, too, needed to return to Japan for resupply of both aircraft and trained aircrews.
89. Babylon Online Dictionary: "tactical victory."

The tactical objective at Coral Sea for the Allies was to stop the MO Strike Force. That objective was achieved. Who, then, suffered the greater losses? In the first carrier-versus-carrier battle in the history of naval warfare, the Japanese lost three carriers to the Allies' one light carrier sunk, one temporarily damaged and lost to aircraft operations, and one whose air wing was temporarily crippled. The loss of *Lexington* was regrettable, but, in truth, she had survived beyond her strategic usefulness, and her own flaws contributed more to her demise than did the Japanese bombs and torpedoes. She was a grand old ship, indeed, and we should always remember that she and her crew were the point of the spear that stopped the Japanese juggernaut and started changing the course of World War II.

EPILOGUE

Follow-up information on some of the interesting figures who have populated this story, arranged alphabetically:

Frank D. Berrien (August 17, 1877–January 31, 1951) was the second captain of CV-2. He graduated from the Naval Academy, Class of
1900, and served in cruisers and battleships until being recalled to the
Academy in 1908 to become the head football coach. Over three sea-
sons, he compiled a record of 21–5–3. In World War I, he earned the
Navy Distinguished Service Medal for what became a famous at-sea
duel between the destroyer he commanded and a German U-boat. He
completed graduate studies at Yale in 1927, attended the Naval War
College, and became a naval aviation observer. After his command of
Lexington, he was stationed at the Naval Hydrographic Office in Boston.
He was elevated to the rank of rear admiral in 1936, after which he
commanded the Third Naval District until his retirement in 1941.

James H. Brett Jr., (October 1, 1905–November 27, 1946) was CO of VT-2
aboard USS *Lexington* at the Battle of the Coral Sea. Lieutenant Commander
Brett graduated from the US Naval Academy, Class of 1928. He won the
Navy Cross twice, for actions on March 10, 1942, and at Coral Sea on
May 7–8, 1942.

Wilson Brown (April 27, 1882–January 2, 1957) graduated from the US Naval
Academy in 1902. Although ostensibly a seagoing officer, Brown spent a great
deal of his career on administrative duty. He was on the staff of Admiral
William Sims in London in World War I and then served as naval aide to both
presidents Coolidge and Hoover. In 1929, he was named commander of the
Naval Base, New London, then commanded the battleship *California* in 1932.
In 1934 he was chief of staff at the Naval War College, was made rear admiral

in 1936, and in 1938 became superintendent of the Naval Academy. In 1941, he was made commander of the Scouting Force, Pacific Fleet, and as World War II broke out he was placed in command of Task Force 11. Brown had some health issues, which led Admiral Nimitz to replace him with Rear Admiral Fitch. Brown was given command (ashore) of the Pacific Fleet Amphibious Force for a short three months, then sent to command the 1st Naval District (Boston). In 1943, it was back to the White House to serve as naval aide to President Roosevelt and later to President Truman. He retired as a vice admiral at the end of World War II.

Elliott Buckmaster (October 19, 1889–October 10, 1976), CO of *Yorktown* at the Battle of the Coral Sea. Buckmaster graduated from the US Naval Academy, Class of 1912. He served in battleships and destroyers until transitioning to naval aviation in 1936, at age forty-seven. He won his aviator's wings and was sent to *Lexington* as XO in 1939. He was promoted to captain and CO of the Naval Air Station, Ford Island, 1940–1941. He assumed command of *Yorktown* in February 1941 and fought her until she was sunk at the Battle of Midway, June 1942. After Midway, Buckmaster was promoted to rear admiral and made commander of naval air primary training. He later commanded the Naval Base San Diego and retired as a vice admiral in 1946. In 1943, he was appointed to commander, 10th Naval District (Puerto Rico) and promoted to vice admiral. He retired on December 1, 1944.

John Gregory Crace (February 6, 1887–May 11, 1968) was commander of Task 44 at the Battle of the Coral Sea. Crace, a native of Australia, joined the Royal Navy as a cadet in 1902. Specializing as a torpedo officer, he steadily moved up through the officer ranks in the Royal Navy and the Royal Australian Navy, moving between the two. In 1939, he was appointed a rear admiral and commander of an Australian squadron. His courageous and essential actions at the Battle of the Coral Sea are detailed in the text. After the battle, he relinquished his sea command in June 1942 and returned to England. He was made vice admiral, then admiral, and commanded the Chatham Naval Dockyard for the remainder of World War II. He was knighted in 1947 and retired.

Wallace M. Dillon (July 18, 1895–April 4, 1965) was XO of *Lexington* until relieved by Mort Seligman on January 18, 1942. Dillon was class of 1918 at the Naval Academy but graduated in 1917 because of World War I. He was an early aviator and after his tour aboard *Lexington* he went to Patrol Wing Two as chief of staff, later promoted to captain. Dillon was the first commanding officer of the light carrier USS *Langley* (CVL-27), August 1943, and was promoted to rear admiral at the end of the war. He retired in 1946.

Robert E. Dixon (1906–October 23, 1981) was CO of VB-2 at the Battle of the Coral Sea. Forever famous for his May 7, 1942, radio message, "Scratch one flattop!"—referring to the sinking of the Japanese light carrier *Shōhō*—"Bob" Dixon went on to win the Navy Cross and served aboard the carriers *Yorktown*, *Enterprise*, *Saratoga*, and *Bunker Hill*. He retired as a rear admiral.

Herbert S. "Ducky" Duckworth (October 23, 1900–May 29, 1990) graduated from the US Naval Academy in 1922. He earned his pilot's wings shortly thereafter and made the very first arrested landing aboard USS *Saratoga*. He commanded VF-2, became the air boss on *Lexington*, and after her sinking was promoted to captain and commanded USS *Cowpens*. From 1947–1948, he commanded the Naval Air Station, Jacksonville. He was promoted to rear admiral and then vice admiral. Duckworth retired to Jacksonville in 1952 and subsequently became president of the Jacksonville Art Museum.

Marion W. Dufilho (May 22, 1916–August 24, 1942) was Butch O'Hare's wingman on the day in February 1942 when O'Hare attained lasting glory defending *Lexington* on his Medal of Honor flight. Dufilho, who graduated from the US Naval Academy in 1938, was killed in action on August 24, 1942, when he was shot down during the Battle of the Eastern Solomons. He was awarded a posthumous Navy Cross, Distinguished Flying Cross, and Purple Heart. The destroyer escort USS *Dufilho*, DE-423, was commissioned in his honor in 1944.

Aubrey W. Fitch (June 11, 1883–May 22, 1978) was the sixth commanding officer of USS *Lexington*. Fitch graduated from the Naval Academy, Class of 1906, and spent the first decade of his career in cruisers, destroyers, and torpedo boats. During World War I, he was the gunnery officer on the battleship *Wyoming*, after which he became an ordnance inspector and then commander of a squadron of mine-laying ships. In 1922, he was assigned to the US Mission in Brazil, then served as executive officer of battleship *Nevada* in 1927. In 1928, he was given command of the stores ship *Arctic*. The 1930s saw Fitch switch to naval aviation. He won his pilot's wings in 1930 and then became commander of USS *Wright*, a seaplane tender, in 1931; CO of USS *Langley*, 1932; commander of Naval Air Station Hampton Roads; staff, Commander Aircraft, Battle Force; CO of *Lexington*, 1936–1937. He attended the Naval War College (1938) and became CO of Patrol Wing 2 (1940), then became commander, Carrier Division 1, just as World War II commenced. He was awarded a Distinguished Service Medal for his activities at Wake Island and Coral Sea. After Coral Sea, the carrier *Saratoga* became his flagship and his task group participated in the Guadalcanal Campaign. In September 1942, Fitch assumed command of all Allied aircraft in the South Pacific. As COMSOPAC, his planes took part in the battles of the Santa Cruz Islands, the second Guadalcanal, and the Solomon campaign. His pilots pioneered night radar bombing and special intelligence photographic aircraft operations—all of which won him a second Navy Distinguished Service Medal. Fitch returned to Washington, DC, in July 1944, to become deputy chief of Naval Operations for Air, receiving a second Legion of Merit for his excellent stewardship. From August 1945 to January 1947, he was superintendent of the Naval Academy and also helped establish the Navy's Department of Aeronautics. Fitch retired, as a full admiral, in July 1947.

James H. Flatley Jr., (June 17, 1906–July 9, 1958) was CO of VF-42 at the Battle of the Coral Sea. Jimmy Flatley graduated from the US Naval Academy in 1929 and earned his wings as a naval aviator in 1931. At Coral Sea, his heroics merited the award of a Navy Cross. He was then ordered back stateside as CO of the new fighter squadron VF-10. He went back to sea in 1943 as CAG for USS *Enterprise*. He compiled an extraordinarily distinguished combat record, earning, in addition to the Navy Cross, the Navy Distinguished Service Medal, Legion of Merit, Distinguished Flying Cross, Bronze Star, Navy Commendation Medal, and Presidential Unit Citation. After the war, he was promoted to rear admiral and was instrumental in founding the Navy Safety Center and pioneering many of the advances in naval air training. He retired in June 1958, and was advanced to vice admiral on the retired list, but died just one month later.

Frank J. "Jack" Fletcher (April 29, 1885–April 25, 1973) was the task force commander for the Allies at the Battle of the Coral Sea. Fletcher graduated from the US Naval Academy in 1906. His early career was spent in battleships and torpedo boats. During the 1914 Battle of Vera Cruz (Mexico), a young Lieutenant Fletcher was awarded the Medal of Honor for his role in safely rescuing 350 refugees from the conflict. Four years later, during World War I, as commanding officer of the destroyer *Benham*, Fletcher was awarded the Navy Cross for his heroic work protecting vital convoys in the North Atlantic. Between the world wars, Fletcher held various senior staff posts ashore, commanded the battleship *New Mexico*, and, in 1941, became a rear admiral and the commander of Cruiser Division 4. Fletcher was a career-long surface officer and yet he was picked ahead of a number of more senior and experienced admirals to head up a carrier-based task force right after Pearl Harbor. He had become close to and had the confidence of both Vice Admiral Halsey and Adm. Chester Nimitz. He was "baptized by fire" in his role as a carrier force commander at Wake Island, Lae-Salamaua, and Coral Sea. These experiences prepared him for his ultimate test: the June 1942 Battle of Midway, a smashing success for the US Navy. Fletcher was promoted to vice admiral immediately after Midway.

Though he never lost a battle, not everything Fletcher did was applauded or appreciated. After successfully putting the marines and their supplies ashore at Guadalcanal in August 1942, Fletcher withdrew his forces to refuel and prepare for a carrier battle he believed was imminent. He acted prudently, in hindsight, but because Guadalcanal was not settled, many marines felt he had "abandoned" them. This action also got him in hot water with Admiral King. In the ensuing Battle of the Eastern Solomon Islands, Fletcher's forces won a victory, but only by a whisker. Fletcher was plagued by the poor performances of several underlings who botched reconnaissance, intelligence, and ground support. Nimitz became critical of Fletcher after the battle for not pursuing the defeated Japanese more aggressively. On August 31, a Japanese submarine fired a torpedo into Fletcher's flagship, USS *Saratoga*. Fletcher received a nasty cut on his forehead that—much to his later embarrassment—merited a Purple Heart. *Saratoga* was forced to withdraw to Pearl Harbor for repairs. Admiral King used the occasion as an excuse to pull Fletcher from his command of TF-61 and push him aside, to commander of the 13th Naval District in Seattle. This was a combat command that included the Alaska Frontier and operations against the Japanese in the Pacific Northwest, but it was definitely a secondary theater. He remained there for the balance of the war. He accepted the surrender of the Japanese forces in Northern Japan on September 9, 1945. After the war, Fletcher was appointed to that sinecure known as the Navy General Board, and even became its chairman. He retired in 1947 with a bump to full admiral in recognition of his valor awards and forty years of exemplary service.

Howell Forgy (January 18, 1908–January 20, 1972) was the senior chaplain aboard the cruiser USS *New Orleans* at the Battle of the Coral Sea. Forgy coined a famous phrase, at Pearl Harbor, when the ammunition party aboard *New Orleans* grew weary. "Praise the Lord and pass the ammunition, boys!" he shouted. His exhortation inspired the men to keep going, and soon thereafter his words were turned into a hit song, one supporting the war effort. He graduated from Muskingum College and Princeton Theological Seminary, and he joined the Chaplain Corps in 1940. Forgy served through the war, reaching the rank of commander. He left the navy in 1946 and moved to Hollister, California, where he led a Presbyterian congregation. He suffered a stroke in 1959 and was forced to retire from active ministry, but he became national chairman of the Pearl Harbor Survivors Association in the early 1960s.

Noel M. Gayler (December 25, 1914–July 14, 2011) was a fighter pilot and XO of VF-2 at the Battle of the Coral Sea. Gayler graduated from the US Naval Academy in 1935. His first assignments were in surface ships before switching to naval aviation in 1940. He earned his pilot's wings and was assigned to fighters with VF-3. Sent to VF-2 as XO, he compiled an incredible record of successful aerial combat in the first months of World War II, earning an amazing three Navy Crosses in four months. His next tours were as fighter project officer and test pilot, as CO of VF-12, and as air operations officer for the 2nd Carrier Task Force. After the war and through the 1950s, he served as a jet fighter squadron commander, an aide to the CNO, CO of a seaplane tender, operations officer for the Pacific Fleet, and naval aide to the secretary of the navy. In the 1960s, Gayler commanded USS *Ranger*, was naval attaché in London, commander of Carrier Division 20, and assistant chief of Naval Operations. He became director of the NSA in 1969 and then, in his final operational command, was CINCPAC from August 1972 to August 1976, when he retired from active duty as a four-star admiral. ADM Gayler, in 1973, was the officer who personally welcomed home the repatriated POWs from the Vietnam War.

Aritomo Gotō (January 23, 1888–October 12, 1942) was the commander of the Main Body Support Force for the IJN at the Battle of the Coral Sea. He was in charge of the cruisers, destroyers, and the light carrier *Shōhō*, all assigned to screen the invasion fleet. Gotō graduated from the IJN Academy in 1910. His early career was spent in destroyers, and he became both a destroyer captain and a destroyer squadron leader. He was promoted to admiral in 1939 and in 1941 was posted to command Cruiser Division 6. Gotō's ships supported the Wake Island offensive and fought at Coral Sea, but were unsuccessful in defending their main asset, *Shōhō*. Gotō's division went on to contest the Guadalcanal operations and fought in the victory at Savo Island, although one of Gotō's cruisers was torpedoed and sunk there. At the Battle of Cape Esperance on October 11, 1942, Gotō's group was surprised by an American naval force and battered badly. Gotō was mortally wounded in the battle and died aboard his flagship the next day.

William E. Hall (October 31, 1913–November 15, 1996) was a scout pilot in VS-2 at the Battle of the Coral Sea. Hall, a naval reserve officer originally from Utah, signed on as a naval aviation cadet and earned his wings in 1940. As a scout pilot at Coral Sea, his incredible valor over two days of flying earned him a Medal of Honor. Seriously wounded on May 8, 1942, he was, after the battle, evacuated to a hospital in Pearl Harbor. While in the hospital, he met and fell in love with a navy nurse, and they were married in September

1942. After he received his Medal of Honor, Hall was an instructor pilot and then served in two staff assignments before leaving the navy as a lieutenant commander at war's end. Hall stayed in the Naval Reserve until retiring in 1960.

William F. "Bull" Halsey (October 30, 1882–August 16, 1959) was commander of Task Force 16 at the time of the Battle of the Coral Sea. Halsey graduated from the US Naval Academy in 1904. He served in a number of battleships and destroyers, earning a Navy Cross in World War I as CO of the destroyer *Shaw*. As a senior captain, desiring promotion to rear admiral, his friend "Ernie" King offered him a career-enhancing tour as CO of the carrier *Saratoga*, but only after he completed an aviation officer's course. At age fifty-two, Captain Halsey enrolled in Pensacola to get his pilot's wings; when he did, he became the oldest naval officer ever to become an aviator. Arguably the most famous navy admiral to come out of World War II, Bull Halsey made many friends as well as many enemies. His first brush with widespread fame occurred when he took his precious carriers to sea in advance of the attack on Pearl Harbor, thus saving the US Navy as an effective fighting force early in the war. Shortly after, he was stymied at Wake by timid leadership. He missed Coral Sea while his group was refueling at Pearl Harbor and then missed the crucial Battle of Midway while seriously ill with a bad skin infection. He recovered his health by mid-1942 and, back in the fight, helped wrest the Pacific from the Japanese. He also fought General MacArthur, Admiral King, Admiral Nimitz, and just about every other senior officer he came across. In the end, he was victorious over friends and foes alike. After the war, Halsey was made a fleet admiral and stayed on active service until March 1947. As a fleet admiral, he never officially retired, nor was he required to do so.

Chūichi Hara (March 15, 1889–February 17, 1964) was commander of the IJN 5th Carrier Division at the Battle of the Coral Sea. Hara graduated from the IJN Academy in 1911. Taller and more "robust" than most Japanese men, he earned the playful nickname "King Kong" from some of his friends. He was an excellent officer who served many years in destroyers and torpedo squadrons. In the mid-1930s he, like Admiral Yamamoto, spent some time in America. Hara was the naval attaché at the Japanese Embassy in Washington, DC, in 1933–1934. After a cruiser command, he was promoted to rear admiral in 1939. With both of his carriers out of action after Coral Sea, Hara missed the Battle of Midway. He was reassigned as commander of the 8th Cruiser Division and fought at the battles of the Eastern Solomons and Santa Cruz. In 1944, Hara was given the Fourth Fleet, which was really command of the Truk

Island garrison—a fleet without ships. Truk was bypassed by the Allies on their march to Japan and as a result became a neglected backwater. All Hara could do was surrender at the end of the war, which he did on September 2, 1945. He was taken to Guam to be tried for war crimes. He was convicted and sentenced to six years in prison. He was released in 1951. Moving to a small house in Tokyo, he spent the remainder of his days helping Japanese servicemen and their families obtain pensions and government relief.

Ralph L. Hauser (February 23, 1914–February 1, 2001) was the CO of the Marine Detachment aboard USS *Lexington* at the Battle of the Coral Sea. Hauser graduated from the University of Iowa in 1935 and then joined the marines. He served with the 4th Marines in Shanghai, trained new marines at Quantico, then served on *Lexington*. It was Hauser's stalwart Marine Detachment that suffered so grievously in the bombing attack on *Lexington* on May 8, 1942. After Coral Sea, Hauser was promoted to major, then lieutenant colonel, and in 1944 he led a battalion in the 3rd Marines that helped recapture Guam. During this action, he was wounded and won the Navy Cross. Hauser completed a twenty-six-year career in the marines as a full colonel in 1961 and then went to George Washington University Law School. After he graduated, he maintained a law practice in Annandale, Virginia, until the early 1980s.

Shigeyoshi Inoue (December 9, 1889–December 15, 1975) was commander of the IJN Fourth Fleet on Rabaul and, thus, the overall commander of the Coral Sea operating area. Inoue graduated from the IJN Academy in 1909. His early years were spent at sea, but he had several important staff, administrative, and attaché assignments, learning both French and German along the way. He was a protégé of Admiral Yamamoto and an ardent advocate of naval aviation. He was made a rear admiral in 1935 and a vice admiral in 1939. In 1940, he was the commander of the Navy Aviation Bureau. When the war started, he was placed in charge of the Guam and Wake invasions. His performance as commander at Coral Sea was a disappointment to Yamamoto, so Inoue was relieved in October 1942 and sent home to Japan to become head of the Japanese Naval Academy. Near the end of the war, he was made a vice minister of the navy and promoted to full admiral. He retired in October 1945 and became a teacher of both English and music to young children.

Stanley Johnston (1900–1963) was an imbedded *Chicago Tribune* correspondent aboard *Lexington* at the Battle of the Coral Sea. Johnston was born in Australia, and as a seventeen-year-old he joined an artillery regiment for service in World War I. He fought in the trenches in France and Gallipoli, was decorated for bravery, and gassed, though not seriously. After the fighting, he returned to Australia and enrolled in the University of Sydney, but he did not graduate. Afflicted with a wanderlust, he ambled around Europe and the Far East, sometimes working as a mining engineer, sometimes as a journeyman correspondent. By 1929 he was in New York, where he met a showgirl originally from Germany, fell in love, and married her. By the late 1930s, Johnston was working in the London Bureau of the *Chicago Tribune* and his wife, Barbara, was employed in Brussels, at the Press Wireless offices. As the Nazis marched across Europe, Johnston, by then a US citizen, helped his wife get out of Belgium via Paris and Portugal. They both ended up in Chicago at Tribune headquarters, where Johnston became close to the publisher, Robert McCormick. "The Colonel," as McCormick liked to be known for his service in World War I, sent Johnston off to cover the war in the Pacific for the *Tribune*. Johnston's first assignment was aboard *Lexington*, where he embarked in April 1942.

As the ride-along began, no one knew, of course, it would be the last sortie for the Lady Lex. In what can only be called period dialogue, Johnston kept meticulous notes and diaries of his adventures aboard the famous ship. Sadly, just about all of that work went down with *Lexington* when she was lost. Johnston had only a few scraps of notes in his pockets as he scrambled off the sinking carrier. He still managed to pull together a manuscript initially published by E. P. Dutton & Co in 1942. The book, *Queen of the Flat-Tops*, though heavily censored at the time, contained wonderful stories and anecdotes from the crew and the battle itself.

While aboard *Lexington*, Johnston became good friends with the ship's XO, Cmdr. Morton Seligman. After *Lexington* was sunk, Johnston and Seligman were rescued by *New Orleans*, and the two were roommates on the same navy troop transport to San Diego. While on board the troop transport, Seligman, by accident or design, gave Johnston access to top-secret messages that showed that the US Navy had broken the Japanese codes. The day after the Battle of Midway, the *Chicago Tribune* published an article by Johnston that indicated that the navy had advance knowledge of what the Japanese fleet would be doing prior to the battle. The firestorm that erupted nearly blew the navy's code-breaking secret into the open.

The Department of the Navy was aghast, and Secretary of the Navy Frank Knox, an old and bitter enemy of his rival newspaperman McCormick, was livid. The furor resulted in a grand jury convened in Chicago to consider charges of treason against Johnston and McCormick. Cooler heads in the Navy Department prevailed. To deflect the story, the navy decided not to show up for the grand jury proceedings. Without the navy's testimony, the case could not go forward. Johnston and Colonel McCormick were off the hook and the story quietly went away. Amazingly, the Japanese never picked up on the coverage and the code breaking went on unabated until the end of the war.

Johnston had performed real heroics aboard *Lexington* as the ship struggled to survive. He personally saved several crewmen from the flames and helped get a number of wounded men off the ship and to safety. He does not mention his actions in his writings. Captain Sherman, Commander Seligman, and several other *Lexington* officers recommended Johnston for a decoration, the Navy and Marine Corps Medal, a high award usually given for noncombat heroics involving rescues. The paperwork was prepared and forwarded, but after the ruckus over the secrets article, any consideration for an award for Johnston was scuttled.

Johnston didn't get much work after that fiasco, becoming toxic in the newspaper business. It didn't much matter. Johnston and his wife, with McCormick's patronage intact, turned their situation into good fortune. Stanley and Barbara moved to McCormick's Cantigny estate in France, where they were put in charge of developing the property's museum and gardens. Johnston became an expert at hybridizing roses and propagated the popular Chicago Peace Rose. He died at Cantigny in 1963. Barbara stayed on as curator, even marrying the next owner of Cantigny after McCormick's death.

Husband E. Kimmel (February 26, 1882–May 14, 1968) was commander in chief, Pacific Fleet, at the time of the Pearl Harbor attack. Kimmel graduated from the US Naval Academy in 1904. His career prior to Pearl Harbor was a very successful one, primarily aboard battleships and destroyers. Kimmel is one of the most controversial and interesting figures of the Second World War. Endless debate has ensued over the years as to what Kimmel knew before Pearl Harbor, what he should have known, or what he wasn't told. His fate was nonetheless sealed as soon as the first Japanese planes flew over the harbor. Kimmel was relieved of his duties ten days after the attack and forcibly retired in early 1942. He spent the rest of his life unsuccessfully trying to rehabilitate his reputation. Long after Kimmel's death in 1999, the US Senate passed a nonbinding resolution to exonerate Kimmel, but nothing has been done since to adopt the resolution formally.

Ernest J. King (November 23, 1878–June 25, 1956) was the third captain of *Lexington*. King graduated fourth in his class of 1901 at the Naval Academy and immediately went into surface ships, primarily cruisers and battleships. During World War I, he served on the staff of the commander of the Atlantic Fleet. In the 1920s, he began a brief career in submarines, and although he commanded a submarine squadron and designed the distinctive submarine officer's insignia, he never qualified as a wearer of the famed "dolphins." In

1926, he was recruited by Adm. William Moffett for duty in naval aviation. King went to Pensacola and earned his pilot's wings at age forty-nine. After a brief stint as Moffett's assistant at the Bureau of Aeronautics (and a subsequent argument over policy with Moffett), he became CO of *Lexington*. After a successful command tour, he attended the Naval War College. In 1933, he became chief of the Bureau of Aeronautics after the death of Admiral Moffett, who had been killed in the crash of the dirigible *Akron*, and was promoted to rear admiral.

In 1936, he was further promoted to vice admiral and became Commander, Aircraft, Battle Force. In this post he showed, during Feet Problem XIX (May 1938), that carrier-based aircraft could successfully conduct an air attack on the Hawaiian Islands—a finding that, to the navy's ultimate regret, went ignored. King was hoping to become CNO, but in 1939 he was assigned to the navy's General Board, a posting widely known as "the graveyard of admirals." The board was where the Navy Department sent admirals whom they deemed no longer eligible for important commands, but who were not yet ready for retirement. King's assignment to this wasteland was most likely in retaliation for his personal foibles. Though able, brilliant, innovative, and successful, he was widely disliked by his peers and just about any officer who had the misfortune to serve under him. His personality was abrasive, domineering, and condescending. He was also a champion imbiber and noted lothario, especially among the wives of his fellow officers. He had one great friend, however, and that was Adm. Harold R. "Betty" Stark who, at the time, was the CNO. Stark, though two years junior to King, believed in him and thought his intelligence was being wasted on the General Board. Stark yanked King out of the boneyard and appointed him commander in chief of the Atlantic Fleet in 1940.

Shortly after Pearl Harbor, he was promoted to full admiral and made commander in chief of the US Fleet. On March 18, 1942, he replaced his friend Betty Stark as CNO. King played a crucial role in World War II, and as a member of the Joint Chiefs of Staff was involved in every major decision on the prosecution of the war. Once the outcome of the war turned favorable, he was elevated to five-star fleet admiral, in December 1944. President Roosevelt, who kept King on even after he reached mandatory retirement age, believed in King completely, even if he once said of him, "He shaves every morning with a blow torch." One of King's six daughters was quoted as saying, "He is the most even-tempered person in the US Navy—he's always in a rage." Military experts still debate King's legacy, but there is no doubt that he was one of the most important and influential figures of World War II. King retired in December 1945 and became president of the Naval Historical

Foundation. A debilitating stroke leveled him in 1947, and he spent the majority of his remaining years in and out of naval hospitals, finally succumbing to a heart attack in Kittery, Maine, in 1956.

Thomas C. Kinkaid (April 3, 1888–November 17, 1972) was the commander of Task Group 17.2, the cruiser force, at the Battle of the Coral Sea. Kinkaid graduated from the US Naval Academy in 1908. His early career was spent in battleships, ordnance engineering, and naval attaché duties in Turkey, Italy, and Yugoslavia. Promoted to rear admiral in 1941, he was ordered to the Pacific at the outbreak of the war. After Coral Sea, he was given command of TF 16, and his ships successfully battled through the Eastern Solomons, the Santa Cruz Islands, and the Aleutians. Promoted to vice admiral in 1943, he became commander of the Southwest Pacific Area and then commander, Seventh Fleet. Promoted to admiral in April 1945, Kinkaid was commander of the Eastern Sea Frontier and the Sixteenth Fleet until his retirement in 1950.

George L. Markle (April 12, 1896–May 9, 1975) was the senior chaplain aboard *Lexington* at the Battle of the Coral Sea. Markle started his military career as a Marine Corps officer in World War I. Afterward, he attended seminary, graduating from Princeton Theological in 1926. He went directly into the Chaplains Corps as a lieutenant. After Coral Sea Markle was promoted to captain, and until 1949 he was the fleet chaplain on the staff of the commander, Service Force, US Pacific Fleet. From 1950–1953, he was the senior (Protestant) chaplain at the US Coast Guard Academy at New London, Connecticut.

Albert Ware Marshall (April 6, 1874–October 8, 1958) was the first captain of *Lexington*. He graduated from the US Naval Academy, Class of 1896, then served in ships for two decades, earning a Navy Distinguished Service Medal for his command of the cruiser USS *Baltimore* in World War I. He became interested in naval aviation and, at the age of fifty-two, became Naval Aviator #3300 in 1926. After brilliantly and successfully commissioning *Lexington*, Marshall went on to several senior commands in naval aviation, retiring as a rear admiral in 1938.

John H. Newton (1881–1948) graduated from the Naval Academy in 1905. He spent his entire career in surface forces, making rear admiral in February 1941. After his command of Task Force 12 at the outbreak of the war, he was assigned as commander, Cruisers, for the Scouting Force. In 1942, he was made deputy commander of the Pacific Ocean Areas; in 1943, deputy commander of the South Pacific Area; then, lastly, commander of the same theater. A capable administrator, he retired shortly after the end of the war.

Chester W. Nimitz (February 24, 1885–February 20, 1966) was commander in chief, Pacific, during the Battle of the Coral Sea. Nimitz graduated from the US Naval Academy in 1905. From graduation through Pearl Harbor, Nimitz served primarily in submarines and battleships. He qualified for his "dolphins" and commanded a submarine flotilla and even became involved in submarine engine design. As a new rear admiral, Nimitz became chief of the Bureau of Navigation in 1939. Ten days after Pearl Harbor, CNO Admiral Stark vaulted Nimitz over a raft of more senior admirals to appoint him CINCPAC. Nimitz went directly from rear admiral to full admiral, skipping the rank of vice admiral. It proved to be an inspired choice. Nimitz skillfully and courageously directed all of the navy's Pacific fleet forces in the face of great challenges over the next four years until victory was wrested from the Japanese. Nimitz was, without question, one of the pivotal and most essential architects of victory in World War II. He was rewarded with the five-star rank of fleet admiral, in 1944, and a total of three Navy Distinguished Service Medals. Nimitz became CNO in December 1945, relieving Admiral King. He served two years as CNO, during which he made one of the most important decisions ever regarding the future of the US Navy: to convert the diesel submarine fleet to nuclear power. Nimitz left the CNO post in December 1947; but, since a fleet admiral's appointment is for life, with full pay and benefits, Nimitz never officially retired.

Edward H. "Butch" O'Hare (March 13, 1914–November 26, 1943) was the US Navy's first ace in World War II and was awarded Naval Aviation's first Medal of Honor. After his legendary exploits, O'Hare became a national hero overnight. He never became comfortable with the attention. After the parades and victory laps stateside, O'Hare was promoted to lieutenant commander and made CO of VF-3, which trained new pilots for combat. He did not get back into the fighting until August 1943, when his squadron (redesignated VF-6) embarked on the new light carrier USS *Independence*. In actions near Marcus and Wake islands, O'Hare earned two Distinguished Flying Crosses. By September, O'Hare was designated CAG on USS *Enterprise*, in charge of an entire air group: three squadrons and one hundred aircraft.

At this point in the war, the Navy ruled the daytime skies. So many IJN carriers and pilots had been eliminated that Japanese air operations became severely curtailed. The only alternative to get back at the Americans was in nighttime operations, resulting in the hurried development of US Navy night fighter tactics. On November 26, 1943, in complete darkness, O'Hare's

Hellcat fighter got involved in a nearly blind shootout between a Japanese Betty bomber and an American Avenger. Neither pilot knew O'Hare was in the middle. O'Hare's aircraft spluttered and dove to the left, toward the sea. Another Hellcat pilot was convinced he saw a parachute and a splash in the water. Neither O'Hare nor his aircraft was ever found. He was declared MIA immediately and KIA one year later. His widow received a posthumous Navy Cross and Purple Heart on November 26, 1944. Chicago's O'Hare Airport is named in Butch's honor and houses a display of memorabilia relating to him in Terminal 2.

John S. Phillips (February 28, 1895–December 17, 1975) was the CO of USS *Neosho* at the Battle of the Coral Sea. Phillips graduated from the US Naval Academy in 1918. He was a surface warfare officer for his entire career and also taught at Northwestern University's NROTC unit and at the Naval Academy prior to World War II. After the sinking of *Neosho*, he was promoted to captain and offered command of another oiler, but he turned it down, with some claiming he was too distraught by the events surrounding *Neosho*'s sinking to go back to sea. Instead, he transferred to naval intelligence. He retired in 1947, and because of his war record at Pearl Harbor, Coral Sea, and his valor decorations, received a "tombstone promotion" to rear admiral. After the war, he pursued his passion for golf, a sport he had played since age fifteen. He became an acknowledged expert on building and keeping greens and was elected President of the Washington DC Golf Association and appointed to the tournament committee of the national senior's championship.

William S. Pye (June 9, 1880–May 4, 1959) was interim commander of the Pacific Fleet after the Pearl Harbor attack. Pye graduated from the US Naval Academy in 1901. He spent the bulk of his career in battleship and destroyer assignments, and as the Japanese attacked Pearl Harbor he was a rear admiral and commander of the Battle Force. It was his battleships that the Japanese sent to the bottom of the harbor, and they did so exactly one day after Pye opined to a group of his officers, on December 6, that "the Japanese will not go to war with the United States. We are too big, too powerful, and too strong." During his short tenure as CINCPAC, he attempted to pull off a relief operation for the besieged garrison at Wake Island but called it off at the last moment, fearing a new Japanese task force was bearing down on his relief force. Pye felt he could not justify the risks involved, and he may have been correct, except that there was no enemy task force in the vicinity. After he was relieved by Admiral Nimitz, Pye was given command of Task Force One, consisting of all the old battleships too tired for war, based in San Francisco.

Pye's days as an operating commander were over. His final command was as president of the Naval War College, from which he officially retired, with three-star rank, in December 1945.

Morton T. Seligman (July 1, 1895–July 9, 1972) was the XO of *Lexington* at the Battle of the Coral Sea. Seligman graduated from the US Naval Academy in 1919. He began his career in ships and early on, as CO of a small surface craft engaged in mine-sweeping operations in the North Sea, he earned a Navy Cross for valor. The award was actually earned after the war was over, but the dangerous work of mine clearing was still considered combat related. In the 1920s, Seligman, like many ambitious officers of his day, was attracted to the glamour of naval aviation. He earned his pilot's wings at Pensacola and became part of the up-and-coming aviator crowd. By 1933, he was XO of a fighter squadron, then CO of VF-1 aboard *Saratoga* the next year. By 1940, he had been promoted to commander and had been CAG aboard USS *Ranger*. The XO's job aboard *Lexington* was next. Seligman was smart, personable, well liked, and an excellent pilot and seemed destined to command his own carrier, attain admiral's stars, and enjoy a superlative career. Instead, his prospects, by late 1942, even after the award of a second Navy Cross for Coral Sea, were in ruins. Admiral King decreed that Seligman would be banned from further promotion, and King made sure Seligman was forcibly retired soon thereafter.

Outside of the loss of *Lexington* herself, and the casualties suffered thereby, the story of Mort Seligman is another tragedy of the Coral Sea drama. Seligman had only two people to blame for his fate, however: himself and Stanley Johnston. (See Johnston's bio on page 206.)

Seligman never revealed if he knew Johnston would publish the story of the breaking of the Japanese codes, but it seems unlikely. It is also unlikely that Seligman would betray his country's most closely guarded secret. But the damage had been done. It was easy for the navy to discover how Johnston had gotten his information, compounded by an eyewitness account from Lt. Cmdr. Robert Dixon, who had also been aboard the transport ship USS *Barnett* and had witnessed Seligman and Johnston working together, poring over some papers that Dixon believed were official navy documents.

Admiral King had him struck from the promotion list for captain and permanently banned from any significant assignments. Seligman was tossed on the beach and never returned to sea duty. He hung around for two years doing very little and was forced into retirement in 1944. Ironically, in retirement he was given a tombstone promotion to captain. This was based on the existing rules, which King couldn't get around, giving Seligman promotion credit for his two Navy Crosses.

Seligman lived near Coronado, California, for another twenty-five years, a naval pariah.

Frederick C. "Ted" Sherman (May 27, 1888–July 27, 1957) was *Lexington*'s tenth and last commanding officer. Sherman graduated from the US Naval Academy in 1910. He served in surface ships, then won his dolphins and a first Navy Cross in submarines, then finally transferred to naval aviation, where he got his wings and two more Navy Cross awards as an aviator, along with three Navy Distinguished Service Medals, a Legion of Merit, and a Navy Commendation Medal. After *Lexington*, he served again with Admiral Fitch in the South Pacific before getting his own flag command as CO, Carrier Division 2. In this assignment, he compiled a brilliant record of operations and strikes against the enemy while losing few aircraft and none of his ships. After a brief shore leave in the States, he was given command of TF 58.3. In the Battle of Leyte Gulf in October 1944, Sherman's carrier group was attacked by nearly two hundred enemy planes. His airmen shot down 167 of those attackers and sank the Japanese super battleship *Musashi* the same day. The next day, his task group played a major role in sinking four IJN carriers and six cruisers and destroyers. On November 11, 1944, Sherman's forces smashed a Japanese convoy at Ormoc Bay in the Philippines, which wiped out fifteen thousand Japanese reinforcing troops along with many ships and harbor installations. In July 1945, he was promoted to vice admiral and became commander of the Fifth Fleet until September 1946. He retired in March 1947 and spent his remaining years in San Diego, where he died of a heart attack in July 1957. He did not accede to higher rank and command because he did not have that many close friends in the navy who could help advance his career. He was also given to plain-speaking in his official reports and correspondence, and his frankness did not win him additional points. Personally, he was aloof, prickly, and abrasive, which didn't help in the clubby atmosphere of the navy of that era.

Felix B. Stump (December 15, 1894–June 13, 1972) was the first commanding officer of USS *Lexington*, CV-16. Stump graduated from the US Naval Academy in 1913. He initially served in gunboats and the battleship *Alabama*. In 1920, he went into naval aviation, and he received his pilot's wings in 1921. He then went to MIT for a master's in aeronautical engineering. Through the 1920s and 1930s, he served in a number of aviation billets ashore and afloat, including CO of VS/B-2 and navigator of USS *Lexington* (CV-2) in 1936–1937. As World War II commenced, he was CO of the venerable old *Langley*, but in early 1942 he was transferred to the staff of the commander in chief of the Asiatic Fleet. In 1943, he assumed command of the new *Lexington*, CV-16, and led her through her initial battles in the South Pacific. He was promoted to rear admiral in 1944 and took command of Carrier Division 24. He also commanded a task group at the Battle of Leyte Gulf, for which he was awarded a Navy Cross. From 1945 to 1948, Stump was chief of Naval Air Technical Training, and from 1948 to 1951 he was commander of Air Forces, Atlantic, and promoted to vice admiral. From 1951 to 1953 he was commander, Second Fleet, and from 1953 until his retirement in 1958 he was CINCPAC and promoted to full admiral. After his retirement, Admiral Stump was CEO of the Freedoms Foundation at Valley Forge. A Spruance Class destroyer was named in his honor, USS *Stump*, DD-978.

Takeo Takagi (January 25, 1892–July 8, 1944) was commander of the IJN Carrier Striking Force at the Battle of the Coral Sea, where he was the senior tactical commander for the IJN on scene. Takagi graduated from the IJN Academy in 1911, the same class as his fellow carrier commander at Coral Sea, Rear Admiral Hara. Takagi was a torpedo expert and spent many prewar years in submarines. As he became more senior, he was also given cruiser and battleship commands. He was promoted to rear admiral in 1938, and when war came he was commanding a cruiser squadron. His cruisers gained a significant victory at the Battle of the Java Sea in March 1942, after which Takagi was promoted to vice admiral and given command of the carriers for the Port Moresby Invasion Force. Admiral Yamamoto blamed Takagi for the strategic losses at Coral Sea and for some of the shame of Midway; but, Takagi still managed to keep the confidence of the Naval Ministry and was even given command of the Sixth Fleet, the Japanese submarine force, in 1943. Despite Takagi's best efforts, his submarines suffered devastating losses during the Gilbert Islands offensive. Many of these losses were due to increasingly adept code cracking by the Americans. Takagi, suspecting something was afoot but not knowing exactly what, flooded the communications channels with orders, many of them bogus, in an attempt to confuse the allies. Unfortunately for the Japanese, they also ended up confusing his own submarine commanders. Takagi vanished during the Saipan invasion in June 1944. It is not clear whether he went down with one of his submarines or if he took his own life in a secluded jungle hideaway. The Naval Ministry posthumously promoted him to full admiral as soon as his death was reported.

David W. Taylor (March 4, 1864–July 28, 1940) was a naval architect and engineer of the United States Navy. He served during World War I as chief constructor of the navy and chief of the Bureau of Construction and Repair. Taylor is best known as the man who constructed the first experimental ship design tank ever built in the United States. He graduated from the US Naval Academy in 1885 at the head of his class, setting a scholarship record that remains unbroken, even today. He also graduated from the Royal Naval College in Greenwich, England, in 1888, setting yet another record for academic achievement.

Taylor was appointed an assistant naval constructor in 1888, and from that point forward spent his career in the navy in duties involving ship engineering and design. After the *Titanic* disaster in 1912, he worked on making ships more seaworthy through better hull construction. On December 14, 1914, a few months after the outbreak of war in Europe, Taylor became chief of the Bureau of Construction and Repair, with the rank of rear admiral. He held that post throughout the war, along with the title of chief constructor of the navy.

Throughout World War I, Taylor supervised the creation of new ships for naval service. For this work, the navy bestowed upon him the Navy Distinguished Service Medal, with the citation: "For exceptionally meritorious service in a duty of great responsibility as Chief of the Bureau of Construction and Repair." The French government made him a commander of the Legion of Honor.

Admiral Taylor retired from active service in 1923. After his retirement, he focused his attention on aeronautics. He played a major role in promoting aviation's technical development, serving on several committees of the National Advisory Committee for Aeronautics (NACA), the precursor of the National Aeronautics and Space Administration. Rear Admiral Taylor also aided in the development of the NC-type flying boat, the first aircraft to make a transatlantic flight.

In 1931, Taylor was awarded the John Fritz Medal, the highest honor in the American engineering profession, "for outstanding achievement in marine architecture, for revolutionary results of persistent research in hull design, for improvements in many types of warships and for distinguished service as chief constructor for the United States Navy during the World War."

Shortly before his death, the Navy's Research and Development community honored Taylor by naming its new ship model basin after him. Constructed at Carderock, Maryland, the facility was dedicated in his presence in 1939.

Taylor died in Washington, DC, on July 28, 1940. In 1942, the destroyer USS *David W. Taylor* (DD-551) was named for him. Today, the Navy's David W. Taylor Award recognizes outstanding scientific achievement in the development of maritime systems, and the Society of Naval Architects and Marine Engineers annually awards the David W. Taylor Medal for "notable achievement in naval architecture and/or marine engineering."[90]

90. Credit for this Taylor background information to commander, Naval Sea Systems Command, Carderock Division, Bethesda, Maryland.

Admiral Wags (1932–1949) was Captain Sherman's faithful black cocker spaniel. Actually, Wags had originally belonged to Sherman's son, but when he went to boarding school, Wags gravitated to "the old man" and the two became close companions. Sherman began taking Wags everywhere, even to sea, and eventually aboard *Lexington*. Wags wore a special collar with two admiral's stars affixed and had a powerful sweet tooth, just like his owner. He was particularly fond of cake. The dog was a favorite with the crew, except perhaps with the swabbies, who had to clean up after him, since Wags was free to do his business anywhere. One thing Wags did not like was the sound of gunfire, and when it occurred he would scurry under the captain's bed. Thus, on the day *Lexington* went down, Admiral Wags was hiding in Sherman's emergency cabin. One of Sherman's marine orderlies was detailed to retrieve Wags. As it became apparent that *Lexington* would not survive, Wags was strapped into a life vest made especially for him, and carefully evacuated from the ship. In the confusion of the rescue, Sherman lost track of Wags. This occasioned, late in the day, a flurry of inter-ship messages from Sherman asking which vessel had ended up in care of his dog. Sherman was on the cruiser *New Orleans*, but Wags was on *Minneapolis*. The two were reunited when both ships arrived in port. Sherman's wife, Fanny Jessop Sherman, wrote a children's book about the adventures of Admiral Wags, published in 1943. Admiral Wags lived a good, long life of seventeen years, passing away in 1949. He was properly buried in the Shermans' backyard in Point Loma, California, accompanied by "full honors."

APPENDIX 1

NAVAL ORDER OF BATTLE, CORAL SEA

Task Force 17—Vice Admiral Frank Jack Fletcher
Task Group 17.2 (Attack Group)—Rear Adm. Thomas C. Kinkaid
cruisers *Minneapolis, New Orleans, Astoria, Chester, Portland*
destroyers *Phelps, Dewey, Farragut, Aylwin, Monaghan*

Task Group 17.3 (Support Group, from Task Force 44)—Rear
    Admiral John Gregory Crace
cruisers *Australia, Chicago, Hobart*
destroyers *Perkins, Walke*

Task Group 17.5 (Carrier Air Group)—Rear Admiral Aubrey Fitch,
    officer in tactical command (OTC)
carrier *Yorktown*
Yorktown Air Group—Lieutenant Commander Oscar Pederson
Fighting 42 (VF-42)—17 F4F Wildcat fighters
Bombing 5 (VB-5)—18 SBD Dauntless dive bombers
Scouting 5 (VS-5)—17 SBD dive bombers
Torpedo 5 (VT-5)—13 TBD Devastator torpedo bombers
carrier *Lexington* (sunk)
Lexington Air Group—Commander William B. Ault
Fighting 2 (VF-2)—21 Wildcat fighters
Bombing 2 (VB-2)—18 SBD dive bombers
Scouting 2 (VS-2)—17 SBD dive bombers
Torpedo 2 (VT-2)—12 TBD torpedo bombers
destroyers *Morris, Anderson, Hammann, Russell*

Task Group 17.6 (Fueling Group)—Captain John S. Phillips
oilers *Neosho* (sunk), *Tippecanoe*
destroyers *Sims* (sunk), *Worden*

Task Group 17.9 (Search Group)—Commander George H. DeBaun
seaplane tender *Tangier* (based at Noumea)
Patrol Squadron 71 (VP-71)—6 PBY-5 Catalinas
Patrol Squadron 72 (VP-72)—6 PBY-5 Catalinas

IJN Fourth Fleet—Vice Admiral Shigeyoshi Inoue
light cruiser *Kashima* (Inoue's flagship, anchored at Rabaul during
    the battle)

Tulagi Invasion Group—Rear Admiral Kiyohide Shima
minelayers *Okinoshima* (Shima's flagship), *Kōei Maru*
transport *Azumasan Maru*
destroyers *Kikuzuki* (sunk), *Yūzuki*
minesweepers *Wa #1* (sunk), *Wa #2* (sunk), *Hagoromo Maru*, *Noshiro
    Maru #2*, and *Tama Maru* (sunk)
subchasers *Toshi Maru #3* and *Tama Maru #8*
400 troops from the 3rd Kure Special Naval Landing Force (SNLF)
    plus a construction detachment from the 7th Establishment Squad.

Support Group/Close Cover Force—Rear Admiral Kuninori Marumo
light cruisers *Tenryū* (Marumo's flagship), *Tatsuta*
seaplane tender *Kamikawa Maru*
Kamikawa Maru air group—12 aircraft
Kiyokawa Maru air group
gunboats *Keijo Maru*, *Seikai Maru*, *Nikkai Maru*

Covering Group/Main Body Support Force—Rear Admiral Aritomo Gotō
light carrier *Shōhō* (sunk)
Shōhō Air Group—Lieutenant Kenjirō Nōtomi
Shōhō Carrier Fighter Unit—8 A6M Zero and 4 Mitsubishi A5M fighters
Shōhō Carrier Attack Unit—6 Nakajima B5N Type 97 torpedo bombers
cruisers *Aoba* (Gotō's flagship), *Kako*, *Kinugasa*, *Furutaka*
destroyer *Sazanami*

Port Moresby Invasion Group—Rear Admiral Sadamichi Kajioka
light cruiser *Yūbari* (Kajioka's flagship)
destroyers *Oite*, *Asanagi*, *Uzuki*, *Mutsuki*, *Mochizuki*, *Yayoi*
1 or 2 unidentified patrol boats
Transport Unit—Rear Admiral Kōsō Abe
minelayer *Tsugaru*
11 transports:
Imperial Japanese Navy (IJN)—*Mogamigawa Maru*, *Chōwa Maru*,
    Goyō Maru, *Akiba Maru*, *Shōka Maru*
Imperial Japanese Army (IJA)—*Asakasan Maru*, *China Maru*,
    Mito Maru, *Matsue Maru*, *Taifuku Maru*, *Hibi Maru*

salvage tugboat *Woshima*

oilers *Hoyo Maru* and *Irō*

minesweepers *W-20* (*Wa #20*), *Hagoromo Maru*, *Noshiro Maru #2*, *Fumi Maru #2*, and *Seki Maru #3*.

Approximately five hundred troops from the 3rd Kure SNLF plus construction specialists from the 10th Establishment Squad on the IJN transports

South Seas Detachment of approximately 5,000 troops on the IJA transports

Carrier Striking Force—Vice Admiral Takeo Takagi

Carrier Division 5—Rear Admiral Chūichi Hara, Officer in Tactical Command

Carrier *Shōkaku*

Shōkaku Air Group—Lieutenant Commander Kakuichi Takahashi

Shōkaku Carrier Fighter Unit—21 A6M Zero fighters

Shōkaku Carrier Bomber Unit—20 Aichi D3A Type 99 dive bombers

Shōkaku Carrier Attack Unit—19 Nakajima B5N Type 97 torpedo bombers

Carrier *Zuikaku* (Hara's flagship)

Zuikaku Air Group—Lieutenant Commander Shigekazu Shimazaki

Zuikaku Carrier Fighter Unit—25 Zero fighters

Zuikaku Carrier Bomber Unit—22 Type 99 dive bombers

Zuikaku Carrier Attack Unit—20 Type 97 torpedo bombers

cruisers *Myōkō* (Takagi's flagship), *Haguro*

destroyers *Ushio*, *Akebono*

destroyers *Ariake*, *Yūgure*, *Shiratsuyu*, *Shigure*

oiler *Tōhō Maru*

Submarine Force—Captain Noburu Ishizaki

Patrol/Scouting Group—*I-21*, *I-22*, *I-24*, *I-28*, and *I-29*

Raiding Group—*Ro-33* and *Ro-34*

25th Air Flotilla (also called the 5th Air Attack Force)— Rear Admiral Sadayoshi Yamada

4th Air Group (based at Rabaul)—17 Mitsubishi G4M Type 1 land attack bombers

Tainan Air Group (based at Lae and Rabaul)—18 A6M Zero and 6 Mitsubishi A5M fighters

Yokohama Air Group (based at Rabaul, Shortland Islands, and Tulagi)—12 Kawanishi H6K reconnaissance and 9 Nakajima A6M2-N fighter aircraft

Genzan Air Group (based at Rabaul)—25 Mitsubishi G3M Type 96 land attack bombers

APPENDIX 2

THE BLUE GHOST

A mere six months after her commissioning, the new USS *Lexington*, CV-16, was in the South Pacific conducting her first combat operations. The Japanese, conducting radio intercepts of their own, were quite confused. They were hearing references to the aircraft carrier "*Lexington*," a ship they had every reason to believe they had sunk well over a year ago in the Coral Sea. Soon thereafter, IJN pilots began making reports concerning a new carrier, mysteriously painted in an ethereal blue-gray, unlike any paint scheme they had yet seen. Sailors aboard CV-16 began hearing the infamous Tokyo Rose refer to them as the "men of the 'Blue Ghost.'" Superstition had decreed that *Lexington* had risen from her watery grave and taken the colors of the ocean that had once washed over her. The men of *Lexington* loved it—the Japanese pilots and sailors who came upon her, not so much.

On December 4, aviators from USS *Essex* (CV-9) and CV-16, jointly attacking Kwajalein Atoll, racked up a total of twenty-eight enemy planes shot from the sky and another nineteen blown up on the ground. They also destroyed a large cargo ship and damaged a light cruiser. USS *Enterprise* (CV-6) and the new USS *Yorktown* (CV-10), part of the same strike force, simultaneously attacked Kwajalein Island and destroyed eighteen float planes and three cargo ships and damaged another cruiser.

During the withdrawal, the Japanese sent attack planes after the American carriers. Twenty-nine more Japanese planes were splashed, but one torpedo plane got through. Its torpedo struck *Lexington* on the aft starboard quarter, killed nine sailors, and knocked out her steering gear. *Lexington* poured out dense smoke from a ruptured oil tank and began turning circles, unable to take steering directions from either the bridge or her emergency steering gear. The rudder was stuck in one position and would not move. Japanese aviators, retiring from their mission, excitedly (and prematurely) reported *Lexington* on fire and sinking—again.

The next day, Tokyo Rose reported the Blue Ghost sunk once and for all, much to the amusement of the crew of CV-16, who were sailing to Pearl

Harbor for emergency repairs. Thirty minutes after the torpedo attack, damage control had stopped the flooding, put out the fires, and, with a jury-rigged hydraulic pump, managed to get the rudder to "zero" so the ship could be steered with her engines.

Lexington was sent on to Bremerton, dry-docked, and repaired. By February 12, 1944, she was once again out of the yards and on her way back to war. On March 8, at Majuro Island in the South Pacific, *Lexington*'s crew were proud to welcome aboard Vice Admiral Marc Mitscher, who made CV-16 the flagship of his mighty Task Force 58.

TF-58, subdivided into several task groups with three to four carriers and support ships in each group, became the primary fast carrier striking force in the Pacific for the balance of the war. At times, the task force was part of Admiral Spruance's Fifth Fleet; at other times, it was under Admiral Halsey's Third Fleet (when it was designated TF-38). *Lexington* was the flagship of this massive, lethal operating group from March through October of 1944.

In April, CV-16 was part of the strike on Truk Island, a powerful Japanese stronghold. Her pilots shot down seventeen enemy fighters and *Lexington* moved on, but not before Tokyo Rose could pronounce her "sunk" once again. Captain Stump, after a valorous and productive tour as CO, was relieved by Capt. Ernest W. Litch.

The Battle of the Philippine Sea took place from June 19 to June 20, 1944, and CV-16 was in the thick of it. Part of this melee has been dubbed "The Great Marianas Turkey Shoot," and a disaster it was for Japanese aviation: somewhere between three hundred and four hundred Japanese planes were shot down in one day. *Lexington* pilots claimed forty-five of these planes.

In July, *Lexington* retired to Eniwetok for some R&R and a restocking of supplies, fuel, and ammunition. In August, using Eniwetok as a base, CV-16 and her air wing conducted raids on Guam, the Palaus, and the Bonins. By September, she was off Luzon completing strikes on selected targets in the Philippines. In October, her last month as flagship to Admiral Mitscher, *Lexington* participated in attacks against Okinawa and Formosa, blasting bases the Japanese could use to defend against the coming attacks to reclaim the Philippines.

All of the foregoing became prelude to what would be the largest naval battle of World War II: the Battle of Leyte Gulf, October 23 to 26, 1944. Stretching over hundreds of miles of open water and four separate mini-battles, Leyte Gulf was a crushing defeat for the Japanese, but also a near disaster for the Allies, narrowly averted by some incredibly brave ship commanders. The United States and Australia lost six warships—including the first ship to be lost to a kamikaze, the escort carrier *St. Loa*—while the Japanese saw twenty-six frontline ships sent to the bottom, including a fleet carrier, three light carriers, three battleships, six heavy cruisers, four light cruisers, and nine destroyers. The single fleet carrier sunk was *Zuikaku*, and she was demolished by *Lexington*'s pilots—sweet vengeance for her predecessor, victimized by the Japanese flattop's planes at Coral Sea.

On November 5, the Blue Ghost suffered one of her darkest days. She was assisting in the continuing bombing raids off Luzon and strikes in Manila Harbor. While the majority of her air wing was off on a mission, a group of kamikazes from a nearby land base took off and headed out to sea. They managed to avoid the Lex's CAP by hiding in some nearby clouds. At 1300, two of the suicide pilots dove on *Lexington*. One of the planes was shot down and fell into the sea off the starboard beam. The second kamikaze, even though hit by several anti-aircraft shells, plowed into the Lex's island superstructure. The pilot had probably been aiming for the bridge, hoping to kill the ship's captain and senior officers and cripple the ship's nerve center. He nearly succeeded. Captain Litch narrowly escaped, but forty-seven of his men were killed and another 127 were wounded. Fires broke out near the crash but were put out in twenty minutes. For the fourth time, Tokyo Rose reported the Blue Ghost a goner.

Damage to *Lexington* looked worse than it actually was. None of the ship's primary systems had been damaged, and the powerplant and flight deck were still fully operational; nonetheless, Lex was sent to Ulithi for repairs. The wounded were transferred to the hospital ship USS *Solace* and the ship-fitters repaired all the damaged areas, although it took the rest of the month of December 1944 to get all the work accomplished.

During January and February of 1945, as flagship of TG 58.2, *Lexington* took part in operations against the Japanese in the Philippines, Saipan, the South China Sea, Hong Kong, and Formosa. During this time, the pilots of her air group were seeing less and less air opposition. The Japanese air forces, army and navy, had been so devastated over the previous few months that their appearances were growing infrequent. As a result, most of the targets attacked by the Lex's airmen were ground-based forces, surface ships, or naval vessels.

Lexington did take a role in the Iwo Jima landings, February 19 to 22, 1945, then sailed north to bomb additional targets around Tokyo before being released to return to Bremerton for an overhaul. She was back in the Pacific by the end of May, ordered to assist the other fast carrier task groups in the continuing bombing campaign against the Japanese homeland. The Empire of Japan was collapsing, but it showed no signs of surrender until the two atomic bombs were dropped on Hiroshima and Nagasaki on August 6 and August 9, respectively. Japan finally surrendered on August 15. At the exact time that the surrender was being announced, a full strike from *Lexington* was on its way to bomb additional targets in Tokyo. Halfway to the target, the pilots were told to turn around, jettison their bombs in a safe area, and return to the ship—the war was over.

The veterans of service aboard the Blue Ghost during her time at war, from 1943 to 1945, like to talk in terms of "storming the Pacific, from Tarawa to Tokyo." Storm, they did: the ship spent twenty-one months in combat during that period, destroying 372 enemy aircraft aloft and another 475 on the ground. The ship's gunners shot down fifteen planes and got credit for five more "assists." *Lexington* and her air wings sank over 300,000 tons of enemy shipping and damaged double that. Her service earned her a Presidential Unit Citation and eleven battle stars. Her crew and airmen won a number of Navy Distinguished Service Medals, Navy Crosses by the score, innumerable Distinguished Flying Crosses and Air Medals, many Silver and Bronze Stars, and buckets full of Purple Hearts.

The immediate postwar years were quiet for the Blue Ghost. She was decommissioned in April 1947 and mothballed in the Navy's Reserve Fleet. The Korean Conflict came and went before *Lexington* was needed; then, in September 1953, she was sent to Puget Sound to be recommissioned and given several upgrades, including an angled deck, hurricane bow, a new island structure, and dual steam catapults. This brought her up to modern status and allowed her to operate the navy's newest jet aircraft.

In August 1955, she shifted to her new home port of San Diego. From late 1955 until December 1963, *Lexington* operated in the Pacific, conducting deployments to the Far East, including duty off Japan, Formosa, Laos, and the Philippines.

Lexington was slated to relieve USS *Antietam* (CVS-36) as the navy's primary training aircraft carrier in late 1962, but that assignment was delayed until December 1963 due to the Cuban Missile Crisis.

From December 1963 until November 8, 1991, *Lexington* sailed the Gulf of Mexico, carrying out her role as the US Navy's principal carrier aircraft training platform. In that period, she logged hundreds of thousands of arrested landings and takeoffs, qualified tens of thousands of naval aviators, and helped them earn their Wings of Gold. The Blue Ghost helped set another navy milestone when, in 1980, she became the first active duty US Navy warship to integrate female members into her crew.

A group of civic and community leaders in Corpus Christi, Texas, late in 1991, formed a commission called "Landing Force 16," an initiative to bring *Lexington* to their community and operate her as a floating museum. For the two-plus decades since, the Blue Ghost has been one of the most popular attractions of the Lone Star State.

BIBLIOGRAPHY

Baldwin, Hanson W. "Navy Sails Far South in Secret War Games." *New York Times*, May 24, 1936.

Combat Narrative: The Battle of the Coral Sea. Washington: Office of Naval Intelligence, US Navy, 1943.

Commander in Chief, US Navy. "Report of Fleet Problem XV." Washington: National Archives, June 1, 1934.

Doyle, David. *USS Lexington CV-2, Squadron at Sea*. Carrolton, TX.: Squadron/Signal Publications, 2013.

Flatley, Lt. Cmdr. James. "US Navy After Action Report," May 7, 1942.

Ford, Lt. Maureen. "Blue Ghost: A half-century of valiant service ends." *All Hands*, March 1992, 4–7.

Hassell, Walter. "USS *Lexington*: Walter Hassell Recalls the Torpedo Attack That Ended Lady Lex." *World War II*, June 2005 (published online June 12, 2006). www.historynet.com/uss-Lexington-walter-hassell-recalls-the-torpedo-attack-that-ended-lady-lex.htm.

Hoehling, Adolph A. *The Lexington Goes Down*. Harrisburg, PA: Stackpole Books, 1971.

Johnston, Stanley. *Queen of the Flat-Tops*. New York: E. P. Dutton & Co., 1942.

Lundstrom, John B. *The First Team: Pacific Naval Air Combat from Pearl Harbor to Midway*. Annapolis, MD: US Naval Institute Press, 1984.

Nofi, Alfred. *To Train the Fleet For War: The US Navy Fleet Problems, 1923–1940*. Newport, RI: Naval War College Press, 2010.

Phillips, CDR John S., US Navy. "U.S.S. Neosho Detail: Engagement of U.S.S. NEOSHO with Japanese Aircraft on May 7, 1942; Subsequent Loss of U.S.S. NEOSHO; Search for Survivors." United States Navy official memorandum, May 25, 1942.

Reese, Lee Fleming. *Men of the Blue Ghost: Historic Events of World War II in the Pacific as Told by the Men Who Lived Them 1943–1946*. San Diego: Lexington Book Co., 1980.

Report of the Commander in Chief. *Records Relating to United States Navy Fleet Problems, I to XXII, 1923–1941*. National Archives.

Reynolds, Clark G. *Admiral John H. Towers: The Struggle for Naval Air Supremacy*. Annapolis, MD: U.S. Naval Institute Press, 1991.

Sherman, Captain Frederick C., US Navy. *Report of Action-Battle of the Coral Sea, May 15, 1942*.

Tillman, Barrett. *SBD Dauntless Units of World War 2*. New York: Osprey Publishing, 1998.

———. *TBD Devastator Units of the US Navy*. New York: Osprey Publishing, 2000.

———. *Wildcat Aces of World War II*. New York: Osprey Publishing, 1995.

US National Archives, College Park, MD.

US Naval Historical Center, Washington Navy Yard, Washington, DC.

US Navy Bureau of Aeronautics (Archives), National Archives, Washington, DC.

US Navy Bureau of Ships (Archives), National Archives, Washington, DC.

USS Lexington CV-16 Association, USS Lexington Museum, Corpus Christi, TX.

USS Lexington Minuteman Club, Hilliard Elliott, (last known) President, Granada Hills, CA.

USS Lexington Museum on the Bay; Corpus Christi, TX.

Walsh, George J. "Guest post #20," USNI blog, July 2011.

Warship Pictorial #33, USS Lexington, CV-2. Tucson, AZ: Classic Warships Publishing, 2009.

Wildenberg, Thomas. *All the Factors of Victory*. Washington: Potomac Books, 2003.

ACKNOWLEDGMENTS

I could not have this wonderful writing life that I love without the faithful, continual, unwavering support that I continue to enjoy from my wonderful muse, my loving partner, Laura Lyons.

Of equal inspiration is my other partner in life, "the Dude," my absolutely terrific and talented son, Pierce. I really do these books as a legacy for him, and for his generation, hoping they and their children will not forget how they got to enjoy their freedoms.

My agent, Nat Sobel, remains my literary guiding light. It was his idea to do this book, and he saw it through the "rough seas" of conceptualization to safe harbor in contract and publishing. I am ever grateful to have Nat on my side. I also want to tip my hat to Nat's exceptional staff, in particular his administrative lead, Adia Wright, who really did the "heavy lifting" to get this book untied from the dock and safely out to sea.

Thank you, Claire Lyons, for your excellent and diligent research at the National Archives and producing those wonderful old drawings of the original *Lexington* plans.

Finally, thanks to my marvelous editor, Elizabeth Demers, who was a steadfast and nurturing presence in getting this manuscript to a successful conclusion. Her insights and suggestions made this book a true "finished product," of which I am very proud.

INDEX